Mythic Women / Real Women

Plays and Performance Pieces by Women

Selected and introduced
by LIZBETH GOODMAN

faber and faber

First published in 2000
by Faber and Faber Limited
3 Queen Square London WC1N 3AU

Photoset by Parker Typesetting Service, Leicester
Printed in England by Clays Ltd, St Ives Plc

The quotation from Eavan Boland's *The Journey*
is reproduced by permission of Carcanet and W. W. Norton.

Second passage on p. 104 is adapted from T. W. Goethe's
Elective Affinities (trans. R. J. Hollingdale),
Penguin, 1971. Passage on pp. 107–8 is adapted from
Gianfranco Draghi, 'Biblon cun Figuris',
Alfabeta, July/August 1987, p. 3.

For all individual copyright notices, original publication,
audio/visual, and all performance requirements, please see
Copyright, Publication, Performing Rights
and Audio/Visual Information

A CIP record for this book
is available from the British Library

ISBN 0–571–19140–1

2 4 6 8 10 9 7 5 3 1

Listen. This is the noise of myth. It makes
the same sound as shadow. Can you hear it?
Eavan Boland, *The Journey*

Contents

Introduction

Contexts

The borders of sexuality and gender have never been quite so persistently, provocatively, publicly, politically challenged as they were in the 1990s. With the coming of the new millennium, the issue of gender has been pushed to the limits: what is it, why and how does it differ from 'sex' or 'sexuality', what has it to do with 'feminism', where does it come from, where is it going, what determines it, can we redirect, repackage, represent it in our lives, our bodies, our images, or our creative work? All these questions have been asked, not only by academics but also by theatre makers, cultural commentators, and public personalities from Madonna (the Material Girl of the 1980s who changed shape multiple times in the nineties) to the Guerrilla Girls to the Riot Grrrls to the Spice Girls. The impact of the 'acts' of all these women is as varied as the women themselves, and of the audiences who interpret their work and accord it a cultural status, covert or explicit.

It has been argued that 'gender reality is performative' (Judith Butler, *Theater Journal* 40: 4 [1988], 527), or that gender is 'real only to the extent that it is performed'. But is not any 'reality' performative, in the sense that any event or state of being comes into public consciousness when it is 'performed' or made to present itself for an audience, even an audience of one? Gender reality is an amorphous and contentious entity; the existential question of what it means to see and be seen frames the debate. The same might be said for the theatre. The survival of the theatre in this age of increasing 'mediazation' and new technological forms has shown that performance in this so-called postmodern and postfeminist age is as much to do with context, with public presentation in a shared space, as it ever was. The theatre is a place where gender issues can be shown to be intricately related to power dynamics: the performance of a play,

ix

poem or story by a woman, in a woman's voice, on stage or some public space, can still be a powerful thing, made more powerful by the presence of an audience. Reading the texts of these works can also make an impact, for individual readers and for those who share the work in classroom or workshop settings.

While the sparks of debate around gender reality have fuelled numerous public fires, a more subtle debate has also been boiling on the back burner: that of the nature of live theatre, or performance, in the new media age. What has shifted most notably in the past few years is the notion of what counts as 'performance'. The traditional play, with characters and a plot and a linear story line, has been refined and deconstructed, rethought and challenged. A book which features women's performance work today must include a wide range of forms and styles, and a wide range of different ways of presenting the amorphous image of the female.

We are looking at performance differently these days, and have been looking at gender issues in increasingly complex ways for decades. This book refocuses the gaze again by offering a range of creative work in which the female characters and personae look out of the pages, from the stage, at contemporary culture.

This book includes eighteen works by a total of twenty-six authors, of whom twenty-five are female: but these authors and their specific cultural conditions and working practices are not the focus here. Instead, focus is on the positioning of women in culture more generally. Each of the pieces included challenges simplistic definitions offered in dictionaries and guides to modern language usage. Each pulls at the seams of what it means to be a woman, putting women centre stage in order to demonstrate the absurdity of the attempt to confine and limit the notion of 'woman' with any easy definition, any single form of representation. Some of the pieces included are plays, or extracts from plays, written for performance in a theatrical setting. Most of these are well suited to film or video or radio/audio adaptation, yet would require a readjustment of the word-image relationship to make that transfer successfully. All the plays work best in live performance; all benefit from the presence of an audience reacting to that performance, looking (and being looked at) from the stage.

The full-length plays are easily identifiable by the layout of dialogue and stage directions (the familiar textual format for dramatic literature). The book also includes a number of poems, a short story, and a few performance pieces which merge forms and cross genres in intriguing ways. Jamaica Kincaid's 'Girl', for instance, is a short story written in the first person: it leaps off the page, demanding to be read aloud as a dramatic monologue which incorporates a number of voices and cultural ways of valuing women and girls. A few of the pieces were written as poems or parts of poetic sequences: Jackie Kay's, Dorothea Smartt's, Kim Morrissey's. While the language is poetic – marked by the rhythms and internal rhymes and assonance of free verse and inflected by the language patterns of the authors (who come, in turn, from Scotland, the Caribbean and the Canadian Prairies) – the work has a theatrical impact when read or performed. The voices of the work demand to be heard; the stories they tell are both familiar and strange; the images conjured in the words and metaphors of the language are ripe for visualization and physicalization.

The collection is presented in alternate patterns of long and short, whole and extracted work. Students and actors may choose to use the collection as presented, or dip in and select work according to subject matter, genre, number of actors, or other practical issues. The collection is also ordered by theme, so that there is a sensible progression from one piece to the next. That progression moves from work depicting one mythic figure, to the 'real' equivalents for women writing today, to settle on the next mythic figure, and so on. The myths build, layer upon layer, one upon another. The common roots of stories are exposed, while the many different interpretations and forms of presentation bear witness to the power of writers, audiences and readers to take hold of any myth and mould it to mean something new.

But what is a mythic figure? The root word 'myth', according to *Fowler's Modern English Usage* (OUP, 1981), derives from Greek legend and is currently used in a general way to refer to 'a purely fictitious narrative usually involving supernatural persons, actions, or events, and embodying some popular idea concerning natural or historical phenomena'. Here, the concept of the 'mythic' clearly relates to fiction. Yet when the concept of myth is applied generally to female figures in drama and in everyday life, some intriguing power dynamics emerge. Feminist critics have, over the years, looked for new ways of putting women centre stage. In the 1970s the focus was often on reading against the grain by looking for ways of re-examining male-created fictions so that the female figures trapped in these stories might come into sharper focus; by the 1980s it was becoming more common to put the stories of male authors aside to write and perform new works which began with female experience. But as we moved through the late 1980s and early 1990s, the concept of a universal female experience was challenged by the representations of black, lesbian and working-class feminists arguing against a totalizing 'female' experience which was often defined implicitly as white, heterosexual and middle class. New stories emerged with a wider range of female characters who did not always agree, who expressed the critical concept of 'difference' in practice and in a wider range of venues: in political parties and universities and on the boards of major companies as well as on the stages of mainstream and fringe theatres. As women's power became more public, a new question began to be asked: were these women 'real' or were they 'monsters' undermining the very heart of the 'nuclear family'? Of course, this 'new' question is actually quite a familiar one which tends to emerge at moments of political and personal uncertainty, so it is not surprising that it should emerge now – along with media furore over AIDS and reproductive rights and privatization of public sector agencies and bodies of all kinds – at the coming of a new millennium. The battle raged, and continues. The gaze continues to shift from the political to the personal, and back again.

This book began back in 1987, when women playwrights from around the UK began responding to the invitation to submit original unpublished work for consideration. Hundreds of scripts arrived over the years, many of them listed in other more academic publications. Reading this wide variety of women's work over the period of a decade – and such a fascinating decade in terms of major shifts in the political, social and artistic representation of women in the UK – provided a rich context for argument about the status of women in theatre. Taking that argument into the academy was one thing, but taking it into the theatre was another. There are, of course, many women writing plays who are interested in and informed by feminist theory and dramatic history; so too are there many women academics who 'also write plays', or perform, or practice theatre-making and creative arts in various ways. Still, there are very different audiences for the work of women writers, in different sectors of the theatre, in the arts world more generally, and in academia – a term used very broadly here to include A-level studies, college, university and drama school training.

That's just in the UK. Yet the period from 1987–99 saw major challenges to the cohesion of the so-called United Kingdom, calling attention to the work of women in the distinct cultural and political realms of Northern Ireland, Scotland, Wales and England. One forum for exchange and debate is the Magdalena Project, directed by Jill Greenhalgh and based in Cardiff, Wales: home to Women's Theatre International gatherings, conferences and performance festivals where women from the UK share their different approaches to performance with women from around the world. The question of whether there might be a 'women's language' or way of using language is one to which Magdalena gatherings inevitably return, as women speak their own languages, often translated, and also perform silent work which communicates through gesture, movement, dance, and shared expressions and sounds.

Then there's the rest of the English-speaking world. The differences in cultural representation, and even vocabulary, for the study of women's artistic work are considerable even between the UK and North America, so the search for plays and performance pieces was extended to Canada and the USA. Next, the search opened out to include women's work in Europe. While a great deal of exciting work has been produced in France, Germany, Greece, Spain and in central and Eastern Europe as well, several performances by women in Italy – Franco Rame and Laura Curino – seemed to be perfectly tailored to the concerns of this volume. The Divina Project, an organization supported by the University of Turin, Italy, and Teatro Settimo, offered the platform for Laura Curino's play *Passion*. At the annual Divina gatherings of the early 1990s, a number of women from the UK (Fiona Shaw, Harriet Walter, Charlotte Keatley, Elizabeth MacLennan and myself) joined Gabriella Giannachi, Barbara Lanati and women in film and theatre from around the world to explore similarities and differences in our working practices and ways of representing ourselves and other women, in and through language, body language and image. At Divina as at Magdalena, and indeed at any international gathering, translation is an issue. While this volume includes two pieces originally written and performed in Italian, the sensitive, poetic translations provided, along with the strong imagery of the texts themselves (which communicate across language and cultural specificity), enable this work to 'speak'. In addition, two selections included in the volume offer the words and ways of using words created by women from the Caribbean: Dorothea Smartt and Jamaica Kincaid. The wide range of women's plays and performance pieces in the Caribbean, Africa and Asia, and in South America and Australia, has begun to receive general recognition. Some valuable collections of this work are now beginning to appear, as are a number of critical studies which help to place that work in context. But all this could not be confined in these covers.

To limit the book to a practical size and focus for classroom and theatre workshop and performance use, it was necessary to be extremely selective, and to include only work which clearly achieves four main objectives:

- a quality of writing which would sustain a reading and analysis of the text as well as performance.
- some formal challenge or innovation in the writing, or some pitting of form against content: experimentation with dialogue, with silence, with verse, with image, with genre.
- some analysis (textual or contextual) of the dynamic tension of gender and power relations, in language, in action, in writing and in everyday life.
- a challenging representation of one or more female characters of uncertain 'mythic' or 'real' status.

The three mythic figures who imposed themselves on these pages from the outset were Mary (the religious icon of the Virgin and her counterpart, Mary Magdalene, merged), Medea and

Medusa. Mary and Medea, in many different incarnations, figure prominently in writing by and about women from a huge variety of cultures, generations, languages and religions. Mary has been reincarnated as the suffering housewife and as the misunderstood sexual being. Medea, the ultimate caricature of the sexual woman and 'bad mommy', has been reclaimed by some as a feminist identity-politician given a bad press for daring to react to abandonment by her unfaithful husband, sacrificing the children she loves in the process. She is all things to all readers: an heroic goddess and a selfish, spiteful woman scorned. She is recreated by each new generation, each looking through the lens of a culture and a period with all its attendant expectations for 'motherly behaviour'.

Medusa is a more cryptic figure: from Greek myth to twentieth-century writings, she has been seen as the ultimate dangerous woman. Yet there is another side to her story. *The Dictionary of Classical Reference in English Poetry* (Cambridge: D. Brewer, 1984, p. 149) introduces Medusa as:

> The mortal sister in the three Gorgons. She was strikingly beautiful and Neptune, who assaulted her in the Temple of Minerva, loved her. For the sacrilege, Minerva changed Medusa's hair into serpents. Medusa was killed by Perseus, who then set her head on his shield where it petrified all who crossed him. From Medusa's blood were held to have come forth Pegasus and the serpents of Africa.

Medusa is first raped and then punished for being raped. But even more striking than this mythic example of 'blaming the victim for the crime' is the way in which the story is conveyed. The language of the passage is passive: it does not imply that Medusa had the power to transform, nor that she had any choice in the matter. This account of Medusa as mythomorphic image takes all of the power of metamorphosis away from her, and grants her instead the responsibility for wreaking havoc in what is defined as an otherwise reasonable and 'real' world (shades of Pandora). The fact that it is Medusa's post-mortem bloodshed which grants her even this power is highly ironic. It says a good deal about the writing of myths, as Brewer was working from established sources.

After her debut in Greek drama, Medusa went underground for long periods, emerging now and then in coded form in feminist critical writing, or in stereotypical form (lesbian, vampire, snake-woman) in horror films and science fiction. She did not feature too prominently in the theatre until feminists, and some lesbian artists in particular, found in her a symbol for masked identity: she who looks but cannot be looked at or seen. Another figure emerged: Cassandra, the visionary who sees but who cannot make herself heard or believed; and connected to Cassandra is Philomele, whose tongue was cut out to prevent her speaking the truth (as was Lavinia's in Shakespeare's *Titus Andronicus*, a text which draws a line back to Ovid's *Metamorphosis* for the origins of Philomele's story). Each of these mythical figures is linked, intertextually, to others past and present: Joan of Arc sees and speaks and is burned for her trouble; Patient Griselda was created variously in Boccacio, Dante and Chaucer as the all-suffering female figure (not too dissimilar to Mary); the women who people Shakespeare's plays, from Lady Macbeth (a version of Medea) to Gertrude and Ophelia in *Hamlet* and the three daughters of *King Lear*; Nabokov's Lolita, the sexually and emotionally abused girl who is presented as 'asking for it', and so on. Once we open Pandora's Box of female archetypes and stereotypes, the mythic figures pour out.

What these figures have in common is a sense of vision: like Medusa, they are all women who are looked at and who seem to look, though we must question the power of the gaze in each case. Can Medusa see anything, as a severed head? Can other female figures in stories and myths see anything which the authors do not put in their field of vision? Where does the mythomorphic power of these figures come from? Selecting these pieces involved a search for an awareness of the gaze: for a self-conscious representation of looking and being looked at, of women's place in cultural production of images of women in forms and sources ranging from mythic stories to modern advertisements, for an acknowledgement of the voyeurism of social relations with regard to gender, sexuality, identity and power. As women recreate these characters, they offer performance pieces which begin with a female point of view – while avoiding the trap of assuming a single, universal 'woman's view' – and which give voice to these characters which otherwise so often remain elusive, mysterious. In giving an identifiable, defiant voice to each 'mythic' character, the writers whose work is gathered here make the characters more 'real'. The point is not to bring myth to life, nor to kill the stories, but to highlight the uneasy distinction between the two, and to show how many erroneous assumptions and gendered uses of language have traditionally defined and carried meaning from one text, culture and generation to the next.

The 'female' is inscribed as 'mythic' in both the context and content of much of what is considered to be 'great literature'. Until recently, for a woman to figure in a story, or get some credit for inspiring or perhaps writing a story, she had to grapple with the concept of myth: perhaps Greek myths offering goddesses and maidens whose bodies are used and often disfigured by gods (Mary, Medea, Medusa, Philomele), but just as often literary versions of 'mythic women': Shakespeare's outnumbered and often silenced female characters, George Bernard Shaw's deliberately demystified 'Saint' Joan, Vladimir Nabokov's invented sexual 'girl' Lolita . . . None of these is a 'real woman'; these are fictional creations, after all, however much they may (or may not) model psychological states of real people. These are characters and as such function at the level of the symbolic. Again, this is not news. The question for readers and writers today is: symbolic of what?

In many dictionaries and guides to language usage, the male is taken for granted as the norm from which the female 'deviates' in language and in representation. So too has the language of plays tended to put women – through their representation in female characters – in a secondary position. Jacques Derrida might have remarked on the absence of a central female referent in traditional drama as 'the transcendental signified' – the male position being assigned an absolute and stable point of reference. Simone de Beauvoir might have referred to the 'otherness' inscribed in references to women and the female, while Hélène Cixous set a new ball rolling with her essay 'The Laugh of the Medusa' (*New French Feminisms,* Harvester Press, 1981). But how do we take these and other theoretical starting points and make them mean something to us today, as we read and study plays, ponder the social relations of gender in our workplaces, or put together plays for the theatre? The key is in looking at the female figures in these plays, and listening to their language, straight on. The plays and performance pieces in this book start from that place known variously as 'the female', though not from the 'feminine' and only sometimes from the explicitly 'feminist'. Written by individuals with a wide range of voices, styles, vernaculars and patterns of language, these pieces offer glimpses through the lenses of 'myth' and 'reality', from the audience to the stage and back again, as if through the reflective shield which allowed 'brave' men to approach the mythic figure of Medusa sideways, without having to look her in the eye. These plays and performance pieces benefit most from a cool, hard stare at the plays, as texts and as performances. Each operates at both the textual and the contextual levels: as literary works to be read and studied, and as performative works to be read aloud, performed, shouted, danced and sung.

Production details of all the plays and performance pieces in the volume are listed in the body of the text. The task here is to say why each text is included, what each adds to the volume and to what uses the texts might be put in the classroom and theatre workshop.

The Texts

Caryl Churchill is one of the world's leading playwrights. She was one of the first women (after Ann Jellicoe) to work extensively at the Royal Court Theatre, London, in the 1970s, and has since developed a reputation as Britain's leading or 'top' female playwright and as a respected and committed socialist. Yet she is, understandably, less interested in these labels and accolades than in creating powerful characters, stories and plays. She has done just that with *Top Girls*. The play depicts a high-flying and rather ruthless career-woman, Marlene, who power-dresses in Margaret Thatcher's signature blue and dedicates herself to moving up the rungs of the social and career ladders. Marlene has left her working-class background and created a new identity, climbing to the post of Managing Director at the Top Girls employment agency. As the play progresses we find that Marlene's professional success rests on an unstable base; her strong exterior belies the emotional bankruptcy of her character and the rejection of those around her, including her own daughter. In the first run of the play in the 1980s, Marlene was sometimes seen as resolutely 'unfeminist', dangerously self-absorbed, extreme. But since then, the play has begun to be seen as prophetic. It has become a modern classic, played on college, amateur and professional stages around the world, for a variety of reasons. The character of Marlene has been variously interpreted as a feminist comment on the unworkable expectations society places on modern-day 'superwomen', a considered exposé of middle-class Tory values, and as a sign of the times. When the play was revived and televised in the 1990s, Margaret Thatcher's impact had changed the scene entirely, and Marlene was seen as less horrid, more familiar. Only ten years in 'real time' made the difference between seeing this character as mythic and even stereotypical, and seeing her as depressingly realistic.

The extract included in this book is taken from the play's opening scene. Marlene has organized a dinner party to celebrate her promotion to the post of Managing Director. She has to organize the party for herself: a sign of her lack of popularity. She has no 'real' friends to invite, so the guests are a collection of female figures drawn from myth, history, art and literature. They include Isabella Bird, Victorian traveller; Lady Nijo, Buddhist nun and Emperor's concubine; Dull Gret, a stout female figure depicted leading the other peasant women to fight off invading devils in the painting *Dulle Griete* (*circa* 1562) by Pieter Brueghel the Elder; Pope Joan, and Patient Griselda. Our extract picks up after Marlene has ordered the first round of drinks from the silent waitress, and after the first two guests have arrived. Marlene introduces the characters to each other, and they all introduce the themes which link them, each mentioning their creation and depiction, or imagined connection to, the lives, narratives and images of men. The stories are painful, filled with sacrifice and lost children, yet Churchill's treatment of the scene is filled with comic pauses and potential. Dull Gret figures as the inarticulate and often silent clown, whose body language is expressive in the scene, and who often steals the show in performance. When Dull Gret finally speaks, the unsayable has been said in a voice no one would have expected, and the extract comes to an end.

This scene experiments with overlapping dialogue: a technique for layering language in the manner of a musical score, with some strains sounding out over others. While the technique is highly artful and immensely difficult to learn and perform, it captures the essence of realistic speech, with the effect of seeming less artful than naturalistic. Overlapping dialogue is an original Churchillian technique, since utilized by many other playwrights. This scene's surreal combination of the mythic and the real, the timeless and the timely, make it one of the most talked about scenes in modern theatre.

To say that Marlene is one of Churchill's most enduring characters is not to suggest that she is at all likeable. She endures as a symbol of the modern superwoman gone wrong; a character in search of status, caught up in a game she cannot win. The character of Marlene in the 1990s is perceived differently than in the 1980s; audience expectations and frames for interpretation have shifted. The character will, no doubt, be viewed quite differently again in the early years of the twenty-first century. In her mutability, Marlene is much like another Churchill creation: *The Skriker* (Nick Hern Books, 1994), the shape-shifting, continually re-emerging female figure of Churchill's 1994 physical theatre production. The Skriker is one minute a homeless woman on the streets of London, and the next a Kelpie, or a Hag . . . changing shape with each encounter. She is dangerous to the extent that she seduces and enchants those she meets. She is Mary, Medea, Medusa all in one. She is the Ubermythic Woman, with a negative capability. But like Medusa, and even like Churchill's less extreme but similarly shape-shifting character Marlene in *Top Girls,* the Skriker is fascinating in her multiplicity, in her possibility, in her endurance and radical edge; the reader and viewer are most entranced, not by her presentation as one thing after another in quick succession, but rather by her many more fully developed personae. Churchill's plays are all, to some extent, shape-shifters: they all experiment with form, refusing to take any traditional notion of 'drama' and work within it. Likewise, all the 'mythic' and 'real' women represented in this book are, in essence, manifestations of the mythic figure which is the Skriker. Marlene in *Top Girls* is, in many ways, an even more powerful shape-shifting figure: Marlene appears on the surface to be constructed in a fairly realistic guise (within what is at times a surrealistic play). Yet because the character is connected to political personalities and social issues, the reading of the character is bound to shift from generation to generation. As the parallels between the character of Marlene and Margaret Thatcher mature, so does the play, and the general notion of the professional woman. The value of each female figure, mythic or real, will shift from age to age.

The second play included in this book is Timberlake Wertenbaker's *The Love of the Nightingale*. Wertenbaker, like Churchill, worked for several years at the Royal Court Theatre (she was Writer in Residence, 1984–5). She has achieved considerable success with several plays representing strong women in compromising situations, though she sees this as an outcome of her work, rather than a deliberate aim. Of all the plays and performance pieces included, this one is the fullest and most faithful reinvention of Greek myth. This is the story of Philomele, the maiden who is lusted after by her sister's husband, Tereus. Tereus rapes her, and later cuts out her tongue to prevent her from telling the tale. Philomele is the 'nightingale' of myth – the bird with the beautiful voice whose sound is so desperately sad. Of the play, Wertenbaker writes that she:

> followed the theme of being silenced. In this case, where there was redemption the silencing inevitably led to violence . . . Although it has been interpreted as being about women, I was actually thinking of the violence that erupts in societies when they have been silenced for too long. Without language, brutality will triumph. I grew up in the Basque country, where the language was systematically silenced, and it is something that always haunts me. (Introduction to *Timberlake Wertenbaker: Plays One*: Faber and Faber, 1995, p. ix.)

Philomele is recreated in a time- and shape-shifted form by American writer Joan Lipkin in *The Girl Who Lost Her Voice*. This short play uses poetic language and experimental form to express the confusion and inner voice of the central character, another young woman who loses her voice. But unlike Philomele, this heroine is more real than mythic from the start. This is the realistic, darkly humorous and introspective story of a modern woman who attends a performance workshop by 'The Famous visiting Performance Artist From New York City'. Expecting to meet this situation with critical aplomb, the woman is stunned into silence by the awesome respect, admiration and desire she feels for this celebrity: for her power with words, for her disdain for other people's discomfort. The woman's loss of voice signals a stream of questions about identity and identification, gender and language and power. Words fail her, and she struggles to pronounce familiar words, uttering only phrases and then silence (like the 'jug jug' of T. S. Eliot's reborn nightingale in *The Waste Land*), crying out to express pain through sound. In the man-made web of language, the loss of this character's voice is the beginning of her journey towards truth.

So we turn from myth to reality and now move to myth treated as reality, in Italian actor Franca Rame's one-woman *Medea*, co-devised and written with Dario Fo. This classic feminist reinterpretation of the Greek myth is communicated to the audience as a report on the state of mind and ravings of the 1970s housewife Medea, who is locked into the mythic story of the woman who kills her children, but within a modern setting. Like other Rame/Fo collaborations, this play is intended to communicate directly to the audience; it is delivered in turns as a conspiratorial sharing of the story with the individuals in the audience who, as Gillian Hanna has pointed out, are meant to leave the theatre having experienced a direct call from the stage to see the 'personal as political' (Methuen, 1993, p. xviii). Franca Rame's version offers Medea a motive and allows the story to be told in her own words, from her own point of view. This Medea is aware of herself and of her role, and is therefore both more understandable – less mystical or mysterious – and more *likeable* than 'traditional' Medeas. The final speech in this version of the myth refers to Medea's awareness of her own exchange value on the open market where men can legally 'trade in' old wives for new. In this light, the end of the Medea myth is transformed from that of grisly murder to that of a positive rebirth of an unstereotyped, demystified woman:

And a terrible howl will echo round the world: Monster . . .
bitch . . . unnatural, cruel mother . . . she-devil. And through
my tears I'll whisper: (*Almost under her breath*)

Die, die, so your blood and bones can give birth to a new
woman! (*At the top of her voice*) die! you must give birth to a
new w-o-o-ma-a-a-n!!

The play, like Lipkin's, ends with a string of letters crying out for
inclusion in a word which might make sense; but language is
empty, does not say what the character needs to say.

Not far away and not many years later, also in Italy, a 'new
woman' is born in Laura Curino's moving comedy, *Passion*. This
play offers not just one 'new woman' but several, in a range of
characters all created and performed by Curino and influenced to
some extent by the work of Rame and Fo, whom Curino
acknowledges as inspiring in her a 'passion' for the theatre. The
play was premiered in 1993, directed by Roberto Tarasco. It
creates the world of Curino's childhood in the working-class
neighbourhood of Settimo, also known as Zone Seven because
this Fiat car-producing area is located seven miles from Turin.
The voices of the play are drawn mainly from Curino's childhood
and young adult life. The versatility and depth of her language
and art are captured in the text of the play, which uses alternating
typefaces to set off the different characters, stories, voices and
dialects. The character sketches are brief but memorable; the
imagery of the play is striking; the limited view from Settimo is
opened into a wide vista of the imagination, with many
references to sight, seeing and being seen.

Layered within the story of 'real women' from Curino's past
and present are some 'mythic' figures, including some fictional
characters Curino has played over the years: Carlota – based on
a character from Goethe's *Elective Affinities* – and most
importantly, Maria (the Virgin Mary) herself, weeping for the
suffering of her son on the cross. The Virgin Mary is not featured
as a character in her own right, but as a part played by the
character Dolores, in a play-within-the-play. Dolores's name is
both a Catholic and a literary reference, meaning 'mother of
sorrows' from 'dolor' meaning 'grief' or 'lamentation'; she is
depicted as an honest woman struggling with language. When

she plays the part of the Madonna in the Passion Play – a performance meditating upon the suffering and death of Christ – she takes the audience with her on a journey from the 'real' to the 'mythic'. *Passion* ends with the artifice of theatre placed squarely in the spotlight of our attention: the working-class character Dolores portrays the Madonna; both are united in the person of Curino, who is the focus of the audience's gaze as lights fade on her troubled face and on the cross. From Medea to Mary and back again.

A martyred mother figure, akin to Mary, is also the subject of *Theresa* by Julia Pascal (1990). But whereas *Passion* frames a highly visual Roman Catholic religiosity and symbolism, *Theresa* provides the story of a Jewish mother, Theresa Steiner, a music professor in Vienna Music Conservatory who is forced to leave her job because 'the Nazis have forbidden Jews to teach gentiles'. She is separated from her son as they each look for ways to become invisible in the prelude to the Holocaust, and she spends the rest of her life (and the rest of the play) trying to find him. At the end of the piece she comes full circle, but no closer to the truth or to her son. This is more a physical theatre piece than a play. This compelling story is told in text fragments and pictures, created by images layered over dance and music: Strauss's 'Blue Danube', to open and end the piece, with many other soundscapes and song fragments setting other moods throughout. This piece is meant to be performed by five actors but there are many parts. Cassandra, the truth-sayer, appears and warns of the rise of the 'little man with the moustache. He wants to break your bones like glass.' No one listens, or at least, not in time. Cassandra shifts shape, becomes another character. The story proceeds. The energy flows, rises and falls like a musical score. The movement of bodies tells part of the story in this physical piece, which opens with an energetic 'jagged' physicality which is revealed to be Jews being made to dance in the streets: not a joyful movement, but desperate, rushed, frenetic. Polish and German phrases weave in and out of the English. This physical performance piece communicates through movement as well as words, and keeps on shifting as the story of Theresa becomes both 'real' and 'mythic', specific and universal.

Cassandra speaks truths which no one will hear. She is, in this sense, a shape-shifted Joan of Arc. Most authors who have treated the figure of Joan have taken this task quite seriously. From myth and legend to G. B. Shaw's dramatic treatment of Joan, to a range of modern feminist reinterpretations, the same range of questions have emerged: is she mad?; is she bad?; is she a saint or a martyr or a lunatic or just a girl who believed in herself and invented voices to say what she wanted to say? If the latter, then she is a metamorphosed version of the nightingale, with a voice no one can hear, speaking truth. In *Trace of Arc* by Scottish writer Ali Smith (1989), the much-debated status of the enigmatic Joan of Arc is re-examined in a comic context.

Smith is an award-winning poet, fiction writer and playwright, known for her ability to treat the dialects of Inverness and Cambridge with equal skill. She weaves comic pauses and silences into the text of her play about – or deliberately not about – Joan of Arc. Joan appears as Conscience, a comic foil to two modern young supermarket assistants. Conscience is heard by one of the girls, but the sensibilities of both are tested as the characters challenge each other's understanding and identities in turn. On the surface a simple play, this text engages with language usage at a complex level. Smith's hallmark is a subtle twist of plot and vocalization, moving quickly from the ridiculous to the sublime: the silly shop assistant becomes visionary and truth-teller, far wiser than her boss, and in some ways even wiser than Conscience (and much funnier too). There is a gentle humour and radical edge to this play which rise and fall in performance, and also a powerful invitation to interpretation – the pauses and words of Conscience spoken to the audience break the frame and invite interaction, response. The play lends itself to re-reading in the challenge to find an appropriate voice for Conscience, to decide whether to listen to her or the 'main characters', especially as the play ends with Conscience/Joan's repeated words: 'Will you listen? Can you hear me?' . . .

We're also asked to listen, and to take sides in *Purple Side Coasters*, written in 1995 by Sarah Daniels. In this, as in her major plays *Masterpieces, Neaptide* and *Beside Herself*, strong female characters are shown at odds with one another and with value systems which label and misrepresent them. This play sets characters against situations of mythic importance yet, as in *Trace of Arc*, part of the action takes place in an everyday public space: a shop. But in this case it's a real shop, a major department store, big enough for people to spend hours in, get lost in, find themselves in. The play presents the realistic, humorous and sad story of two contrasting female figures: Deb, the working-class mother struggling to keep her temper when funds and time are tight, and Susannah, the middle-class mother who thinks she understands, but doesn't. Deb in turn thinks she understands Susannah, but doesn't. They both ought to know better. Years before their accidental reunion in a department store, the two met in the ward of a mental institution where they had both been 'sectioned' for post-partum depression and suspected 'puerperal psychosis' (misheard by Deb in a moment of confusion as 'purple side coasters'). Whilst inside the two became friends, supporting each other and finding ways to amuse and nurse each other back to sanity with laughter. But their friendship does not seem likely to stand the test outside in the real world, where class difference matters more when 'performed' in public spaces. Like several of Daniels's plays and also like Churchill's *Top Girls*, this play experiments with shifting time frames. The real-time scenes in the department store are contrasted with flashback and memory scenes of the two women in hospital together, and at home with their respective partners before being admitted. As this play was written for radio performance, some of the characters' lines situate physical locale more explicitly than it is necessary to do for stage or video performance. Musical cues set the scenes as well.

Daniels's writing is sharp and witty; the contrasts of mood and tone work to powerful effect, as do the contrasts between visual and verbal images and perceptions in the play. The language which these 'real' women use gives them some sense of community and identity, even in their isolation. In the ward, the identity of patients is stripped away and all are levelled by the stigma of their near-'Medea' syndrome. Susannah, the well-educated and articulate 'type' unaware of her own prejudices and tendency to try to fix things with money, is symptomatically verbal in her symptoms – her depression expresses itself in panic attacks, choking, hyperventilating. Deb, whose language skills play second fiddle to her flamboyant expressionism and ill-timed honesty, is a visual character, with symptoms which express themselves in the compulsive need to take photos of everything she sees, with a camera she cannot afford. Irresistible set-ups and punchlines pepper Daniels's plays, even when she deals with serious themes such as the threat of motherly violence and the destabilizing impact of psychiatric treatment. This play is no exception. From the title to the final empty promise the women make, the play offers a glimpse of the class divides of contemporary English life, with all its enticing and infuriating expressions in language.

Generations, by Jackie Kay, is a poem which has considerable theatrical impact when read aloud. The poem is very much about identity, about mothers and daughters, and about knowing, or needing to know, where you come from. In this sense, it sits comfortably next to Daniels's play – variations on a theme. But whereas the 'real women' in Daniels's play take on 'mythic' proportions when placed in the levelling, identity-removing context of the mental ward (where the individual woman's crisis is linked to a more 'universal' female situation, a collective 'hysteria' of 'Womankind'), the voices of Kay's poems never lose their specificity. These voices are based on the imagined words of 'real people'. In fact, the voices in this poem are Jackie Kay's and her birth mother's. Originally part of the collection *The Adoption Papers*, which related Kay's personal story of a search for her roots, *Generations* is a dialogue between mother and daughter, lost to each other and imagining each other into existence. Kay was born in Edinburgh, daughter of a nineteen-year-old white mother from the Scottish Highlands working in Aberdeen and a black father from Nigeria who had returned to his country before the child (the poet) was born. The poem deals as much with racial prejudice as with class or gender dynamics.

The cycle of poems is told from three points of view: Jackie Kay's (in childhood and as an adult, in memory and in fantasy), her birth mother's and her adoptive mother's. Alternating typefaces are used to signal shifts in the narrative voice (as in *Passion*). What is most striking about *Generations* is its visual imagery; set against the exterior landscapes of Scotland and London we find the internal landscapes of two women's imaginations: the images each has conjured of the other over the years. The words of the piece carry the imagery; it is not necessary to illustrate the poem, as the mind's eyes of the audience will do so. Yet the poem could be richly illustrated, either in multimedia performance with a slide-projected or video set of changing images behind or indeed on the body of the performer(s), or with body language and gesture. The last few lines of the poem signal the author's desire, not to see her birth mother's face or even to be seen by her, but to hear her voice, to find a connection through the voicing of a shared lineage or bloodline, expressed in simple gestures such as talking with her hands.

Kay's poem offers images of motherhood too complex to simplify as either 'Mary'- or 'Medea'-like. *Mary Medusa*, by Shawna Dempsey and Lorri Millan, attempts to boil down both archetypes to their bare essence. This multimedia performance piece explores the mythic images of Mary and Medusa alongside one another, pointing out their similarities and differences in comic style. All of the characters are versions of Medusa, all played by Shawna Dempsey. Her snake-like locks remain in place throughout the performance, as Dempsey presents herself in a wide variety of guises. The subtitle of this piece is 'A Testimonial' – readers and viewers are invited to read a personal statement in this fantastic story. But whereas Kay's 'testimonial' is sensitively and poetically phrased, this piece deals with similar subjects – the search for identity, issues of lineage and not fitting in – with extreme juxtapositions and absurd style. In this highly visual performance piece (short prose passages intended to be read aloud or performed), the narrative voice details a surreal world where ' realism' gives way to flights of fancy, and the reader or listener is never quite sure where s/he stands.

This piece reads like a comic book, and it is easy to imagine the images which might fill each box of the strip. Yet the still images would not be enough – the story comes to life when it is told. And that is precisely the point, for this is the story of a woman whose identity is challenged, who decides to become a man, is then challenged again, and decides to 'reject the concept of gender altogether'. The piece is full of references to seeing and being seen (she would 'get up in the morning and look in the

mirror only to face a blank image'), but in recounting the story of
rape by her friend's husband it also brings the figure of Philomele
back into focus. Whereas Wertenbaker's Philomele has her
tongue cut out and Lipkin's narrator loses her voice, Dempsey
makes a positive statement: 'I stopped talking.' The narrator
defines herself at the outset as a good girl from Goodland –
described as a backwater town in rural Manitoba, Canada,
'where miracles don't happen' – raised to see herself as a
Christian and also a descendant of the Greek gods and
goddesses: mythic connections all. The narrator, Mary,
transforms into Philomele, then Medusa. Finally she declares
herself a 'new woman'; she triumphs as did Rame's Medea, and
also Churchill's Marlene (both hollow victories, but triumphs
over the stereotype of the passive female, at least). She is the
goddess most feared and revered. Mary/Medusa – the comic,
composite figure which Dempsey embraces – is mythic beyond all
proportion, and is also disturbingly, hilariously 'real'. The only
visible sign of her mythic status is her snake-like hair. She wears it
with pride, and yet she knows that it may one day let her down,
as Perseus and his modern-day 'real' counterparts are still out
there, looking for something to hold on to.

   Medusa? Medusa Black!, by Dorothea Smartt, begins with an
image of snake-like hair, her 'afrikan dreads' or dreadlocks. The
hair is a key image for Medusa, as it was for the biblical
(mythical) Samson: a source of power and symbol of strength,
always linked to the possibility of loss: of power, of strength, of
control of the image. Smart reclaims Medusa's hair as an
empowering image, something to hold on to. Her locks are the
central threads of the poem, which are seen as essential to black
identity. She mocks the urge to straighten, to wax, to undo the
locks and make them 'white'. To be unruly is to be strong, to defy
definition and take mythic strength as a weapon in 'real' life. In
this piece, the voice and the eye are given equal weight.
Performance for Smartt is a space where she can exercise her
Bajan voice. Seeing Edward Braithwaite's *Mother Poem*
performed aloud, hearing that voice, made her suddenly realize
that there were people who spoke like her parents; that in art she
could find words she'd always known. *Medusa? Medusa Black!*
was the first piece in which she used her Bajan voice so blatantly,

and also one of the first highly visual pieces she performed. The poem came together as a performance piece when first Ingrid Pollard and then Sherlee Mitchell (photographers) provided images. The image of the mask which dominates the piece in performance has immense significance for Smartt; to her it represents 'being someone you're not – sometimes for protection, sometimes out of fear of sanction'. Smartt had studied Greek mythology in her youth, but returned to the image of Medusa when in 1985/86, living in south London, the neighbourhood children looked at her dreadlocks and called her first 'The Witch' and then 'Medusa'. Utilizing her full powers of selective interpretation, she decided to think of this as a powerful name. Turning the insult to a compliment, she saw a way to attach a rich symbolism and sensuality to her hair, empowering it to empower her. The transformative power of the hair – as symbol of strength, as fashion statement, as political badge – is highly sexual.

The theme linking much of the work discussed so far is sexuality. The themes of the 'mythic' and the 'real' bring women's sexualities and representations of sexuality into stark relief. As soon as we focus on images of women and concepts of women, the link between identity and gender is made, and we are only a short step away from the rich, complex, shape-shifting subject of sexuality.

Of all the pieces in this collection, the theme of sexuality is perhaps least explicit in *Girl* by Jamaica Kincaid. Yet the very heart of this story – prose employing poetic imagery and language, which benefits from performance – is a young girl's effort to understand the coded instructions passed down to her regarding appropriate feminine decorum. This is not a handbook to ladylike behaviour written by and for the white middle classes, but is rather a list of instructions handed down from the mother or unidentified elder female figure to the young girl of the title. Alternating typefaces are used once more to indicate the change in voice. What is interesting here is the proportion of the main type (the elder woman's voice) as compared to the italics (the girl's voice). The girl has only two fragments of lines: interjections which reflect her personality to some extent (earnest, trying to do right) and also reflect the speed of the diatribe (the girl's objections are included several lines after the instructions to which she objects – she is having trouble getting a word in edgewise). Inscribed in this stream of consciousness narrative are two personalities: the elder woman keen to set a good model for the younger generation, offering practical advice on seemingly simple tasks, and the younger woman or girl trying to take it all in and make it mean something to her in the 'real' world. Beneath the upper layer of instructions, though, is a subtext: a code for maintaining status by observing 'proper' sexual conduct. The end reference to the danger of being 'the kind of woman who the baker won't let near the bread' says it all. The piece could be performed by two voices, or by multiple voices, one for each line, so long as the two lines in italics (the girl's) are performed by the same voice. The piece takes on a different meaning when the entire speech is delivered by one voice: one meaning when the performer is an older woman and another when a girl plays the part. Casting and context will inflect and inform the text of this performance piece considerably.

Kim Morrissey's linked poems from the sequence called *Poems for Men Who Dream of Lolita* deal much more directly with sexuality and with the identity of a young girl. In this work, though, the voice of female guidance is missing altogether; at first this girl is not even aware that what is happening to her is unusual. In the first poem, dated Tuesday 6 June 1947, Mr Humbert tells the young girl not to tell mother; 'tell her what?' comes the reply. The four poems are all written from the perspective of the young Dolores, the abused girl taken advantage of by an older man in Nabokov's novel, *Lolita*. Dolores (recall the name in Curino's *Passion*) is an apt name for the sad, suffering girl who grows up too quickly. Her friends, she tells us, call her Dolly, but he calls her Lolita. And Lolita speaks to us, the readers of the poems. The force of her words and the images they conjure remind us to keep looking; we are fixed in Lolita's gaze and see her tears. Her eyes are the focus in the first poem, then her name, then a mirror, and then her eyes again. In encouraging readers to see Lolita's eyes, as well as to see through them, Morrissey reclaims Dolores from Nabokov and from those who have found vicarious pleasure in reading of this girl's abuse.

The poems are disturbing, vivid, intense. The verse is spare, direct, intended to hurt. There is no looking away from the image the poems create: the girl who looks in the mirror and cannot find herself, but who knows that she has no choices, that she will be left, that she has become the 'sore' he 'picked red, never wanting it to heal'. Morrissey takes on the mother's role, giving voice to the character so that she might heal. As readers and viewers of this work in performance we become the community helping that healing to continue.

Lift and Separate, by Victoria Worsley, rejects images of women in myth, history, and fiction alike, taking a lingerie catalogue as its starting point. Worsley is known in the UK for her innovative physical performance work with Tattycoram, an all-woman performance troupe which trained in critical thought at Oxford University and in physical expression in Paris, before teaming up as a professional company dedicated to devising imaginative recreations of mythic and literary female figures. Their first piece was a collaboration with performance artist Annie Griffin: *The Very Tragical History of Mary Shelley, Her Husband, and Famous Friends* concerned itself with the ways in which 'women are looked at and treated on stage', in Griffin's words. Several performances later, their *Three Sisters in I Want to Go to Moscow* (1988) experimented with a reframing of both the sibling relations and stage dynamics of Chekhov's play. In 1989 the group disbanded, but Worsley continued to experiment with Tattycoram collaborator Caroline Ward on physical theatre pieces such as *Make Me a Statue* (1989/90): an exploration of the art and life of sculptor Camille Claudel (commonly known as Auguste Rodin's lover). Worsley formed her own company, Jade, in 1992.

One of the first products of her new phase of single-authored work was a commission for the Soho Poly's '(Small) Objects of Desire' series: *Lift and Separate* (1993). In this piece, Worsley's training in textual deconstruction and physical communication are both employed to effect. The piece is a linked vignette of visual images connected to a 'found text': pages 174 and 175 of the Burlington Lycra Warehouse's mail-order catalogue for Spring/Summer 1996. In choosing these two pages from a catalogue as her starting point, Worsley appears to begin with something connected to a particular time and place, something 'real'. Yet in reading the fine print, we discover that this is not a catalogue which arrived through the letterbox, bur rather a catalogue of ideas, anticipating fashions of the future. The collection is for 1996, but the catalogue was 'found' by Worsley on display at the Victoria and Albert Museum display on 20th Century Design, in good time for the play to be written and performed in 1993. Time-shifting, image-changing again.

While Worsley wrote this script on her own, a number of female figures appear. The central figure is simply called The Woman, while the models who appear in varying degrees of dress are called by number and colour: Apricot (1), Black (2), etc. They alternate costumes and lines in quick succession, and Caryl Churchill's technique of overlapping dialogue is employed (signalled by a solidus in the text between two lines of speech, as in *Top Girls*). The performance is visual, colourful, evocative. It is also highly amusing, as the concept of the bra which will 'lift and separate' is enacted while the interior monologues of the models are heard by the audience. Women are positioned deliberately as problematic sites of representation – subjects and objects, depending on who looks, from what angle and for what reason – by a writer concerned with demystifying the mystique of image-consciousness. What the women wear is everything, and nothing. The universality of clothes-consciousness is undercut, quite literally, by the ludicrous nature of the 'Wonderbra', by underwear.

Faith and Dancing (1996), written and performed by Lois Weaver, begins in another place entirely – the American South – but underwear creeps into the story here too. A mother shows her daughter how to hang laundry: 'The most important thing to remember is category. Hang things in groups. Sheets with sheets, towels with towels and underwear together always on the back line. Keep in mind that people can see these details of your life . . . can see how you manage your private affairs in the way you hang out your laundry.' This might be the 1950s American version of Jamaica Kincaid's advice to her 'Girl', while the same advice would surely have been rejected by the models in Worsley's lingerie play. But in Weaver's semi-autobiographical solo performance, the advice rings home – it carries a weight of authenticity, authority, and also a sense of impending danger, like a storm about to break. In fact, the performance makes continual reference to the weather: the twister is always about to come, the weather about to change, as Weaver shifts and dances her way through the years of sexual awakening.

Weaver was Artistic Director of Gay Sweatshop in 1995–6, and is known internationally as one third of the lesbian performance company Split Britches (with Peggy Shaw and Deborah Margolin). Her work is renowned for its daring leaps of imagination, for the beauty of text and image juxtaposed to both serious and comic effect. Weaver's solo work on *Faith and Dancing*, subtitled 'Mapping Femininity And Other Natural Disasters', takes us to the American landscape of her childhood in Virginia: the name of her home state and also of her mother. Or rather, Virginia is the name of the mother character referred to in the performance; it is not always clear which parts of this piece are 'fact' and which are 'fiction', a necessary ambiguity separating this performance piece from the genres of autobiography or personal poetry. The form of the piece is prose, interspersed with minimal stage directions and some detailed descriptions of the visual tableaux. The opening images are familiar: Weaver wears the ruby slippers from *The Wizard of Oz*, and refers to corn bread scattered on the ground, reminiscent of *Hansel and Gretel* – both stories about little girls trying to find their way home. But here *Faith and Dancing* leaves childhood fiction with happy endings, and gets much more complicated. Weaver tells a story which is both her story and a more general story into which we might all imagine ourselves at various points; it is a story of growing up, discovering sexuality, developing identity and learning to view home as the place where we can't necessarily be ourselves. The text twists around the concept that any sense of community will grow and shift from the local and familial into a larger and less familiar global landscape of connections, mapped over unfamiliar terrain. In playing herself as a young girl (with shades of Dorothy and Gretel) and also capturing a sense of her mother and the inspiringly independent neighbour woman in the performance, Weaver embodies the mythic associations of these real women and connects them to the bodies and imaginations of real women and men in the audience, through the use of her own body and voice on stage.

The next selection, *Digging for Ladies* by Jyll Bradley, is an extract from a longer play, originally performed in London in 1996. This version was revised as a free-standing short performance piece, first performed in an Italianate garden in Sissinghurst, Kent (south-east England) in 1997. The piece is written for outdoor performance, and is site-specific (designed for the gardens of stately homes) but flexible (it can be played in any garden). The main players are four female gardeners. They are, specifically, amateur gardeners competing through overblown language and comic physical theatre for the attention of audiences and for their place in the gardens as 'budding professionals'. Bradley has worked with Scarlet Theatre, a physical performance group, and tends in her writing to use the theatre space as a forum for experiment with poetic language and imagery. This piece revels in words. The language is delicious: from the naming of the women as the performance begins, to the declaration of 'many representations and grievances', through to the incantatory, repeated line 'I graze and graze the lawns' which brings the piece to a close. This is heightened poetic language, not intended to be read literally. This is language making fun and commenting upon itself in performance: metatheatre. The energy of the piece communicates freely, and the comic portrayal of these absurd female characters – a group of four women who appear on location in formal landscaped gardens and vie for employment as gardeners – calls out for visual representation. The piece works on its own as a comic scene, ideal for workshop with actors or students. It adds another layer to the reading if you know that the 'playing fields of her rejection' are the gardens of Sissinghurst, created by a 'real' woman of mythic stature: Vita Sackville-West, in her attempt at a 'conquest of nature'. Sexuality and its pruning, grazing, taming and conquest are explored in indirect references to Sackville-West throughout the piece . . . whilst those who know of the relationship between Sackville-West and Virginia Woolf (paragon of a 'room of one's own') will read yet more between the lines of this piece.

Bradley sees this performance piece as 'drawing on the rich relationship between female literature, class and gardening; it follows the journeys of four budding gardeners, each desirous of an apprenticeship that will take them on to the 'playing fields' of erotic enlightenment. In Bradley's words: 'I am interested in the concept of the "amateur" in performance as a particular English aesthetic: "amateur" because the endeavour of the women to be gardeners and to do their performance – their desire to do and be – is the fuel for the play, and the fuel for their desire.' In making the characters so funny, Bradley allows them to be both overtly desirous in a sexualized sense and also desexualized by the comedy. The more you know about Vita Sackville-West and Virginia Woolf, the more absurd this intentionally overly reverential tribute to their creative and erotic 'endeavours' becomes. Another literary reference is readable between the lines of this piece as well: a passing knowledge of Shakespeare enriches this scene, as readers may notice that the four female gardeners of Bradley's creation play their parts as working-class dreamers with a carefree creativity reminiscent of the 'rude mechanicals' in *A Midsummer Night's Dream*. The performance piece works without these references; it is readable and enjoyable on many levels, and is offered here as an excellent source for verbal experimentation with the sensual sounds and feel of language on the tongue.

So too is the extract included from Bryony Lavery's play *Ophelia,* written and first performed in 1996 in a production directed by Rosemary Hill. This piece is particularly well suited to teaching purposes, as the text introduces numerous characters from Shakespeare as well as a number of servants and players who do not appear in Shakespeare. It offers a large number of parts for women and some for men, rendering the piece suitable for experimentation in large classroom or workshop settings. In fact, the need for giving strong voices and story lines to a variety of female parts was the starting point for the play. Lavery was approached by actors who were 'fed up with the paucity of women's roles in the many Shakespeare plays they performed', and who 'wanted a big play of their own'. While her extensive career in British theatre has produced a long list of plays offering strong parts for women, and while she has co-written and performed a number of gender-bending lesbian pantomimes as well as writing for more 'mainstream' stage and broadcast outlets (including a major adaptation of *Wuthering Heights*), Lavery's work had, until 1996, managed to steer clear of Shakespeare. She had written about the absence of good women's roles in Shakespeare, but had not set out to write any herself. *Ophelia* engages not only with Shakespeare's language and characters but also with the Shakespeare myth: the cultural industry which venerates the Bard and protects a 'traditional' approach to British performance. Performance brings out the nuances of the text of *Ophelia,* when regional accents and the voices of women of different ages mix and mingle, and when the bodies of women on stage speak the play emphatically in the context of live performance.

Ophelia is an experimental play which tells the story of *Hamlet* but gives priority to the parts of the story which affect Ophelia and the other female characters (including a few created by Lavery). The play does not exactly show us Ophelia's point of view, or at least, not explicitly. But it does show us what happens backstage, behind closed doors, to Ophelia and the other female characters: what makes them act as they do, what frightens them, angers them, motivates them. The play does not restrict itself to *Hamlet*: it opens with the cast of players from the play-within-the-play gathered in the scene of carnage which ends Shakespeare's tragedy. Lavery's version picks up there, and moves back and forth in time, weaving in and out of the story of the Prince of Denmark to explore the stories of the many other characters whose lives are intermingled with Hamlet's. Servants figure prominently in this play; the noble characters converse with them as often as with each other, and so we see the nobles through the eyes of the workers. Their point of view provides a below-stairs perspective on the events of the play. As readers and audience members we are called upon to witness Ophelia's need for freedom as she runs on the beach escaping enclosure in the towers of Elsinore; we witness her respect for knowledge and for book learning when offered by a female scholar, her rejection of the teachings of her brother Laertes (who mingles book learning with incestuous molestations), her appeals to Polonius for help and protection (all misunderstood and so unmet), her witness of the Ghost of the late King Hamlet (which only she sees), her manipulation by the needy Queen Gertrude, her dawning attraction to Hamlet and her confused sense of rejection. All this is recorded by the female scribes who appear to write the untold stories which will not be recorded among the descriptions of 'great men' and tragic events which are recorded in Shakespeare's play. To avoid her own tragic death Ophelia writes a new version of the story. Female scribes record the gossip of the palace, the conversations of servants and courtiers below stairs, the seedier side of the tale (including the invention of a reason for Ophelia's emotional distress: the secret sexual abuse she endures from her brother). The scribes, and Ophelia as a woman who writes her own story within the play, offer the subtexts of Shakespeare's text, appealing to her audience to rewrite the stories we all know, to look and see what the classic texts do not say. All that sounds quite serious: but the play is, above all, irreverent, funny: an achievement of verse competing with prose, a feast of language as sensuous to the ear as to the eye. The last scene included here leaves us, with the female scribes, in a tower. There, the next play, *Lear's Daughters*, opens.

Lear's Daughters is the 'prequel' or 'play before the play' of *King Lear*. Though based on the story of Lear, it offers parallels of the Medea myth in its depiction of princesses who must learn their value in the marriage market. This play, based on an idea by Elaine Feinstein and written in workshop by members of the Women's Theatre Group for its first run in 1987, has been billed as 'the story of women growing up in the kingdoms of their fathers'. What the play offers is a set of female characters created out of the subtext of Shakespeare's *King Lear*: they are the people who live in the margins of the original, given centre stage in their own play. Like Lavery's *Ophelia* this play functions as a feminist rewriting of a 'classic' or canonical text. The play focuses on Lear's daughters as they might have seen themselves: as 'three daughters, locked in a room with two mothers, dead or gone missing and a Father, waiting outside; three princesses, sitting in a tower with two servants, behind the door and a King holding the crown.' Aside from the three princesses, only two other characters are represented by performers on stage: Nanny and Fool. Other characters such as Lear and the dead Queen are only referred to and represented by various props and gestures. Nanny is a very prim, 'feminine' substitute mother for the three princesses. Fool, however, is androgynous: not clearly female or male, masculine or feminine. Even in a world reduced to five people, one of them cannot be pinned down – nothing is certain.

The princesses look to Nanny, and to a lesser extent also to Fool, for guidance in relation to marriage and sexuality. But the stakes are raised when Regan finds herself pregnant. Locked in a tower with her two sisters, she finds more concern for her relative position in the family hierarchy – as potential inheritor of the kingdom – than she does interest in the unborn child. A pregnant princess will not inherit; nor will she be married off to the most eligible prince. The nurse gives Regan a herbal brew. Regan's labour is induced; the foetus is stillborn. As Regan aborts the foetus, her sisters watch, as does the audience of the play in performance. But Regan has the last word: in the closing scene, each of the three sisters delivers a brief image-based speech which crystallizes her perception and interpretation of the events in the two plays which created and now confine them (*Lear's Daughters* and *King Lear*). Goneril speaks about being Lear's daughter rather than being her own woman; Cordelia speaks about the power which is inscribed in language. In between, Regan – the second daughter who was also, almost, a mother – speaks of a 'veil being pulled from her eyes' when she realized what women endure to survive in the world of men. She speaks as Mary, Medea and Medusa, the good girl transformed by the need to survive in a world without mothers, without safety.

We've come full circle: from the mother who succeeds in the modern business world by giving up her child (Churchill's Marlene) to the mother who aborts in order to preserve her financial worth (Regan, second daughter to Lear). Yet in between these two bleak and sadly realistic, though hopefully not representative, portraits flow many currents of conflicting images: mothers and daughters, lovers, strong women, women in need of support, mythic women and real women. Each is a challenge to look at, to consider and re-present.

Lear's Daughters may be the easiest play in this collection to use in a classroom or workshop situation; students and actors can begin with something they probably know – *King Lear* – and then build on the familiar to move towards the less familiar in the voices of the women. But all the plays and performance pieces included here can be used in any number of ways. Each benefits from being read aloud; all can be studied and enjoyed as texts too. Common themes can be traced, mythic figures can be found and connected to other figures, other myths, or to real people whose stories also deserve telling. Each play offers layered images and stories, resources for performance and for study. Each can be juxtaposed with any of the others, in any order and for any reason, practical or theoretical. Some benefit from performance by women; some release new potential meanings when performed by men, or by mixed companies. Double and triple bills for performance suggest themselves in each comparison of the texts; possible essay topics abound as well. Each new contextualizing of the plays and each individual interpretation will open up new possibilities. Whether or not gender reality 'really' is performative, the issue can be put to the test with these plays and performance pieces, the full potential of which can only be realized when readers and actors engage with them through their own eyes and ears, for their own reasons, in their own time.

Lizbeth Goodman
Oxford

Top Girls

CARYL CHURCHILL

The following extract begins part-way through the first act of the play. Marlene, who has just been promoted at the 'Top Girls' employment agency, has invited a group of women from myth and history to join her at a celebratory dinner.

Caryl Churchill has written for the stage, television and radio. Her stage plays include *Owners*, *Objections to Sex and Violence*, *Light Shining in Buckinghamshire*, *Vinegar Tom*, *Traps*, *Cloud Nine*, *Three More Sleepless Nights*, *Top Girls*, *Fen*, *Softcops*, *A Mouthful of Birds* (with David Lan), *Serious Money*, *Ice Cream*, *Mad Forest*, *Lives of the Great Poisoners*, *The Skriker*, a translation of Seneca's *Thyestes* and *Blue Heart*.

Note on characters

Isabella Bird (1831–1904) lived in Edinburgh, travelled extensively between the ages of 40 and 70.

Lady Nijo (b.1258) Japanese, was an Emperor's courtesan and later a Buddhist nun who travelled on foot through Japan.

Dull Gret is the subject of the Brueghel painting, *Dulle Griet*, in which a woman in an apron and armour leads a crowd of women charging through hell and fighting the devils.

Pope Joan, disguised as a man, is thought to have been Pope between 854–856.

Patient Griselda is the obedient wife whose story is told by Chaucer in The Clerk's Tale of *The Canterbury Tales*.

Note on layout

A speech usually follows the one immediately before it BUT:

1 When one character starts speaking before the other has finished, the point of interruption is marked /. For example:

Isabella This is the Emperor of Japan? / I once met the Emperor of Morocco.

Nijo In fact he was the ex-Emperor.

2 A character sometimes continues speaking right through another's speech. For example:

Isabella When I was forty I thought my life was over. / Oh I was pitiful. I was

Nijo I didn't say I felt it for twenty years. Not every minute.

Isabella sent on a cruise for my health and I felt even worse. Pains in my bones, pins and needles . . . etc.

3 Sometimes a speech follows on from a speech earlier than the one immediately before it, and continuity is marked*. For example:

Griselda I'd seen him riding by, we all had. And he'd seen me in the fields with the sheep*.

Isabella I would have been well suited to minding sheep.

Nijo And Mr Nugent riding by.
Isabella Of course not, Nijo, I mean a healthy life in the open air.
Joan *He just rode up while you were minding the sheep and asked you to marry him?
where 'in the fields with the sheep' is the cue to both 'I would have been' and 'He just rode up'.

Top Girls was first performed at the Royal Court Theatre, London, on 28 August 1982 with the following cast:

Marlene Gwen Taylor
Isabella Bird / Joyce / Mrs Kidd Deborah Findlay
Lady Nijo / Win Lindsay Duncan
Dull Gret / Angie Carole Hayman
Pope Joan / Louise Selina Cadell
Patient Griselda / Nell / Jeanine Lesley Manville
Waitress / Kit / Shona Lou Wakefield

Directed by Max Stafford Clark
Designed by Peter Hartwell

Act One	Restaurant. Saturday night.
Act Two	
Scene One	'Top Girls' Employment agency. Monday morning.
Scene Two	Joyce's back yard. Sunday afternoon.
Scene Three	Employment agency. Monday morning.
Act Three	Joyce's kitchen. Sunday evening, a year earlier.

4

Marlene Magnificent all of you. We need some more wine, please, two bottles I think, Griselda isn't even here yet, and I want to drink a toast to you all.

Isabella To yourself surely, / we're here to celebrate your success.

Nijo Yes, Marlene.

Joan Yes, what is it exactly, Marlene?

Marlene Well it's not Pope but it is managing director.*

Joan And you find work for people.

Marlene Yes, an employment agency.

Nijo *Over all the women you work with. And the men.

Isabella And very well deserved too. I'm sure it's just the beginning of something extraordinary.

Marlene Well it's worth a party.

Isabella To Marlene.*

Marlene And all of us.

Joan *Marlene.

Nijo Marlene.

Gret Marlene.

Marlene We've all come a long way. To our courage and the way we changed our lives and our extraordinary achievements.

They laugh and drink a toast.

Isabella Such adventures. We were crossing a mountain pass at seven thousand feet, the cook was all to pieces, the muleteers suffered fever and snow blindness. But even though my spine was agony I managed very well.

Marlene Wonderful.

Nijo Once I was ill for four months lying alone at an inn. Nobody to offer a horse to Buddha. I had to live for myself, and I did live.

Isabella Of course you did. It was far worse returning to Tobermory. I always felt dull when I was stationary. / That's why I could never stay anywhere.

Nijo Yes, that's it exactly. New sights. The shrine by the beach, the moon shining on the sea. The goddess had vowed to save all living things. / She would even save the fishes. I was full of hope.

Joan I had thought the Pope would know everything. I thought God would speak to me directly. But of course he knew I was a woman.

Marlene But nobody else even suspected?

The Waitress brings more wine.

Joan In the end I did take a lover again.*

Isabella In the Vatican?

Gret *Keep you warm.

Nijo *Ah, lover.

Marlene *Good for you.

Joan He was one of my chamberlains. There are such a lot of servants when you're a Pope. The food's very good. And I realized I did know the truth. Because whatever the Pope says, that's true.

Nijo What was he like, the chamberlain?*

Gret Big cock.

Isabella Oh Gret.

Marlene *Did he fancy you when he thought you were a fella?

Nijo What was he like?

Joan He could keep a secret.

Marlene So you did know everything.

Joan Yes, I enjoyed being Pope. I consecrated bishops and let people kiss my feet. I received the King of England when he came to submit to the church. Unfortunately there were earthquakes, and some village reported it had rained blood, and in France there was a plague of giant grasshoppers, but I don't think that can have been my fault, do you?*

Laughter.

The grasshoppers fell on the English Channel and were washed up on shore and their bodies rotted and poisoned the air and everyone in those parts died.

Laughter.

Isabella *Such superstition! I was nearly murdered in China by a howling mob. They thought the barbarians ate babies and put them under railway sleepers to make the tracks steady, and ground up their eyes to make the lenses of cameras. / So

Marlene And you had a camera!

Isabella they were shouting, 'child-eater, child-eater'. Some people tried to sell girl babies to Europeans for cameras or stew!

Laughter.

Marlene So apart from the grasshoppers it was a great success.

Joan Yes, if it hadn't been for the baby I expect I'd have lived to an old age like Theodora of Alexandria, who lived as a monk. She was accused by a girl / who fell in love with her of being the father of her child and –

Nijo But tell us what happened to your baby. I had some babies.

Marlene Didn't you think of getting rid of it?

Joan Wouldn't that be a worse sin than having it? / But a Pope with a child was about as bad as possible.

Marlene I don't know, you're the Pope.

Joan But I wouldn't have known how to get rid of it.

Marlene Other Popes had children, surely.

Joan They didn't give birth to them.

Nijo Well you were a woman.

Joan Exactly and I shouldn't have been a woman. Women, children and lunatics can't be Pope.

Marlene So the only thing to do / was to get rid of it somehow.

Nijo You had to have it adopted secretly.

Joan But I didn't know what was happening. I thought I was getting fatter, but then I was eating more and sitting about, the life of a Pope is quite luxurious. I don't think I'd spoken to a woman since I was twelve. The chamberlain was the one who realized.

Marlene And by then it was too late.

Joan Oh I didn't want to pay attention. It was easier to do nothing.

Nijo But you had to plan for having it. You had to say you were ill and go away.

Joan That's what I should have done I suppose.

7

Marlene Did you want them to find out?

Nijo I too was often in embarrassing situations, there's no need for a scandal. My first child was His Majesty's, which unfortunately died, but my second was Akebono's. I was seventeen. He was in love with me when I was thirteen, he was very upset when I had to go to the Emperor, it was very romantic, a lot of poems. Now His Majesty hadn't been near me for two months so he thought I was four months pregnant when I was really six, so when I reached the ninth month / I

Joan I never knew what month it was.

Nijo announced I was seriously ill, and Akebono announced he had gone on a religious retreat. He held me round the waist and lifted me up as the baby was born. He cut the cord with a short sword, wrapped the baby in white and took it away. It was only a girl but I was sorry to lose it. Then I told the Emperor that the baby had miscarried because of my illness, and there you are. The danger was past.

Joan But Nijo, I wasn't used to having a woman's body.

Isabella So what happened?

Joan I didn't know of course that it was near the time. It was Rogation Day, there was always a procession. I was on the horse dressed in my robes and a cross was carried in front of me, and all the cardinals were following, and all the clergy of Rome, and a huge crowd of people. / We set off from

Marlene Total Pope.

Joan St Peter's to go to St John's. I had felt a slight pain earlier, I thought it was something I'd eaten, and then it came back, and came back more often. I thought when this is over I'll go to bed. There were still long gaps when I felt perfectly all right and I didn't want to attract attention to myself and spoil the ceremony. Then I suddenly realized what it must be. I had to last out till I could get home and hide. Then something changed, my breath started to catch, I couldn't plan things properly any more. We were in a little street that goes between St Clement's and the Colosseum, and I just had to get off the horse and sit down for a minute. Great waves of pressure were going through my body, I heard sounds like a cow lowing, they came out of my mouth. Far away I heard people screaming, 'The Pope is ill, the Pope is dying.' And the baby just slid out onto the road.*

Marlene The cardinals / won't have known where to put themselves.
Nijo Oh dear, Joan, what a thing to do! In the street!
Isabella *How embarrassing.
Gret In a field, yah.

They are laughing.

Joan One of the cardinals said, 'The Antichrist!' and fell over in a faint.

They all laugh.

Marlene So what did they do? They weren't best pleased.
Joan They took me by the feet and dragged me out of town and stoned me to death.

They stop laughing.

Marlene Joan, how horrible.
Joan I don't really remember.
Nijo And the child died too?
Joan Oh yes, I think so, yes.

Pause.
   The Waitress enters to clear the plates. They start talking quietly.

Isabella (*to Joan*) I never had any children. I was very fond of horses.
Nijo (*to Marlene*) I saw my daughter once. She was three years old. She wore a plum-red / small-sleeved gown. Akebono's
Isabella Birdie was my favourite. A little Indian bay mare I rode in the Rocky Mountains.
Nijo wife had taken the child because her own died. Everyone thought I was just a visitor. She was being brought up carefully so she could be sent to the palace like I was.
Isabella Legs of iron and always cheerful, and such a pretty face. If a stranger led her she reared up like a bronco.
Nijo I never saw my third child after he was born, the son of Ariake the priest. Ariake held him on his lap the day he was born and talked to him as if he could understand, and cried. My fourth child was Ariake's too. Ariake died before he was

9

born. I didn't want to see anyone, I stayed alone in the hills. It was a boy again, my third son. But oddly enough I felt nothing for him.

Marlene How many children did you have, Gret?

Gret Ten.

Isabella Whenever I came back to England I felt I had so much to atone for. Hennie and John were so good. I did no good in my life. I spent years in self-gratification. So I hurled myself into committees, I nursed the people of Tobermory in the epidemic of influenza, I lectured the Young Women's Christian Association on Thrift. I talked and talked explaining how the East was corrupt and vicious. My travels must do good to someone beside myself. I wore myself out with good causes.

Marlene Oh God, why are we all so miserable?

Joan The procession never went down that street again.

Marlene They rerouted it specially?

Joan Yes they had to go all round to avoid it. And they introduced a pierced chair.

Marlene A pierced chair?

Joan Yes, a chair made out of solid marble with a hole in the seat / and it was in the Chapel of the Saviour, and after he was

Marlene You're not serious.

Joan elected the Pope had to sit in it.

Marlene And someone looked up his skirts? / Not really?

Isabella What an extraordinary thing.

Joan Two of the clergy / made sure he was a man.

Nijo On their hands and knees!

Marlene A pierced chair!

Gret Balls!

Griselda arrives unnoticed.

Nijo Why couldn't he just pull up his robe?

Joan He had to sit there and look dignified.

Marlene You could have made all your chamberlains sit in it.*

Gret Big one, small one.

Nijo Very useful chair at court.

Isabella *Or the laird of Tobermory in his kilt.

They are quite drunk. They get the giggles.
  Marlene notices Griselda.

Marlene Griselda! / There you are. Do you want to eat?

Griselda I'm sorry I'm so late. No, no, don't bother.

Marlene Of course it's no bother. / Have you eaten?

Griselda No really, I'm not hungry.

Marlene Well have some pudding.

Griselda I never eat pudding.

Marlene Griselda, I hope you're not anorexic. We're having
  pudding, I am, and getting nice and fat.

Griselda Oh if everyone is. I don't mind.

Marlene Now who do you know? This is Joan who was Pope in
  the ninth century, and Isabella Bird, the Victorian traveller, and
  Lady Nijo from Japan, Emperor's concubine and Buddhist
  nun, thirteenth century, nearer your own time, and Gret who
  was painted by Brueghel. Griselda's in Boccaccio and Petrarch
  and Chaucer because of her extraordinary marriage. I'd like
  profiteroles because they're disgusting.

Joan Zabaglione, please.

Isabella Apple pie / and cream.

Nijo What's this?

Marlene Zabaglione, it's Italian, it's what Joan's having, / it's
  delicious.

Nijo A Roman Catholic / dessert? Yes please.

Marlene Gret?

Gret Cake.

Griselda Just cheese and biscuits, thank you.

Marlene Yes, Griselda's life is like a fairy-story, except it starts
  with marrying the prince.

Griselda He's only a marquis, Marlene.

Marlene Well everyone for miles around is his liege and he's
  absolute lord of life and death and you were the poor but
  beautiful peasant girl and he whisked you off. / Near enough a
  prince.

Nijo How old were you?

Griselda Fifteen.

Nijo I was brought up in court circles and it was still a shock.
  Had you ever seen him before?

Griselda I'd seen him riding by, we all had. And he'd seen me in the fields with the sheep.*

Isabella I would have been well suited to minding sheep.

Nijo And Mr Nugent riding by.

Isabella Of course not, Nijo, I mean a healthy life in the open air.

Joan *He just rode up while you were minding the sheep and asked you to marry him?

Griselda No, no, it was on the wedding day. I was waiting outside the door to see the procession. Everyone wanted him to get married so there'd be an heir to look after us when he died, / and at last he announced a day for the wedding but

Marlene I don't think Walter wanted to get married. It is Walter? Yes.

Griselda nobody knew who the bride was, we thought it must be a foreign princess, we were longing to see her. Then the carriage stopped outside our cottage and we couldn't see the bride anywhere. And he came and spoke to my father.

Nijo And your father told you to serve the Prince.

Griselda My father could hardly speak. The Marquis said it wasn't an order, I could say no, but if I said yes I must always obey him in everything.

Marlene That's when you should have suspected.

Griselda But of course a wife must obey her husband. / And of course I must obey the Marquis.*

Isabella I swore to obey dear John, of course, but it didn't seem to arise. Naturally I wouldn't have wanted to go abroad while I was married.

Marlene *Then why bother to mention it at all? He'd got a thing about it, that's why.

Griselda I'd rather obey the Marquis than a boy from the village.

Marlene Yes, that's a point.

Joan I never obeyed anyone. They all obeyed me.

Nijo And what did you wear? He didn't make you get married in your own clothes? That would be perverse.*

Marlene Oh, you wait.

Griselda *He had ladies with him who undressed me and they had a white silk dress and jewels for my hair.

Marlene And at first he seemed perfectly normal?

Griselda Marlene, you're always so critical of him. / Of course he was normal, he was very kind.

Marlene But Griselda, come on, he took your baby.

Griselda Walter found it hard to believe I loved him. He couldn't believe I would always obey him. He had to prove it.

Marlene I don't think Walter likes women.

Griselda I'm sure he loved me, Marlene, all the time.

Marlene He just had a funny way / of showing it.

Griselda It was hard for him too.

Joan How do you mean he took away your baby?

Nijo Was it a boy?

Griselda No, the first one was a girl.

Nijo Even so it's hard when they take it away. Did you see it at all?

Griselda Oh yes, she was six weeks old.

Nijo Much better to do it straight away.

Isabella But why did your husband take the child?

Griselda He said all the people hated me because I was just one of them. And now I had a child they were restless. So he had to get rid of the child to keep them quiet. But he said he wouldn't snatch her, I had to agree and obey and give her up. So when I was feeding her a man came in and took her away. I thought he was going to kill her even before he was out of the room.

Marlene But you let him take her? You didn't struggle?

Griselda I asked him to give her back so I could kiss her. And I asked him to bury her where no animals could dig her up. / It

Isabella Oh my dear.

Griselda was Walter's child to do what he liked with.*

Marlene Walter was bonkers.

Gret Bastard.

Isabella *But surely, murder.

Griselda I had promised.

Marlene I can't stand this. I'm going for a pee.

Marlene goes out.
    The Waitress brings dessert.

Nijo No, I understand. Of course you had to, he was your life. And were you in favour after that?

Griselda Oh yes, we were very happy together. We never spoke about what had happened.

Isabella I can see you were doing what you thought was your duty. But didn't it make you ill?

Griselda No, I was very well, thank you.

Nijo And you had another child?

Griselda Not for four years, but then I did, yes, a boy.

Nijo Ah a boy. / So it all ended happily.

Griselda Yes he was pleased. I kept my son till he was two years old. A peasant's grandson. It made the people angry. Walter explained.

Isabella But surely he wouldn't kill his children / just because –

Griselda Oh it wasn't true. Walter would never give in to the people. He wanted to see if I loved him enough.

Joan He killed his children / to see if you loved him enough?

Nijo Was it easier the second time or harder?

Griselda It was always easy because I always knew I would do what he said.

Pause. They start to eat.

Isabella I hope you didn't have any more children.

Griselda Oh no, no more. It was twelve years till he tested me again.

Isabella So whatever did he do this time? / My poor John, I never loved him enough, and he would never have dreamt . . .

Griselda He sent me away. He said the people wanted him to marry someone else who'd give him an heir and he'd got special permission from the Pope. So I said I'd go home to my father. I came with nothing / so I went with nothing. I

Nijo Better to leave if your master doesn't want you.

Griselda took off my clothes. He let me keep a slip so he wouldn't be shamed. And I walked home barefoot. My father came out in tears. Everyone was crying except me.

Nijo At least your father wasn't dead. / I had nobody.

Isabella Well it can be a relief to come home. I loved to see Hennie's sweet face again.

Griselda Oh yes, I was perfectly content. And quite soon he sent for me again.

Joan I don't think I would have gone.

Griselda But he told me to come. I had to obey him. He wanted me to help prepare his wedding. He was getting married to a young girl from France / and nobody except me knew how to arrange things the way he liked them.

Nijo It's always hard taking him another woman.

Marlene comes back.

Joan I didn't live a woman's life. I don't understand it.

Griselda The girl was sixteen and far more beautiful than me. I could see why he loved her. / She had her younger brother with her as a page.

The Waitress enters.

Marlene Oh God, I can't bear it. I want some coffee. Six coffees. Six brandies. / Double brandies. Straightaway.

Griselda They all went in to the feast I'd prepared. And he stayed behind and put his arms round me and kissed me. / I felt half asleep with the shock.

Nijo Oh, like a dream.

Marlene And he said, 'This is your daughter and your son'.

Griselda Yes.

Joan What?

Nijo Oh. Oh I see. You got them back.

Isabella I did think it was remarkably barbaric to kill them but you learn not to say anything. / So he had them brought up secretly I suppose.

Marlene Walter's a monster. Weren't you angry? What did you do?

Griselda Well I fainted. Then I cried and kissed the children. / Everyone was making a fuss of me.

Nijo But did you feel anything for them?

Griselda What?

Nijo Did you feel anything for the children?

Griselda Of course, I loved them.

Joan So you forgave him and lived with him?

Griselda He suffered so much all those years.

Isabella Hennie had the same sweet nature.

Nijo So they dressed you again?

Griselda Cloth of gold.

Joan I can't forgive anything.

Marlene You really are exceptional, Griselda.

Nijo Nobody gave me back my children.

Nijo cries. The Waitress brings brandies.

Isabella I can never be like Hennie. I was always so busy in England, a kind of business I detested. The very presence of people exhausted my emotional reserves. I could not be like Hennie however I tried. I tried and was as ill as could be. The doctor suggested a steel net to support my head, the weight of my own head was too much for my diseased spine. / It is dangerous to put oneself in depressing circumstances. Why should I do it?

Joan Don't cry.

Nijo My father and the Emperor both died in the autumn. So much pain.

Joan Yes, but don't cry.

Nijo They wouldn't let me into the palace when he was dying. I hid in the room with his coffin, then I couldn't find where I'd left my shoes, I ran after the funeral procession in bare feet, I couldn't keep up. When I got there it was over, a few wisps of smoke in the sky, that's all that was left of him. What I want to know is, if I'd still been at court, would I have been allowed to wear full mourning?

Marlene I'm sure you would.

Nijo Why do you say that? You don't know anything about it. Would I have been allowed to wear full mourning?

Isabella How can people live in this dim pale island and wear our hideous clothes? I cannot and will not live the life of a lady.

Nijo I'll tell you something that made me angry. I was eighteen, at the Full Moon Ceremony. They make a special rice gruel and stir it with their sticks, and then they beat their women across the loins so they'll have sons and not daughters. So the Emperor beat us all / very hard as usual – that's not it,

Marlene What a sod.

Nijo Marlene, that's normal, what made us angry, he told his attendants they could beat us too. Well they had a wonderful time. / So Lady Genki and I made a plan, and the ladies all hid

The Waitress has entered with coffees.

Marlene I'd like another brandy please. Better make it six.

Nijo in his rooms, and Lady Mashimizu stood guard with a stick
at the door, and when His Majesty came in Genki seized him
and I beat him till he cried out and promised he would never
order anyone to hit us again. Afterwards there was a terrible
fuss. The nobles were horrified. 'We wouldn't even dream of
stepping on your Majesty's shadow.' And I had hit him with a
stick. Yes, I hit him with a stick.

Joan
Suave, mari magno turbantibus aequora ventis,
e terra magnum alterius spectare laborem;
non quia vexari quemquamst iucunda voluptas,
sed quibus ipse malis careas quia cernere suave est.
Suave etiam belli certamina magna tueri
per campos instructa tua sine parte pericli.
Sed nil dulcius est, bene quam munita tenere
edita doctrina sapientum templa serena, /
despicere unde queas alios passimque videre
errare atque viam palantis quaerere vitae,

Griselda I do think – I do wonder – it would have been nicer if
Walter hadn't had to.

Isabella Why should I? Why should I?

Marlene Of course not.

Nijo I hit him with a stick.

Joan
certare ingenio, contendere nobilitate,
noctes atque dies niti praestante labore
ad summas emergere opes retumque potiri.
O miseras / hominum mentis, o pectora caeca!*

Isabella Oh miseras!

Nijo *Pectora caeca.

Joan
qualibus in tenebris vitae quantisque periclis
degitur hoc aevi quodcumquest! / nonne videre
nil aliud sibi naturam latrare, nisi utqui
corpore seiunctus dolor absit, mente fruatur

Joan subsides.

Gret We come into hell through a big mouth. Hell's black and
red. / It's like the village where I come from. There's a river and
Marlene (*to Joan*) Shut up, pet.
Isabella Listen, she's been to hell.
Gret a bridge and houses. There's places on fire like when the
soldiers come. There's a big devil sat on a roof with a big hole
in his arse and he's scooping stuff out of it with a big ladle and
it's falling down on us, and it's money, so a lot of the women
stop and get some. But most of us is fighting the devils. There's
lots of little devils, our size, and we get them down all right and
give them a beating. There's lots of funny creatures round your
feet, you don't like to look, like rats and lizards, and nasty
things, a bum with a face, and fish with legs, and faces on
things that don't have faces on. But they don't hurt, you just
keep going. Well we'd had worse, you see, we'd had the
Spanish. We'd all had family killed. My big son die on a wheel.
Birds eat him. My baby, a soldier run her through with a
sword. I'd had enough, I was mad, I hate the bastards. I come
out my front door that morning and shout till my neighbours
come out and I said, 'Come on, we're going where the evil
come from and pay the bastards out.' And they all come out
just as they was / from baking or washing in their
Nijo All the ladies come.
Gret aprons, and we push down the street and the ground opens
up and we go through a big mouth into a street just like ours
but in hell. I've got a sword in my hand from somewhere and I
fill a basket with gold cups they drink out of down there. You
just keep running on and fighting / you didn't stop for nothing.
Oh we give them devils such a beating.
Nijo Take that, take that.
Joan
Something something something mortisque timores
tum vacuum pectus – damn.
Quod si ridicula –
something something on and on and on and something
   splendorem purpureai.
Isabella I thought I would have a last jaunt up the west river in
China. Why not? But the doctors were so very grave. I just
went to Morocco. The sea was so wild I had to be landed by

ship's crane in a coal bucket. / My horse was a terror to me a
Gret Coal bucket, good.
Joan
   nos in luce timemus
   something
   terrorem.
Isabella powerful black charger.

Nijo is laughing and crying.
   Joan gets up and is sick in a corner.
   Marlene is drinking Isabella's brandy.

So off I went to visit the Berber sheikhs in full blue trousers and
great brass spurs. I was the only European woman ever to have
seen the Emperor of Morocco. I was seventy years old. What
lengths to go to for a last chance of joy. I knew my return of
vigour was only temporary, but how marvellous while it lasted.

End of Act One

The Love of the Nightingale

TIMBERLAKE WERTENBAKER

Timberlake Wertenbaker was resident writer at the Royal Court Theatre in 1984–5. Plays include *The Third* (King's Head), *Case to Answer* (Soho Poly), *New Anatomies* (ICA), *Abel's Sister* (Royal Court, Theatre Upstairs), *The Grace of Mary Traverse* (Royal Court, main stage), *Our Country's Good* (Royal Court, main stage, West End and Broadway), winner of the Laurence Olivier Play of the Year Award in 1988 and New York Drama Critics' Circle Award for Best New Foreign Play in 1991, *The Love of the Nightingale* (Royal Shakespeare Company's Other Place, Stratford-upon-Avon), which won the 1989 Eileen Anderson Central TV Drama Award, *Three Birds Alighting on a Field* (Royal Court, main stage), which won the Susan Smith Blackburn Award and Writers' Guild Award in 1992, *The Break of Day* (Out of Joint Production, Royal Court and touring, 1995) and *After Darwin* (Hampstead Theatre, 1998). She wrote the screenplay of *The Children* based on Edith Wharton's novel, and a BBC2 film entitled *Do Not Disturb*. Translations include Marivaux's *False Admissions and Successful Strategies* for Shared Experience, Marivaux's *La Dispute*, Jean Anouilh's *Leocadia*, Maurice Maeterlinck's *Pelleas and Melisande* for BBC Radio, Ariane Mnouchkine's *Mephisto*, adapted for the RSC in 1986, Sophocles' *The Theban Plays* (RSC, 1991), Euripides' *Hecuba* (San Francisco, 1995), Eduardo de Fillippo's *Filumena* (Peter Hall Company at the Piccadilly Theatre, 1998) and Pirandello's *Come tu mi vuoi*.

The Love of the Nightingale was first performed by the Royal Shakespeare Company at the Other Place, Stratford-upon-Avon, on 28 October 1988. The cast was as follows:

Male chorus David Acton, Stephen Gordon, Richard Haddon Haines, Patrick Miller, Edward Rawle-Hicks
First Soldier Patrick Miller
Second Soldier David Acton
Procne Marie Mullen
Philomele Katy Behean
King Pandion Richard Haddon Haines
The Queen Joan Blackham
Tereus Peter Lennon

Female chorus
Hero Cate Hamer
Iris Claudette Williams
June Joan Blackham
Echo Joanna Roth
Helen Jill Spurrier

Actors in the Hippolytus play
Aphrodite Claudette Williams
Phaedra Cate Hamer
The Nurse Jill Spurrier
Female Chorus Joanna Roth
Hippolytus Edward Rawle-Hicks
Theseus David Acton
Male Chorus Stephen Gordon

The Captain Tony Armatrading
Niobe Jenni George
Servant Joanna Roth
Itys Nicholas Besley/Alexander Knott

Directed by Garry Hynes
Lighting by Geraint Pughe
Music by Ilona Sekacz

Note on the Chorus
The Chorus never speak together, except the one time it is
specifically indicated in the text.

SCENE ONE

Athens. The Male Chorus

Male Chorus War.

Two Soldiers come on, with swords and shields.

First Soldier You cur!
Second Soldier You cat's whisker.
First Soldier You flea's foot.
Second Soldier You particle. (*Pause.*) You son of a bitch.
Second Soldier You son of a bleeding whore.
First Soldier You son of a woman! (*Pause.*) I'll slice your
drooping genitalia.
Second Soldier I'll pierce your windy asshole.
First Soldier I'll drink from your skull. (*Pause.*) Coward!
Second Soldier Braggard.
First Soldier You worm.
Second Soldier You – man.

They fight.

Male Chorus And now, death.

The First Soldier kills the Second Soldier.

Second Soldier Murderer!
First Soldier Corpse!
Male Chorus We begin here because no life ever has been
untouched by war.
Male Chorus Everyone loves to discuss war.
Male Chorus And yet its outcome, death, is shrouded in silence.
Male Chorus Wars make death acceptable. The gods are less
cruel if it is man's fault.
Male Chorus Perhaps, but this is not our story. War is the

inevitable background, the ruins in the distance establishing place and perspective.

Male Chorus Athens is at war, but in the palace of the Athenian king Pandion, two sisters discuss life's charms and the attractions of men.

SCENE TWO

Procne, Philomele.

Procne Don't say that, Philomele.

Philomele It's the truth: he's so handsome I want to wrap my legs around him.

Procne That's not how it's done.

Philomele How can I know if no one will tell me? Look at the sweat shining down his body. My feet will curl around the muscles of his back. How is it done, Procne, tell me, please? If you don't tell me, I'll ask Niobe and she'll tell me all wrong.

Procne I'll tell you if you tell me something.

Philomele I'll tell you everything I know, sweet sister. (*Pause.*) I don't know anything.

Procne You know yourself.

Philomele Oh, yes, I feel such things, Procne, such things. Tigers, rivers, serpents, here, in my stomach, a little below. I'll tell you how the serpent uncurls inside me if you tell me how it's done.

Procne That's not what I meant. Philomele, I'm going to marry soon.

Philomele I envy you, sister, you'll know everything then. What are they like? Men?

Procne Look: they fight.

Philomele What are they like: naked?

Procne Spongy.

Philomele What?

Procne I haven't seen one yet, but that's what they told me to prepare me. They have sponges.

Philomele Where?

Procne Here. Getting bigger and smaller and moving up and down. I didn't listen very carefully, I'll know soon enough.

Philomele, when I am married, will you want to come and visit me?

Philomele Yes, sister, yes. I'll visit you every day and you'll let me watch.

Procne Philomele! Can't you think of anything else?

Philomele Not today. Tomorrow I'll think about wisdom. It must be so beautiful. Warm ripples of light.

Procne I think most of it you can do on your own. The sponge. I think it detaches.

Philomele I wouldn't want to do it on my own. I want to run my hands down bronzed skin. Ah, I can feel the tiger again.

Procne If I went far away, would you still want to come and visit me?

Philomele I will cross any sea to visit you and your handsome husband, sister. (*Pause.*) When I'm old enough, I won't stop doing it, whatever it is. Life must be so beautiful when you're older. It's beautiful now. Sometimes I'm so happy.

Procne Quiet, Philomele! Never say you're happy. It wakes up the gods and then they look at you and that is never a good thing. Take it back, now.

Philomele You taught me not to lie, sister.

Procne I wish I didn't have to leave home. I worry about you.

Philomele Life is sweet, my sister, and I love everything in it. The feelings. Athens. You. And that brave young warrior fighting to protect us. Oh!

Procne Philomele? Ah.

Philomele He's dead.

Philomele Crumpled. Procne, was it my fault? Should I have held my tongue?

Procne Athens is at war, men must die.

Philomele I'm frightened. I don't want to leave this room, ever.

Procne You must try to become more moderate. Measure in all things, remember, it's what the philosophers recommend.

Philomele Will the philosophers start speaking again after the war? Procne, can we go and listen to them?

Procne I won't be here.

Philomele Procne, don't go.

Procne It's our parents' will. They know best. (*Pause.*) You will come to me if I ask for you, you will?

Philomele Yes.

Procne I want you to promise. Remember you must never break a promise.

Philomele I promise. I will want to. I promise again.

Procne That makes me happy. Ah.

SCENE THREE

The palace of King Pandion. King Pandion, the Queen, Tereus, Procne, Philomele, the Male Chorus.

Male Chorus Athens won the war with the help of an ally from the north.

Male Chorus The leader of the liberators was called Tereus.

King Pandion No liberated country is ungrateful. This is a rule. You will take what you want from our country. It will be given with gratitude. We are ready.

Tereus I came not out of greed but in the cause of justice, King Pandion. But I have come to love this country and its inhabitants.

Queen (*to King Pandion*) He wants to stay! I knew it! (*Pause.*)

King Pandion Of course if you wish to stay in Athens that is your right. We can only remind you this is a small city. But you must stay if you wish.

Tereus No. I must go back north. There has been trouble while I've conducted this war. What I want – is to bring some of your country to mine, its manners, its ease, its civilized discourse.

Queen (*to King Pandion*) I knew it: he wants Procne.

King Pandion I can send you some of our tutors. The philosophers, I'm afraid, are rather independent.

Tereus I have always believed that culture was kept by the women.

King Pandion Ours are not encouraged to go abroad.

Tereus But they have a reputation for wisdom. Is that false?

Queen Be careful, he's crafty.

King Pandion It is true. Our women are the best.

Tereus So.

Queen I knew it.

Pause.

King Pandion She's yours, Tereus. Procne –
Procne But, Father –
King Pandion Your husband.
Procne Mother –
Queen What can I say?
King Pandion I am only sad you will live so far away.
Philomele Can I go with her?
Queen Quiet, child.
Tereus (*to Procne*) I will love and respect you.
Male Chorus It didn't happen that quickly. It took months and much indirect discourse. But that is the gist of it. The end was known from the beginning.
Male Chorus After an elaborate wedding in which King Pandion solemnly gave his daughter to the hero, Tereus, the two left for Thrace. There was relief in Athens. His army had become expensive, rude, rowdy.
Male Chorus Had always been, but we see things differently in peace. That is why peace is so painful.
Male Chorus Nothing to blur the waters. We look down to the bottom.
Male Chorus And on a clear day, we see our own reflections.

Pause.

Male Chorus In due course, Procne had a child, a boy called Itys. Five years passed.

SCENE FOUR

Procne and her companions, the Female Chorus: Hero, Echo, Iris, June, Helen.

Procne Where have all the words gone?
Hero She sits alone, hour after hour, turns her head away and laments.
Iris We don't know how to act, we don't know what to say.
Hero She turns from us in grief.
June Boredom.

Echo Homesick.

Hero It is difficult to come to a strange land.

Helen You will always be a guest there, never call it your own, never rest in the kindness of history.

Echo Your story intermingled with events, no. You will be outside.

Iris And if it is the land of your husband can you even say you have chosen it?

June She is not one of us.

Hero A shared childhood makes friends between women.

Echo The places we walked together, our first smells.

Helen But an unhappy woman can do much harm. She has already dampened our play.

June Mocked the occupation of our hours, scorned.

Iris What shall we do?

Helen I fear the future.

Procne Where have the words gone?

Echo Gone, Procne, the words?

Procne There were so many. Everything that was had a word and every word was something. None of these meanings half in the shade, unclear.

Iris We speak the same language, Procne.

Procne The words are the same, but point to different things. We aspire to clarity in sound, you like the silences in between.

Hero We offered to initiate you.

Procne Barbarian practices. I am an Athenian: I know the truth is found by logic and happiness lies in the truth.

Hero Truth is full of darkness.

Procne No, truth is good and beautiful. See . . . (*Pause.*) I must have someone to talk to.

June We've tried. See . . .

Hero She turns away.

Procne How we talked. Our words played, caressed each other, our words were tossed lightly, a challenge to catch. Where is she now? Who shares those games with her? Or is she silent too?

Echo Silent, Procne, who?

Procne My sister. (*Pause.*) My friend. I want to talk to her. I want her here.

Hero You have a family, Procne, a husband, a child.

Procne I cannot talk to my husband. I have nothing to say to my son. I want her here. She must come here.

Hero It's a long way and a dangerous one for a young girl.

Helen Let her be, Procne.

Procne I want my sister here.

Helen She could come to harm.

Procne Tereus could bring her, she'll be safe with him.

Echo Tereus.

Helen Dangers on the sea, he won't want you to risk them.

Procne He can go alone. I'll wait here and look after the country.

Echo Tereus.

Hero Will your sister want to come to a strange land?

Procne She will want what I want.

Helen Don't ask her to come, Procne.

Procne Why not?

Hero This is no country for a strange young girl.

Procne She will be with me.

Hero She won't listen.

Helen I am worried. It is not something I can say. There are no words for forebodings.

Hero We are only brushed by possibilities.

Echo A beating of wings.

June Best to say nothing. Procne? May we go now?

Procne To your rituals?

June Yes, it's time.

Procne Very well, go.

They go.

This silence . . . this silence . . .

SCENE FIVE

The theatre in Athens. King Pandion, Tereus, Hippolytus, Theseus.

King Pandion Procne has always been so sensible. Why, suddenly, does she ask for her sister?

Tereus She didn't explain. She insisted I come to you and I did what she asked.

King Pandion I understand, Tereus, but such a long journey . . . Procne's not ill?

Tereus She was well when I left. She has her child, companions.

King Pandion Philomele is still very young. And yet, I allowed Procne to go so far away . . . What do you think, Tereus?

Tereus You're her father.

King Pandion And you, her husband.

Tereus I only meant Procne would accept any decision you made. It is a long journey.

Aphrodite enters.

Aphrodite I am Aphrodite, goddess of love, resplendent and mighty, revered on earth, courted in heaven, all pay tribute to my fearful power.

King Pandion Do you know this play, Tereus?

Tereus No.

King Pandion I find plays help me think. You catch a phrase, recognize a character. Perhaps this play will help us come to a decision.

Aphrodite I honour those who kneel before me, but that proud heart which dares defy me, that haughty heart I bring low.

Tereus That's sound.

King Pandion Do you have good theatre in Thrace?

Tereus We prefer sport.

King Pandion Then you are like Hippolytus.

Tereus Who?

King Pandion Listen.

Aphrodite Hippolytus turns his head away. Hippolytus prefers the hard chase to the soft bed, wild game to foreplay, but chaste Hippolytus shall be crushed this very day.

Aphrodite exits. The Queen and Philomele enter.

Philomele We're late! I've missed Aphrodite.

King Pandion She only told us it was going to end badly, but we already know that. It's a tragedy.

Enter Phaedra.

Queen There's Phaedra. (*to Tereus*) Phaedra is married to Theseus, the King of Athens. Hippolytus is Theseus' son by his previous mistress, the Amazon Queen, who's now dead, and so Phaedra's stepson. Phaedra has three children of her own.

Phaedra Hold me, hold me, hold up my head. The strength of my limbs is melting away.

Philomele How beautiful to love like that! The strength of my limbs is melting away. Is that what you feel for Procne, Tereus?

Queen Philomele! (*to Tereus*) Phaedra's fallen in love with Hippolytus.

Tereus Her own stepson! That's wrong.

King Pandion That's what makes it a tragedy. When you love the right person it's a comedy.

Phaedra Oh, pity me, pity me, what have I done? What will become of me? I have strayed from the path of good sense.

Tereus Why should we pity her? These plays condone vice.

King Pandion Perhaps they only show us the uncomfortable folds of the human heart.

Phaedra I am mad, struck down by the malice of the implacable god.

Philomele You see, Tereus, love is a god and you cannot control him.

Queen Here's the nurse. She always gives advice.

The Nurse enters.

Nurse So: you love. You are not the first nor the last. You want to kill yourself? Must all who love lie? No, Phaedra, the god has stricken you, how dare you rebel? Be bold, and love. That is god's will.

Tereus Terrible advice.

Philomele No, Tereus, you must obey the gods. Are you blasphemous up there in Thrace?

King Pandion Philomele, you are talking to a king.

Tereus And to a brother, let her speak, Pandion.

Nurse I have a remedy. Trust me.

King Pandion Procne has asked for you. She wants you to go back with Tereus to Thrace.

Philomele To Thrace? To Procne? Oh, yes.

King Pandion You want to leave your parents? Athens?

Philomele I promised Procne I would go if she ever asked for me.

King Pandion You were a child.

Tereus We have no theatre or even philosophers in Thrace, Philomele.

Philomele I have to keep my word.

Tereus Why?

Philomele Because that is honourable, Tereus.

Queen Listen to the chorus. The playwright always speaks through the chorus.

Female Chorus Love, stealing with grace into the heart you wish to destroy, love, turning us blind with the bitter poison of desire, love, come not my way. And when you whirl through the streets, wild steps to unchained rhythms, love, I pray you, brush not against me, love, I beg you, pass me by.

Tereus Ah!

Philomele I would never say that, would you, brother Tereus? I want to feel everything there is to feel. Don't you?

Tereus No!

King Pandion Tereus, what's the matter?

Tereus Nothing. The heat.

Phaedra Oh, I am destroyed for ever.

Philomele Poor Phaedra.

Tereus You pity her, Philomele?

Queen Hippolytus has just heard in what way Phaedra loves him. He's furious.

Hippolytus Woman, counterfeit coin, why did the gods put you in the world? If we must have sons, let us buy them in the temples and bypass the concourse of these noxious women. I hate you women, hate, hate and hate you.

Philomele This is horrible. It's not Phaedra's fault she loves him.

Tereus She could keep silent about it.

Philomele When you love you want to imprison the one you love in your words, in your tenderness.

Tereus How do you know all this, Philomele?

Philomele Sometimes I feel the whole world beating inside me.

Tereus Philomele . . .

Phaedra screams offstage, then staggers on.

34

Queen Phaedra's killed herself and there's Theseus just back from his travels.

Theseus My wife! What have I said or done to drive you to this horrible death? She calls me to her, she can still speak. What prayers, what orders, what entreaties do you leave your grieving husband? Oh, my poor love, speak! (*He listens.*) Hippolytus! Has dared to rape my wife!

Tereus Phaedra has lied! That's vile.

Philomele Why destroy what you love? It's the god.

Theseus Father Poseidon, great and ancient sea-god, you once allotted me three wishes. With one of these, I pray you now, kill my son.

Queen That happens offstage. A giant wave comes out of the sea and crashes Hippolytus's chariot against the rocks. Here's the male chorus.

Male Chorus Sometimes I believe in a kind power, wise and all-knowing but when I see the acts of men and their destinies, my hopes grow dim. Fortune twists and turns and life is endless wandering.

King Pandion The play's coming to an end, and I still haven't reached a decision. Queen . . .

Male Chorus What I want from life is to be ordinary.

Philomele How boring.

Queen Hippolytus has come back to Athens to die. He's wounded. The head.

Female Chorus Poor Hippolytus, I weep at your pitiful fate. And I rage against the gods who sent you far away, out of your father's lands to meet with such disaster from the sea-god's wave.

King Pandion That's the phrase. Philomele, you must not leave your father's lands. You'll stay here.

Philomele But, Father, I'm not Hippolytus. You haven't cursed me. And Tereus isn't Phaedra, look. (*She laughs.*)

Tereus I have expert sailors, I don't think we'll crash against the rocks.

King Pandion It's such a long journey.

Tereus We must go soon, or she'll fall ill with worry.

King Pandion When?

Tereus Tomorrow.

Hippolytus Weep for me, weep for me, destroyed, mangled, trampled underfoot by man and god both unjust, weep, weep for my death.

Philomele Ah.

Tereus You're crying, Philomele.

Philomele I felt, I felt – the beating of wings . . .

King Pandion You do not have to go.

Philomele It's the play, I am so sorry for them all. I have to go. My promise . . .

King Pandion (*to Queen*) It's only a visit, Philomele will come back to us.

Queen Where is she going?

King Pandion To Thrace! Weren't you listening?

Male and Female Chorus (*together*) These sorrows have fallen upon us unforeseen.

Male Chorus Fate is irresistible.

Female Chorus And there is no escape.

King Pandion And now we must applaud the actors.

SCENE SIX

A small ship, sailing north. The Male Chorus, Philomele, Tereus, the Captain.

Male Chorus The journey north:
Row gently out of Piraeus on a starlight night. Sail around Cape Sounion with a good wind, over to Kea for water and provisions. Kea to Andros, a quiet sea. Up the coast of Euboea to the Sporades: Skiathos, Paparethos, Gioura, Pathoura. Skirt the three fingered promontory of the mainland: Kassandra, Sithounia and Athos of the wild men and into the Thracian sea. The dawns, so loved by the poets.

Male Chorus Rosy fingered, female.

Male Chorus The dawns get colder and colder as we sail north.

Pause.

Male Chorus Philomele wonders at the beauty of the sea.

Male Chorus Tereus wonders at Philomele's beauty.

Male Chorus We say nothing. And when the order comes.

Male Chorus Such an order.

Male Chorus Six Athenian soldiers have been sent to accompany Philomele. They stand on the deck, watching. On a dark night, they disappear.

Pause.

Male Chorus In the cold dawns, Tereus burns.

Male Chorus Does Philomele know? Ought we to tell her? We are here only to observe, journalists of an antique world, putting horror into words, unable to stop the events we will soon record.

Male Chorus And so we reach the lonely port of Imeros. It is dark, there is no welcome.

Male Chorus We are not expected.

Male Chorus No moon in the sky.

Male Chorus This is unpropitious.

Male Chorus But that we already knew. Could we have done something? And now?

Male Chorus We choose to be accurate, and we record:

SCENE SEVEN

The Captain, Philomele, Niobe.

Philomele Where are we now, Captain?

Captain Far north of Athens, miss.

Philomele I know that, Captain. How far are we from Thrace?

Captain A few days, perhaps more. It depends.

Philomele On you?

Captain No. On the sea.

Philomele Isn't that a fire over there?

Captain Yes.

Philomele That means we're not far from the coast, doesn't it?

Captain Yes, it does.

Philomele Look how high the fire is. It must be a mountain, Captain.

Captain Yes, it is.

Philomele What is it called, Captain, what is it like? I would like to know about all these lands. You must tell me.

Captain That would be Mount Athos, miss.

Philomele Why don't we anchor there, Captain, and climb the mountain?

Captain You wouldn't want to go there, miss.

Philomele Why not, is it ugly?

Captain No, but wild men live there, very wild. They kill all women, even female animals are not allowed on that mountain.

Philomele Why not?

Captain They worship male gods. They believe all harm in the world comes from women.

Philomele Why do they believe that? (*Pause.*) You don't agree with them, do you, Captain?

Captain I don't know, miss.

Philomele If you don't disagree, you agree with them, Captain, that's logic.

Captain Women are beautiful.

Philomele But surely you believe that beauty is truth and goodness as well?

Captain That I don't know. I would have to think about it.

Philomele I'll prove it to you now, I once heard a philosopher do it. I will begin by asking you a lot of questions. You answer yes or no. But you must pay attention. Are you ready?

Captain I think so.

Philomele And when I've proved all this, Captain, you will have to renounce the beliefs of those wild men.

Captain I might.

Philomele You have to promise.

Tereus enters.

Tereus Why are the sails up, Captain?

Captain We have a good wind, Tereus.

Tereus Take them down.

Captain We could be becalmed further north and then my men will have to row. They're tired, Tereus.

Tereus We're sailing too fast, it's frightening Philomele.

Philomele I love to feel the wind, Tereus.

38

Tereus Why aren't you asleep?

Philomele It's such a beautiful night. I was watching the fires on
Athos.

Tereus Athos? Yes, the hooded men.

Philomele The Captain was telling me about them.

Tereus Lower the sails, Captain.

Captain But Tereus –

Tereus This isn't a battle, we have time.

Exit the Captain.

Niobe I'll take Philomele down with me, my lord.

Tereus Not yet. (*Pause.*) Come and talk to me, Philomele.

Niobe Entertain his lordship, Philomele.

Silence.

Tereus Well. You were talking easily enough when I came
above.

Philomele Tell me about my sister, Tereus.

Tereus I've already told you.

Philomele Tell me more. How does she occupy her time?

Tereus I don't know. She has women with her.

Philomele What do they talk about?

Tereus What women talk about. I didn't ask you to grill me,
Philomele. Talk to me. Talk to me about the night.

Philomele The night?

Pause.

Tereus The night. Something! What were you saying to the
captain?

Philomele I was asking him questions, Tereus.

Silence. The Sailors sing a song, softly.

Philomele How well they sing.

Pause.

Tereus Do you want to be married, Philomele?

Niobe Oh, yes, my lord. Every young girl wants to be married.
Don't you, Philomele?

Philomele Niobe, go to bed, please.

Niobe No, I can't. I mustn't. I will stay here. I must.

Philomele Why?

Niobe It wouldn't be right . . . A young girl. A man.

Philomele I am with my brother, Niobe.

Tereus You can go, Niobe.

Niobe Yes, yes. Well . . . I will go and talk to the sailors.
Although what they will say to an old woman . . . no one
wants to talk to an old woman. But so it is . . . I'm not far, I'm
not far. The Queen said I was not to go far . . .

Pause.

Tereus You're beautiful.

Philomele Procne always said I was. But the Athenians admired
her because of her dignity. Has she kept that in all her years?

Tereus In the moonlight, your skin seems transparent.

Philomele We used to put water out in the full moon and wash
our faces in it. We thought it would give us the skin of a
goddess. I still do it in memory of my sister. Does she still let
out that rhythmical laugh when she thinks you're being
foolish? Always on one note, then stopped abruptly. Does she
laugh with her women?

Tereus I don't know . . .

Philomele Does she laugh at you?

Tereus Philomele.

Philomele Yes, brother.

Tereus What sort of man do you want to marry? A king?

Philomele Why not? A great king. Or a prince. Or a noble
captain.

Tereus Not necessarily from Athens?

Philomele No. As long as he is wise.

Tereus Wise?

Philomele But then, all kings are wise, aren't they? They have to
be or they wouldn't be kings.

Tereus You are born a king. Nothing can change that.

Philomele But you still have to deserve it, don't you?

Tereus Would you marry a king from the north? Like your
sister? Would you do as your sister in all things?

Philomele What do you mean? Oh, look, they're making fun of
Niobe. Niobe! Here!

Niobe They say I would be beautiful if I were young and if I were beautiful then I would be young, no one is kind to an old woman, but I don't mind, I've seen the world. You made his lordship laugh, Philomele, I heard it, that's good. All is well when power smiles, that I know.

Tereus Philomele wants to marry a king from the north.

Niobe Why yes, a man as great and brave as you.

Philomele I am happy for my sister and that is enough for me.

Niobe Sisters, sisters . . .

Tereus If Procne were . . .

Niobe I had sisters . . .

Philomele Procne.

Tereus To become ill . . .

Philomele What are you saying, Tereus? Wasn't she well when you left? Why didn't you tell me? Why are we going so slowly? Tell the captain to go faster.

Tereus I didn't say that, but if . . .

Niobe Yes, I had many sisters.

Tereus Things happen.

Niobe Too many . . .

Philomele My love will protect her, and yours too, Tereus.

Tereus Yes . . . But should . . .

Niobe They died.

Philomele Niobe!

Niobe I only want to help. I know the world. Old women do. But I'll be quiet now, very quiet.

Philomele Sister. We will be so happy.

Tereus Philomele.

SCENE EIGHT

The Male Chorus.

Male Chorus What is a myth? The oblique image of an unwanted truth, reverberating through time.

Male Chorus And yet, the first, the Greek meaning of myth, is simply what is delivered by word of mouth, a myth is speech, public speech.

Male Chorus And myth also means the matter itself, the content of the speech.

Male Chorus We might ask, has the content become increasingly unacceptable and therefore the speech more indirect? How has the meaning of myth been transformed from public speech to an unlikely story? It also meant counsel, command. Now it is a remote tale.

Male Chorus Let that be, there is no content without its myth. Fathers and sons, rebellion, collaboration, the state, every fold and twist of passion, we have uttered them all. This one, you will say, watching Philomele watching Tereus watching Philomele, must be about men and women, yes, you think, a myth for our times, we understand.

Male Chorus You will be beside the myth. If you must think of anything, think of countries, silence, but we cannot rephrase it for you. If we could, why would we trouble to show you the myth?

We row Philomele north. Does she notice the widening cracks in that fragile edifice, happiness? And what about Procne, the cause perhaps, in any case the motor of a myth that leaves her mostly absent?

SCENE NINE

Procne and the Female Chorus.

Hero Sometimes I feel I know things but I cannot prove that I know them or that what I know is true and when I doubt my knowledge it disintegrates into a senseless jumble of possibilities, a puzzle that will not be reassembled, the spider web in which I lie, immobile, and truth paralysed.

Helen Let me put it another way: I have trouble expressing myself. The world I see and the words I have do not match.

June I am the ugly duckling of fact, so most of the time I try to keep out of the way.

Echo Quiet. I shouldn't be here at all.

Iris But sometimes it's too much and I must speak. Procne.

Procne What are you women muttering about this time? Something gloomy, no doubt.

Iris Procne, we sense danger.

Procne You always sense something, and when I ask you what, you say you don't know, it hasn't happened yet, but it will, or it might. Well, what is it now? What danger? This place is safe. No marauding bands outside, no earthquake, what? What?

Hero I say danger, she thinks of earthquakes. Doesn't know the first meaning of danger is the power of a lord or master.

Helen That one is always in someone's danger.

Echo In their power, at their mercy.

June All service is danger and all marriage too.

Iris Procne, listen to me.

Procne What now?

Hero The sky was so dark this morning . . .

Procne It'll rain. It always rains.

Iris Again.

Hero I was not talking meteorologically. Images require sympathy.

Echo Another way of listening.

Iris Procne.

Procne Yes, yes, yes.

Hero Your sister is on the sea.

Procne She's been on the sea for a month. Have you just found that out?

Helen But the sea, the sea . . .

Hero And Tereus is a young man.

Echo Tereus.

Procne He'll move that much more quickly. Tell me something I don't know.

Hero When it's too late, it's easy to find the words.

Iris Procne.

Procne Leave me alone.

Iris If you went down to the seaport. Met them there.

Echo A welcome . . .

Procne I promised Tereus I would stay here and look after his country. I will wait for him here.

Iris Procne.

Procne Enough of your nonsense. Be silent.

Helen Silent.

Echo Silent.

SCENE TEN

The Male Chorus, First Soldier, Second Soldier, Tereus.

Male Chorus We camp on a desolate beach. Days pass.
First Soldier Why are we still here?
Second Soldier Tereus has his reasons.
First Soldier I want to go home.
Second Soldier We can't until we have the order.
First Soldier It's no more than four days' walk to the palace. Why are we still here?
Second Soldier I told you: because we haven't been ordered to move.
First Soldier Why not?
Second Soldier You ask too many questions.
Male Chorus Questions. The child's instinct suppressed in the adult.
Male Chorus For the sake of order, peace.
Male Chorus But at what price?
Male Chorus I wouldn't want to live in a world that's always shifting. Questions are like earthquakes. If you're lucky, it's just a rumble.
First Soldier Why don't we ask Tereus if we can go home? I want to see my girl.
Second Soldier He wants to see his wife.
First Soldier How do you know?
Second Soldier He would, wouldn't he?
First Soldier Then why are we here?
Second Soldier Ask him.
First Soldier Why don't you?
Male Chorus More days pass. We all wait.
First Soldier Why don't we talk to him together? Respectful, friendly.
Second Soldier And say what?
First Soldier Ask him if he's had any news of home. Tell him how nice it is. And spring's coming.
Second Soldier I'd leave out the bit about spring.
First Soldier Why?
Second Soldier Ready? (*Pause.*) Not today. He's worried.

First Soldier What about me?

Second Soldier You're not a king. His worry is bigger than yours.

First Soldier Why?

Second Soldier It's more interesting.

Male Chorus Days.

Male Chorus Days.

Second Soldier Tereus?

Tereus Yes.

Second Soldier He wants to speak to you.

Tereus Speak.

First Soldier Speak.

Second Soldier Euh?

Pause. Tereus turns away.

First Soldier Why are we here?

Second Soldier What are we waiting for?

First Soldier Why aren't we going home?

Second Soldier Why haven't any messengers been sent to tell everyone we're safe?

First Soldier We want to go home.

Second Soldier We've had enough.

Pause.

Tereus I have my reasons.

Male Chorus An old phrase, but it buys time. More days.

First Soldier What reasons?

Second Soldier Yes, what reasons?

Tereus You must trust me. (*Pause.*) Am I not your leader?

Second Soldier Yes, Tereus, but –

Tereus My knowledge is greater than yours, that is my duty, just as yours is to trust me. Think: when you fight wars with me, you see only part of the battle, the few enemies you kill, or your own wounds. Sometimes this seems terrible to you, I know, but later you see the victory and the glory of your country. That glory, fame, I have seen all along.

Second Solder Yes, Tereus, but.

First Soldier Where's the enemy?

Tereus I have information.

Male Chorus More days.

Second Soldier Why do we have to wait so long?

First Soldier For what?

Second Soldier It's this waiting makes me afraid. I'd rather something happened, anything.

Tereus I know this is difficult for you. (*Pause.*) It's difficult for me. (*Pause.*) You're experienced soldiers, responsible citizens, I trust you not to risk the safety and honour of your country because you don't understand yet. Trust me and you'll understand all in time.

Male Chorus In time . . .

Male Chorus What hasn't been said and done in the name of the future? A future always in someone else's hands. We waited, without the pain of responsibility for that promised time, the good times. We asked no more questions and at night, we slept soundly, and did not see:

SCENE ELEVEN

Philomele, Niobe, Tereus.

Tereus Philomele.

Philomele (*to Niobe*) Why does he follow me everywhere? Even Procne left me alone sometimes.

Niobe Don't make him angry!

Philomele Let's ignore him.

Tereus Philomele.

Philomele It's spring. Look at these flowers, Niobe, we have them in the woods near Athens. I'll bring some to Procne.

Tereus Philomele.

Philomele And here is some wild thyme, and that is xorta. Procne loves its bitter taste.

Tereus Philomele.

Philomele What is this plant, Niobe? Smell it. It's salty, never seen it before. Procne will know.

Tereus Philomele!

Philomele Quiet, brother, you're disturbing the butterflies. Procne would not like that.

Tereus Procne. Procne. Procne is dead. (*Silence.*) There is a
mountain not far from the palace. She climbed it with her
women to see if she could catch sight of the sea. On a clear day
you can look at the sea from there. She climbed to the top, but
there was a tall rock and she said she would climb that as well,
to see us, to welcome the ship. The women begged her not to,
no one would follow her. The rock is slippery and on the other
side drops straight into the river below. She climbed, climbed
higher to welcome her sister and stood there, waving, safe, the
women thought. But then she seemed to grow dizzy, she cried
out and suddenly fell, down the rock, down the cliff, into the
river swollen now because of the winter rains. They are still
looking for her body, it was carried with the torrent. Perhaps
better not to find it.

Niobe Yes, better. Never look at a battered body, it is worse than
the death that came to it.

Tereus Mourn, Philomele, mourn with me. She was my wife.

Philomele Procne.

Tereus Procne.

Niobe Procne.

Philomele begins to cry and scream. Tereus takes her in his arms.

Tereus Sister, beloved sister. My sister.

Philomele Procne. No! I want to see her body!

Chorus Nor did we see, still sleeping:

SCENE TWELVE

Philomele, the Captain, Niobe.

Philomele How long have we been in this place forsaken by the
gods, Captain?

Captain Almost a full month, Philomele.

Philomele Why? (*Pause.*) I can't mourn my sister here. Let me at
least remember her where she lived all those years. Why do we
wait and wait, for what?

Captain There may be trouble. Tereus keeps these things to
himself.

Philomele And you, Captain, where will you go?

Captain I'm waiting for orders.

Philomele South?

Captain Perhaps.

Philomele You won't say, you've been asked not to say, why?

Captain You ask too many questions, Philomele.

Philomele And you ask none, why? (*Pause.*) Do you love the sea?

Captain Sometimes.

Philomele I used to watch you at night, standing on your deck, an immense solitude around you. You seemed a king of elements, ordering the wind.

Captain No, you guess the wind, you order the sails. The winds have names, they're godlike, man obeys.

Philomele I never understood obedience, Captain philosophical.

Captain You're a woman.

Philomele Does that make me lawless? Do you have a wife?

Captain No, no.

Philomele Why not?

Niobe (*muttering*) Girl without shame. After a captain when she could have a king.

Philomele Take me with you.

Captain Take you. Where?

Philomele On the sea. South . . . Wherever . . .

Captain You're laughing at me, Philomele. Tereus . . .

Philomele Frightens me. Since Procne's accident. Perhaps before. His eyes wander, have you noticed? In Athens the philosophers used to talk about wandering eyes. I forget exactly what they said, but it was not good. Yes, the eyes are the windows of the soul – Tereus has a nervous soul.

Captain You shouldn't speak like that. Not to me. My job is to obey him.

Philomele Again! What about your obedience to the elements, and desire, isn't that a god too?

Captain Philomele . . .

Philomele You touched my hand on the ship once, by mistake, and once I fell against you, a wave, you blushed, I saw it, fear, desire, they're the same, I'm not a child. Touch my hand again: prove you feel nothing.

She holds out her hand. The Captain hesitates and touches it.

Philomele So – I was right. Take me with you.
Captain We will ask Tereus.
Philomele We will ask the gods within us. Love . . .
Captain . . . your power . . .
Philomele Not mine . . . Between us, above us.

She takes his hand and puts it on her breast. Tereus enters.

Tereus Traitor! Traitor! Traitor! (*He kills the Captain.*) A young
  girl, defenceless. I'll cut off your genitals. Go to the
  underworld with your shame around your neck. (*Pause.*) Be
  more careful, Philomele.
Male Chorus (*carrying the body off*) We saw nothing.

SCENE THIRTEEN

Moonlight. The beach. Philomele.

Philomele Catch the moonlight with your hands. Tread the
  moonlight with your toes, phosphorescence, phosphorescence,
  come to me, come to me, tell me the secrets of the wine-dark
  sea. (*Pause.*) I am so lonely. (*Pause.*) Procne, come to me.
  (*Pause. She waits.*) Procne, Procne, sister. Help me. Catch the
  lather of the moonlight. Spirits, talk to me. Oh, you gods, help
  me.

Tereus enters. Philomele senses this.

(*softly*) Phosphorescence, phosphorescence, tell me the secrets of
  the wine-dark sea . . .
Tereus (*softly*) Philomele, what are you doing?
Philomele Catching the lather of the sea. Moonlight, moonlight.
Tereus I only wish you well . . .
Philomele Let me bury my sister.
Tereus I told you, we never found the body.
Philomele Take me to the gorge, I will find it.
Tereus Nothing left now, weeks –
Philomele I will find the bones.
Tereus Washed by the river.

Philomele Let me stand in the river.

Tereus It's dangerous.

Philomele I don't want to stay here.

Tereus You have everything you want, you loved the spot when
we first came.

Philomele Then . . . Tereus, I want to see my sister's home, I
want to speak to the women who were with her. I want to
know the last words she said, please, please take me there.
Why are we here? What is the point of talking if you won't
answer the question? (*Silence. She turns away.*) Moonlight,
moonlight . . .

Tereus Philomele, listen to me.

Philomele Light the shells, light the stones, light the dust of old
men's bones . . .

Tereus Philomele!

Philomele Catch the lather of the sea . . .

Tereus Do you remember that day in the theatre in Athens? The
play?

Philomele Evanescence, evanescence . . .

Tereus Philomele, I am telling you. (*Pause.*) I love you.

Philomele I love you too, brother Tereus, you are my sister's
husband.

Tereus No, no. The play. I am Phaedra. (*Pause.*) I love you. That
way.

Silence.

Philomele It is against the law.

Tereus My wife is dead.

Philomele It is still against the law.

Tereus The power of the god is above the law. It began then, in
the theatre, the chorus told me. I saw the god and I loved you.

Philomele Tereus. (*Pause.*) I do not love you. I do not want you. I
want to go back to Athens.

Tereus Who can resist the gods? Those are your words.
Philomele. They convinced me, your words.

Philomele Oh, my careless tongue. Procne always said – my
wandering tongue. But, Tereus, it was the theatre, it was hot,
come back to Athens with me. My parents – Tereus, please, let
me go back to Athens.

Tereus The god is implacable.

Philomele You are a king, you are a widower. This is – frivolous.

Tereus You call this frivolous. (*He seizes her.*)

Philomele Treachery.

Tereus Love me.

Philomele No.

Tereus Then my love will be for both. I will love you and love myself for you. Philomele, I will have you.

Philomele Tereus. Wait.

Tereus The god is out.

Philomele Let me mourn.

Tereus Your darkness and your sadness make you all the more beautiful.

Philomele I have to consent.

Tereus It would be better, but no, you do not have to. Does the god ask permission?

Philomele Help. Help me. Someone. Niobe!

Tereus So, you are afraid. I know fear well. Fear is consent. You see the god and you accept.

Philomele Niobe!

Tereus I will have you in your fear. Trembling limbs to my fire.

He grabs her and leads her off. Niobe appears.

Niobe So it's happened. I've seen it coming for weeks. I could have warned her, but what's the point? Nowhere to go. It was already as good as done. I know these things. She should have consented. Easier that way. Now it will be all pain. Well I know. We fought Athens. Foolish of a small island but we were proud. The men – dead. All of them. And us. Well – we wished ourselves dead then, but now I know it's better to live. Life is sweet. You bend your head. It's still sweet. You bend it even more. Power is something you can't resist. That I know. My island bowed its head. I came to Athens. Oh dear, oh dear, she shouldn't scream like that. It only makes it worse. Too tense. More brutal. Well I know. She'll accept it in the end. Have to. We do. And then. When she's like me she'll wish it could happen again. I wouldn't mind a soldier. They don't look at me now. All my life I was afraid of them and then one day they stop looking and it's even more frightening. Because what makes you invisible is death coming quietly. Makes you pale, then unseen. First, no one turns, then you're not there. Nobody goes to my island any more. It's dead too. Countries are like women. It's when they're fresh they're wanted. Why did the Athenians want our island? I don't know. We only had a few lemon trees. Now the trees are withered. Nobody looks at them. There. It's finished now. A cool cloth. On her cheeks first. That's where it hurts most. The shame. Then we'll do the rest. I know all about it. It's the lemon trees I miss, not all those dead men. Funny, isn't it? I think of the lemon trees.

SCENE FOURTEEN

The palace of Tereus. Procne and the Female Chorus.

Procne If he is dead then I want to see his body and if he is alive then I want to see him. That is logical. Iris, come here. Closer. There. (*Pause.*) Iris, I have seen you look at me with some kindness. You could be my friend, possibly? What is a friend? A friend tells the truth. Will you be my friend? No, don't turn away, I won't impose the whole burden of this friendship. One gesture, one gift. One question. Will you be my friend to the tune of one question? Ah, you don't say no. Iris, answer me. Is Tereus dead? (*Pause.*) Iris, please, pity. One yes, one no. Small words and yet can turn the world inside out. (*Pause.*) I have learned patience. It is the rain. (*Pause.*) The inexorable weight of a grey sky. I can wait. (*Silence.*) It's only one word. Very well, don't. And when I kill myself, it will be for you to bring news of my death, Iris. You don't believe me? Athenians don't kill themselves. But I can be Thracian too. I have been here long enough. Go now.

Iris No.

Procne He is not dead.

Iris No.

Procne But then, why? (*Pause.*) Yes, my promise. (*Pause.*) Thank you.

My sister? No, of course, another question. If there is one, might there not be two? (*She addresses the women.*) My

husband is not dead. Who will tell me where he is? Why? You
have husbands among his men. Don't you ask yourselves
questions? What sirens have entangled them in what melodies?
Is that it? But no, he is not dead, so he is not drowned. Turned
into a wild beast by the power of a witch, is that it? You've
heard barking in the forest and recognized your husbands?
Don't dare say, the shame of it; my husband is a dog. All fleas,
wagging tail and the irrational bite, well, is that it? Weeks,
weeks and no one speaks to me. (*Pause.*) Even a rumour would
do. *Where are your men? Where is mine? Where is Tereus?*

Tereus and the Male Chorus enter.

Tereus Here. (*Pause.*) A delay.
Procne (*very still*) A delay. (*Pause.*) There's blood on your
hands.
Tereus A wild beast. Or a god in disguise. Unnameable.
Procne My sister?
Tereus (*after a brief pause*) Not here.
Procne No. (*Pause.*) Drowned?

Pause.

Tereus But I am here.
Procne Yes.

*She opens her arms. The Male Chorus comes forward, hiding
Tereus and Procne.*

Male Chorus Home at last.
Male Chorus We said nothing.
Male Chorus It was better that way.

SCENE FIFTEEN

*Philomele, Niobe. Philomele is being washed by Niobe, her legs
spread out around a basin. Her head is down.*

Niobe There. Nothing left. It's a weak liquid, it drops out
quickly. Not like resin.
Philomele I can still smell it. Wash me.

Niobe It's your own smell, there's nothing left.

Philomele It's the smell of violence. Wash me.

Niobe It's the smell of fear.

Philomele Wash me.

Niobe Some women get to like the smell. I never did. Too much like fishing boats. I like the smell of pines.

Philomele I want to die. Wash me.

Niobe You will, when it's time. In the meantime, get him to provide for you. They don't like us so much afterwards, you know. Now he might still feel something. We must eat. Smile. Beg.

Philomele Beg? Was it my fault?

Niobe I don't ask questions. Get some coins if you can.

Philomele Goddesses, where were you?

Niobe Stop worrying about the gods and think of us. Don't make him angry. He might still be interested. That would be excellent.

Philomele You. You are worse than him. (*She pours the dirty water over Niobe.*) Filth. Here. Drink his excretions.

Niobe Don't be so mighty, Philomele. You're nothing now. Another victim. Grovel. Like the rest of us.

Philomele No.

Niobe Be careful. Worse things can happen. Keep low. Believe me. I know. Keep silent.

Philomele Never.

Niobe Here's the King. Hold back your tongue, Philomele.

Tereus enters.

Tereus Now I wish you didn't exist.

Pause.

Philomele When will you explain, Tereus?

Tereus Explain?

Philomele Why? The cause? I want to understand.

Tereus I don't know what to do with you . . .

Philomele Me . . . (*Pause.*) I was the cause, wasn't I? Was I? I said something. What did I do? (*Pause.*) Something in my walk? If I had sung a different song? My hair up, my hair down? It was the beach. I ought not to have been there. I ought

54

not to have been anywhere. I ought not to have been . . . at all
. . . then there would be no cause. Is that it? Answer.

Tereus What?

Philomele My body bleeding, my spirit ripped open, and I am
the cause? No, this cannot be right, why would I cause my own
pain? That isn't reasonable. What was it then, tell me, Tereus,
if I was not the cause? (*Pause.*) You must know, it was your
act, you must know, tell me, why, say. (*Pause.*) It was your act.
It was you. I caused nothing. (*Short pause.*) And Procne is not
dead. I can smell her on you. (*Pause.*) You. You lied. And you.
What did you tell your wife, my sister, Procne, what did you
tell her? Did you tell her you violated her sister, the sister she
gave into your trust? Did you tell her what a coward you are
and that you could not, cannot bear to look at me? Did you tell
her that despite my fear, your violence, when I saw you in your
nakedness I couldn't help laughing because you were so
shrivelled, so ridiculous and it is not the way it is on the
statues? Did you tell her you cut me because you yourself had
no strength? Did you tell her I pitied her for having in her bed a
man who could screech such quick and ugly pleasure, a man of
jelly beneath his hard skin, did you tell her that? (*Pause.*) And
once I envied her happiness with her northern hero. The leader
of men. Take the sword out of your hand, you fold into a
cloth. Have they ever looked at you, your soldiers, your
subjects?

Tereus That's enough.

Philomele There's nothing inside you. You're only full when
you're filled with violence. And they obey you? Look up to
you? Have the men and women of Thrace seen you naked?
Shall I tell them? Yes, I will talk.

Tereus Quiet, woman.

Philomele You call this man your king, men and women of
Thrace, this scarecrow dribbling embarrassed lust, that is what
I will say to them, you revere him, but have you looked at him?
No? You're too awed, he wears his cloak of might and virility
with such ease you won't look beneath. When he murdered a
virtuous captain because a woman could love that captain,
that was bravery, you say. And if, women of Thrace, he wants
to force himself on you, trying to stretch his puny manhood to

your intimacies, you call that high spirits? And you soldiers, you'll follow into a battle a man who lies, a man of tiny spirit and shrivelled courage? Wouldn't you prefer someone with truth and goodness, self-control and reason? Let my sister rule in his place.

Tereus I said that was enough.

Philomele No, I will say more. They will all know what you are.

Tereus I warn you.

Philomele Men and women of Thrace, come and listen to the truth about this man –

Tereus I will keep you quiet.

Philomele Never, as long as I have the words to expose you. The truth, men and women of Thrace, the truth –

Tereus cuts out Philomele's tongue.

SCENE SIXTEEN

Philomele crouched in a pool of blood. Niobe.

Niobe Now truly I pity Philomele. She has lost her words, all of them. Now she is silent. For good. Of course, he could have killed her, that is the usual way of keeping people silent. But that might have made others talk. The silence of the dead can turn into a wild chorus. But the one alive who cannot speak, that one has truly lost all power. There. I don't know what she wants. I don't know what she feels. Perhaps she likes being silent. No responsibility.

Philomele seizes her, tries to express something.

I don't know what she wants. She can no longer command me. What good is a servant without orders? I will go. I don't know what she wants.

Tereus enters. Philomele stands still. Silence.

Tereus You should have kept quiet. (*Pause.*) I did what I had to. (*Pause.*) You threatened the order of my rule. (*Pause.*) How could I allow rebellion? I had to keep you quiet. I am not sorry.

56

Except for your pain. But it was you or me. (*Long pause.*) You are more beautiful now in your silence. I could love you. You should have allowed the god to have his way. You should have kept quiet. I was the stronger. And my desire. Niobe, you will look after her. This to ease the pain. (*He gives Niobe money, then goes to Philomele.*) Why weren't you more careful? Let me kiss those bruised lips. You are mine. My sweet, my songless, my caged bird

He kisses her. She is still.

SCENE SEVENTEEN

Tereus' palace. Procne, Itys, Tereus.

Procne I wouldn't want to be young again. Time flows so gently as you get older. It used to feel broken by rocks. Five years since my sister died. Tomorrow. I will light a candle towards the sea, as I do every year. But the pain flickers now, almost out. Will you come with me this time, Tereus?

Tereus No.

Procne I used to be angry that you would not mourn my sister. Why should you mourn her? You hardly knew her. Your aunt, Itys. You would have liked her. She was full of laughter.

Itys I have uncles. They're strong.

Procne She could speak with the philosophers. She was bold and quick.

Itys What's a philosopher?

Procne A man who loves wisdom.

Itys What is wisdom?

Procne It brings peace.

Itys I don't like peace. I like war.

Procne Why?

Itys So I can be brave. I want to be a great captain. Lead thousands into battle. Like Mars.

Procne Mars is a god.

Itys What is a god?

Procne Like us. But doesn't die.

Itys Why can't I be a god?

Procne You have to be born one.

Tereus But you'll be a king, Itys. That's almost as good.

Procne A wise king, like your father.

Itys (*turning round with his spear in hand*) I'll fight this way. I'll fight that way. I'll fight this way. I'll fight this way. (*He runs out.*)

Procne I am happy, as there was to be only one, that we have a son. (*Pause.*) Aren't you?

Tereus Yes.

Procne You're quiet. (*Pause.*) Over the years you have become quiet. I used to be afraid of you, did you know? But we shall grow old in peace. I wish more people came to visit this country. Then we could show our hospitality. No one comes here. Why? (*Silence.*) And if a god came to visit, he would find us sitting here, content, and perhaps turn us into two trees as a reward, like Baucis and Philemon. Would you like that?

Tereus Not yet.

Procne Ha. I love to see you smile. (*Pause.*) And tomorrow is the feast of Bacchus. I will go out this time. I will go out with the women of this country. You see how I become Thracian. (*Pause.*) You're going? Of course, you must. The evening is soft, look, stars too. We do not have many evenings together. I was frightened of your evenings when we were first married. That is why I sent you to Athens for my sister. I am a woman now. I can take pleasure in my husband.

She approaches Tereus, but he puts her away from him and leaves. When he is gone, she holds the bottom of her stomach.

Desire. Now. So late. Oh, you gods, you are cruel. Or, perhaps, only drunk.

She begins to dress as a member of the Bacchae, as does the Female Chorus. Music.

SCENE EIGHTEEN

Music. The stage fills with Bacchae. Niobe enters leading Philomele, who carries two huge dolls. Behind her, the Servant carries a third doll.

Niobe No place safe from the Bacchae. They run the city and the woods, flit along the beach, no crevass free from the light of their torches. Miles and miles of a drunken chain. These people are savages. Look at their women. You never see them and when you do, breasts hanging out, flutes to their mouths. In my village, they'd be stoned. Out of the way, you, out of the way.

Servant We could move faster without those big dolls, Niobe.

Niobe She wouldn't go without them. Years she's been sewing, making them, painting faces. Look. Childlike pastime for her, what can I say? It's kept her still. And she's quiet anyway. Tereus said, get her out, quickly, into the city. She'll be lost there. Another madwoman, no one will notice. Could have cut off her tongue in frenzied singing to the gods. Strange things happen on these nights, I have heard.

Servant Very strange. Niobe. But she was better in the hut.

Niobe No. It gives her a little outing. She's only seen us and the King for five years.

Servant He doesn't come much any more.

Niobe No. They all dream of silence, but then it bores them.

Servant Who is she, Niobe?

Niobe No one. No name. Nothing. A king's fancy. No more.

Servant I feel pity for her, I don't know why.

Niobe Look, some acrobats. The idiot will like it. Look. Look. See the acrobats. Now that's like my village. Except I believe they're women. Shame on them. But still, no harm in watching.

She thrusts Philomele to the front of a circle, watching. A crowd gathers around. The Acrobats perform. Finish. As they melt back into the crowd, the empty space remains and Philomele throws the dolls into the circle. Niobe grabs one of them and tries to grab Philomele, but she is behind the second doll. Since the dolls are huge, the struggle seems to be between the two dolls. One is male, one is female and the male one has a king's crown.

A mad girl, a mad girl. Help me.

But the crowd applauds, makes a wider circle and waits in silence. The rape is re-enacted in a gross and comic way, partly because of Niobe's resistance and attempt to catch Philomele. Philomele does most of the work with both dolls. The crowd laughs. Philomele then stages a very brutal illustration of the cutting of the female doll's tongue. Bloody cloth on the floor. The crowd is very silent. Niobe still. Then the Servant comes inside the circle, holding the third doll, a queen. At that moment, Procne also appears in the front of the crowd's circle. She has been watching. The Procne doll weeps. The two female dolls embrace. Procne approaches Philomele, looks at her and takes her away. The dolls are picked up by the crowd and they move off. A bare stage for a second. Then Procne and Philomele appear, Procne holding on to Philomele, almost dragging her. Then she lets go. Philomele stands still. Procne circles her, touches her. Sound of music very distant. Then a long silence. The sisters look at each other.

Procne How can I know that was the truth? (*Pause.*) You were always wild. How do I know you didn't take him to your bed? You could have told him lies about me, cut out your own tongue in shame. How can I know? You won't nod, you won't shake your head. I have never seen him violent. He would not do this. He had to keep you back from his soldiers. Desire always burnt in you. Did you play with his sailors? Did you shame us all? Why should I believe you? (*She shakes Philomele.*) Do something. Make me know you showed the truth. (*Pause.*) There's no shame in your eyes. Why should I believe you? And perhaps you're not Philomele. A resemblance. A mockery in this horrible drunken feast. How can I know? (*Silence.*) But if it is true. My sister. Open your mouth.

Philomele opens her mouth, slowly.

To do this. He would do this. (*Pause.*) Is that what the world looks like? (*Pause.*) Justice. Philomele, the justice we learned as children, do you remember? Where is it? Come, come with me.

The Bacchae give wine to Procne and Philomele.

Do this.

Philomele drinks.

Drink. Oh, we will revel. You, drunken god, help us. Help us.

They dance off with the Bacchae.

SCENE NINETEEN

Two Soldiers.

First Soldier It's almost dawn. Let's go.

Second Soldier He used to stay by the palace until the sun was up.

First Soldier What is he afraid of? An invasion of Amazons? They're all in there.

Second Soldier Our enemies know this is a strange night.

First Soldier I never liked this festival. All these drunken women. My girl's in there. And she'll never tell what happens. I tell her about the war. Well. Most of it. Let's go.

Second Soldier We can't.

First Soldier There's no law on these nights.

Second Soldier Do you want to look in?

First Soldier They'd kill us.

Second Soldier That window, there. We could see through the shutters.

First Soldier It's supposed to be a mystery. A woman's mystery. That's what my girl says. Give me a break.

Second Soldier You could sit on my shoulders. Make sure your girl's behaving.

First Soldier It's all women in there.

Second Soldier It's all men in a war.

First Soldier You mean, she – they – no.

Second Soldier Have a look.

First Soldier If she – I'll strangle her. So that's what a mystery is. Let me see. (*The First Soldier climbs on to the Second Soldier's shoulder.*)

Second Soldier Can you see?

First Soldier Steady.

Second Soldier I'm holding your legs. Can you see?

First Soldier Yeah.

Second Soldier Well?

First Soldier It's just a lot of women.

Second Soldier We know that, stupid. What are they doing?

First Soldier Drinking.

Second Soldier And?

First Soldier Oh.

Second Soldier What?

First Soldier Oh, you gods.

Second Soldier Well? What are they doing? Exactly? What?

First Soldier (*jumping down, laughing*) Nothing.

He does a dance with the Second Soldier.

Dancing. Lots of wine. They've swords and lances.

Itys has appeared.

What are you doing here?

Itys I saw you.

First Soldier No men, no boys on the street. Go home.

Itys I saw you looking.

Second Soldier That's Itys. Tereus's son. Why aren't you asleep?

Itys I saw you. I'm going to tell my father when he gets back.

First Soldier Nothing wrong with looking.

Itys Mother said no one's to see.
I'll tell her, she'll tell Father. He'll be angry.

Second Soldier Don't you want to see?

Itys It's not allowed.

Second Soldier Aren't you a prince? A king's son? You let women tell you what is and is not allowed?

Itys You shouldn't have looked.

First Soldier It's just women.

Second Soldier Why don't you see for yourself? A king has to be informed.

First Soldier You can sit on my shoulders.

Second Soldier Do you know how to sit on somebody's shoulders? Are you strong enough?

Itys Of course I know.

Second Soldier You sure? It's difficult.

First Soldier We'll hold you.

Second Soldier No, we won't. You have to climb all by yourself. Like a man. Can you do it?

Itys I'll show you. (*He climbs on the shoulders of the Second Soldier.*)

Second Soldier Good. You'll make a soldier yet. You're too small to reach the window, aren't you?

Itys No, I'm not.

Second Soldier I think you are.

Itys stretches himself to the window and looks. Pause.

Itys Oh.

First Soldier Still dancing, the women?

Itys They drink more than my father.

First Soldier But only once a year.

Itys There's Mother.

First Soldier What is she doing?

Itys Why should I tell you?

Second Soldier Quite right, boy. What about the other women?

Itys There's one I've never seen before. She looks like a slave. That's my sword. That slave girl. A slave, a girl slave holding my sword. Let me down.

Second Soldier Where are you going?

Itys To stop them.

First Soldier No.

Second Soldier Wait.

Itys runs off.

First Soldier Let's go.

Second Soldier Let me look. (*He climbs.*) He's there. They've stopped. They're looking at him. It's all right. Procne is holding him. Shows him to the slave girl. He looks up. They've all gone still. He laughs. Oh! (*He drops down.*)

First Soldier What happened?

Second Soldier I'm drunk. I didn't see anything. It didn't happen. The god has touched me with madness. For looking. I'm seeing things. I didn't see anything. Nothing. Nothing. Nothing. Let's go. I didn't see anything. There's Tereus. I don't know anything. I wasn't here.

They run off.

SCENE TWENTY

The Female Chorus. Procne. Philomele.

Hero Without the words to demand.

Echo Or ask. Plead. Beg for.

June Without the words to accuse.

Helen Without even the words to forgive.

Echo The words that help to forget.

Hero What else was there?

Iris To some questions there are no answers. We might ask you now: why does the Vulture eat Prometheus' liver? He brought men intelligence.

Echo Why did God want them stupid?

Iris We can ask: why did Medea kill her children?

June Why do countries make war?

Helen Why are races exterminated?

Hero Why do white people cut off the words of blacks?

Iris Why do people disappear? The ultimate silence.

Echo Not even death recorded.

Helen Why are little girls raped and murdered in the car parks of dark cities?

Iris What makes the torturer smile?

Echo We can ask. Words will grope and probably not find. But if you silence the question.

Iris Imprison the mind that asks.

Echo Cut out its tongue.

Hero You will have this.

June We show you a myth.

Echo Image. Echo.

Helen A child is the future.
Hero This is what the soldiers did not see.

Itys comes running in.

Itys That's my sword. Give me my sword.
Procne Itys.
Itys Give me my sword, slave, or I'll kick you. Kill you all. Cut off your heads. Pick out your eyes.

Itys goes for Philomele. Procne holds him. Philomele still has the sword. Philomele brings the sword down on his neck. The Female Chorus close in front. Tereus enters.

Tereus It's daylight at last. The revels are over. Time to go home.

Silence. No one moves.

We're whitewashing the streets. All that wine. Poured like blood. It's time for you to go home.

No one moves.

Stupefied? You should hold your wine better. You've had your revels. Go on. Stagger home. Procne, tell your women to go home.

Philomele is revealed. Hands bloodied. There is a silence.

I had wanted to say.
Procne Say what, Tereus?
Tereus If I could explain.
Procne You have a tongue.
Tereus Beyond words.
Procne What?
Tereus When I ride my horse into battle, I see where I am going. But close your eyes for an instant and the world whirls round. That is what happened. The world whirled round.

Pause.

Procne What kept you silent? Shame?
Tereus No.
Procne What?
Tereus I can't say. There are no rules.

Procne I obeyed all rules: the rule of parents, the rule of marriage, the rules of my loneliness, you. And now you say. This.

Long pause.

Tereus I have no other words.
Procne I will help you find them.

The body of Itys is revealed.

If you bend over the stream and search for your reflection, Tereus, this is what it looks like.
Tereus Itys. You.
Procne I did nothing. As usual. Let the violence sweep around me.
Tereus She –
Procne No. You, Tereus. You bloodied the future. For all of us. We don't want it.
Tereus Your own child!
Procne Ours. There are no more rules. There is nothing. The world is bleak. The past a mockery, the future dead. And now I want to die.
Tereus I loved her. When I silenced her, it was from love. She didn't want my love. She could only mock, and soon rebel, she was dangerous.
I loved my country. I loved my child. You – this.
Procne You wanted something and you took it. That is not love. Look at yourself. That is not love.
Tereus How could I know what love was? Who was there to tell me?
Procne Did you ask?
Tereus Monsters. Fiends. I will kill you both.

Tereus takes the sword of Itys. The Female Chorus comes forward.

Hero Tereus pursued the two sisters, but he never reached them. The myth has a strange end.
Echo No end.
Iris Philomele becomes a nightingale.
June Procne a swallow.

66

Helen And Tereus a hoopoe.
Hero You might ask, why does the myth end that way?
Iris Such a transformation.
Echo Metamorphosis.

The birds come on.

SCENE TWENTY-ONE

Itys and the birds.

Philomele (*the nightingale*) And now, ask me some more
  questions.
Itys I wish you'd sing again.
Philomele You have to ask me questions first.

Pause.

Itys Do you like being a nightingale?
Philomele I like the nights and my voice in the night. I like the
  spring. Otherwise, no, not much, I never liked birds, but we
  were all so angry the bloodshed would have gone on forever.
  So it was better to become a nightingale. You see the world
  differently.
Itys Do you like being a nightingale more than being Philomele?
Philomele Before or after I was silenced?
Itys I don't know. Both.
Philomele I always felt a shadow hanging over me. I asked too
  many questions.
Itys You want me to ask questions.
Philomele Yes.
Itys Will you sing some more?
Philomele Later.
Itys Why doesn't Procne sing?
Philomele Because she was turned into a swallow and swallows
  don't sing.
Itys Why not?
Philomele Different job.
Itys Oh. (*Pause.*) I like it when you sing.

Philomele Do you understand why it was wrong of Tereus to cut
out my tongue?

Itys It hurt.

Philomele Yes, but why was it wrong?

Itys (*bored*) I don't know. Why was it wrong?

Philomele It was wrong because –

Itys What does wrong mean?

Philomele It is what isn't right.

Itys What is right?

The nightingale sings.

Didn't you want me to ask questions?

Fade.

The Girl Who Lost Her Voice

JOAN LIPKIN

Born in Chicago, Illinois, Joan Lipkin is the Artistic Director of That Uppity Theatre Company in St Louis, Missouri, where she founded the Alternate Currents/Direct Currents and Women Centerstage Series, The Disability Project and the Nadadada Festival, in addition to developing much of her work. She is also a Visiting Artist-in-Residence at Washington University, where she teaches courses that survey and devise contemporary solo and ensemble performance. Her plays include *Small Domestic Acts* (pub. in *Amazon All Stars*, Applause Books), *Some of My Best Friends Are . . .* and *He's Having Her Baby* (with Tom Clear), among others. A playwright, director, screen and fiction writer, teacher and social activist, her award-winning work has been presented in the United States, Canada, Great Britain, Ireland, Australia and Asia.

The Girl Who Lost Her Voice was first performed in St Louis, Missouri.

It was an ordinary enough day, I think, the day my voice left. A grey St Louis November day looking too quickly to feel like winter, when the branches of the already bare trees shivered in protest against the sky.

If I can trust my memory. That's the thing, you see. Nothing seems like solid ground since the day my voice left. And ordinary . . . isn't.

I raced to the university late, I think, where the Famous Visiting Performance Artist from New York City was scheduled to show us how it was done.

She was little but talked big. About farting and eating pussy and how hung over she was. A couple of people were shocked into leaving. I could see the voltage spark on impact, tightening their mouths and straightening their spines. I was shocked into staying, rooted to the spot. Could barely edge my chair closer to smell the courage rising off her pale minow skin like fine steam.

She played a cool game, sitting cross-legged in her size six combat boots, drinking her coffee without cream. But I noticed her nails were bitten to the quick and her left eye winked even when there was no joke in the room.

I looked at the poem that she was and thought, I want what you've got. Have got to get me some of that. Does it come with the black leather jacket? Do they sell it bottled on the subway?

One woman bridled at the words and a squabble flared up faster than a flash fire. The Famous Visiting Performance Artist from New York City looked cool. Bored even as she shot back a few words in her direction, extinguishing the flame.

'Well, now, what *is* the big deal?' she asked. 'The way I see it, you're either eating pussy or having it done. Whether they wear a dick or not. And if you're *not* having it done,' she chuckled, 'well, then, lady, I do feel sorry for you.'

As that flame sputtered, the woman next to me sighed. 'I can't hear a word she's saying,' she confided to her neighbour on the left. 'My heart is beating so loud. Do you think she'd, well . . . go out with me if I asked?'

My heart was beating loudly, too. Although for another reason, I think. It thumped behind my eyes and in my ears. I felt a different drumming, strange yet not unfamiliar. At the base of my throat and in between my legs. What if I *had* been late, heavy-lidded, for much of my life? My wake-up call sat maybe ten feet away, pissing off the provost and jumpstarting my sleepy self.

Hair. Heart. Teeth. Toes. Clit. Cleft.

I had pulses I scarcely knew had places.

> And they beat – – – Say anything.
> And they beat – – – Do anything.
> And they beat – – – Say. *Say.*
> And they beat – – – Say. *Say.*

The Famous Visiting Performance Artist from New York City laughed. Even her laugh issued a challenge. Bouncing from wall to wall, taking up space, more than her polite share. Letting us know that even if they were paying, she intended to run the show, and to enjoy herself.

'I like to talk dirty,' she said, staring down the department head whose beard couldn't quite hide his blush. 'I make a habit of it. Separates the men from the boys right away, so to speak. Now we can get down to work.'

Work? Nobody had said that we were actually going to *do* anything.

'Come on, come on!' She clapped her hands impatiently, gathering us in a circle for some silly ass theatre game she had learned in the seventies. 'Let's say you're in the desert. Haven't had anything to drink for days. There's an airplane overhead but in order to be seen, you have to call out adjectives.'

The man behind me groaned. 'Adjectives. Just adjectives,' she said, waving away questions with one nailbitten hand. 'I don't want to hear any nouns.'

> Beat. *Beat.*
> Beat. *Beat.*
> Beat. *Beat.*
> Beat. *Beat.*

72

Some assistant professor from Comp Lit who wasn't willing to look foolish suddenly remembered a class he had to teach or a meeting he couldn't miss. And a senior from Fine Arts developed the most terrible cough.

Whatever he had was catching. There was an airplane alright but not exactly the one she had described. I blinked at the swoosh of comings and goings as people hurried to gather their luggage of pens and pencils, books and bookbags. The room had more traffic than Lambert Field.

I wanted to wrap my arms around the Famous Visiting Performance Artist from New York City like a chainlink security fence. I wanted to be able to say things that made people run from or stay in a room. I wanted to trip the goddamned graduate student racing for the exit.

'I'm used to it,' she said, answering our unspoken question. 'They like to come, look at the lesbian in the cage. Especially the . . . *academics*.' She paused and spit out the word, spraying disdain and cigarette smoke in equal measure. 'They like to come and look. So they can, I don't know, write a paper or something and say they've had their experience.' She laughed and suddenly looked tired enough to sleep through next week. 'I used to mind but now I don't. Because it leaves the rest of us. The ones that want to get down with words.'

Pause.

Beat. *Beat.*

Pause.

Beat. *Beat.*

'So. Who wants to go first?'

She looked at us, measuring. She looked at us, testing.

The people who would want to go first, well, the people who usually went first, had already left the room. We all stared at each other. The diminishing and defiant ragtaggle of teachers and students, brazen passersby and people who just heard that there might be food later. Some of us were desperate for something, others merely curious. Still, this was no easy curious. Thinking there was no way to be right, no one was in a hurry to be wrong.

Pause.
Beat. *Beat.*
Pause.
Beat. *Beat.*

Anna gave her a break, about the time when she had probably decided that we were wasting hers. Anna went first. 'Anna,' she said, counting adjectives like groceries on the tips of her unfurled fingers. 'Responsible,' she said, listing. 'Organized.'

Blue-eyed . . . Aquarian . . . Studious . . . Funny . . . Shy. The words tiptoed around the room as people struggled to name themselves. What self to name? And in the moment of naming, what selves to leave behind?

Messy . . . Clean . . . Ambitious . . . Blonde . . . Male . . .

The words tiptoed around the room and stopped short at my door.

Pause.
Beat. *Beat.*
Pause.
Beat. *Beat.*

'Well?' The Famous Visiting Performance Artist from New York City looked at me. I looked at her skinny freckled arms folded around her body and the place that her belly wasn't. I reached into the vast grab bag of words floating by and grabbed with great deliberation.

'Round,' I said to be funny.

'Round,' I said to be teacher's pet.

'Round,' I said, stalling for time.

She leaned forward and I saw the lines under her eyes, the ones you couldn't see in all the newspaper photos and magazines. 'That's good,' she said, laughing. 'That's tasty.' And then everyone else laughed, too. 'So what's next?'

'R-o-u-n-d-d-d-d,' I said once more, warming to my audience, and building on the buttery word that filled my mouth like a Parker House roll.

But as I pursed my lips and backed up to get a good steam going, the word turned sharply on me and snapped in another direction.

74

'R-r-r-r-*ow*.'

I tried again.

'R-r-r-r-*ow*.'

And again.

'R-r-r-r-*ow*.'

'*Ow*?'

Wha the – – –   Wha the – – –   Wha the – – –
Why this?   Why me?   Why now?

But,
therewasnotimetoasknotimetoasknotimetoaskwhy.

Sudden as a sneeze, the ground cracked open. I was falling through a trapdoor, hurtling fast towards nowhere. Nowhere that I *knew*. What is the sound of terror? What shape the unknown? What what what is the way you say stop?! I reached for the word that had been my friend just moments ago.

'*Ow*-n-d.'

I moved in towards the sound.

It closed in for the kill, splintered faster than my screaming selves.

owwwwww
owwwwwwww
owwwwwwwwww

'That's good,' I heard her say from somewhere beyond my reach.
'That's good,' I heard her say from somewhere beyond my grasp.
'Stay with that.'

'*Owwwwwwwww*!!!!'

I moaned up from my belly, from between my toes.

'*Owwwwwwwww*!!!!'

I stumbled halfway to sobbing.

'But . . . that's not an adjective,' someone said.
'And this is, you know, really kind of weird,' said someone else.

She sprang to her feet, standing for the first time all afternoon. From where my head hung heavy over my shoes, I could feel the air shift in the room.

'Ssshh,' she said sharply. Then, 'Ssshh,' she said, softening. 'Give us another one. Tell us what's next.'

Pause.
Beat. *Beat.*
Pause.
Beat. *Beat.*

'Tell us a name,' she said, trying hard to sound casual. 'Or a joke or a song. Just say something.'

But my voice had gone mute. Was it because they laughed, even though I had wanted them to? Had I been too clever for my own good? Was the crime in wanting to to be clever? And in wanting to be clever, had I betrayed myself? Tossed aside a self meant to remain hidden, protected? Or could I just not find a follow-up to my own punchline?

I scanned in desperation for words that punctuated my days like walking the dog or watching the six o'clock news. Dangling still over some dark, endless pit, I reached for words, ordinary-one-creme-two sugar-words that linked arms with each other because they knew the value of cooperation.

Words like . . .

Hello my name is – – – Would you like some more – – – Do you know what time it – – – How much is that – – – Did you have a nice – – – Could I please – – – Could I please – – – Could I please – – –

Words I swore never to take for granted again. Words I would avow every vowel if only they'd lay neatly on my tongue once more.

But there was no answer. Only the drumming that was loud and grew louder still.

Beat. *Beat.*
Beat. *Beat.*
Beat. *Beat.*
Beat. *Beat.*

Okay. Sounds. Sounds then. The building blocks for their more elegant cousins. I pushed and pushed again for something that would not come. Far from a silent universe, I heard the thumping of my heart and the rasp of my breath as the room went red then black then red again.

Beat. *Beat.*

Beat. *Beat.*

Beat. *Beat.*

Beat. *Beat.*

I lurched forward, past a rush of open mouths and stunned faces.

She ran after me, The Famous Visiting Performance Artist from New York City. Shedding her black leather jacket in the run to meet me, panting, outside the circle of her celebrity. 'Wait! Wait!'

But where I was going, she couldn't follow.

I looked into her eyes as she turned into another country on a distant, fading shore. There was no excuse to mutter. Speaking seemed another lifetime, so far away, for once, I had no shame.

Out the door, through the urban galaxy, I stumbled. I walked backwards as bones crumbled, concrete to ash beneath my feet.
Over
 the raging body of my father and Saturday afternoons in
 Sunday school.
Over
 my mother's admonitions and the teacher calling on
 someone else.
Over
 the sudden end of day and my confusing desires.
Over
 my budding breasts and the dangerous slip into night.
Over
 the crazy lady panhandling on the street and the man
 driving past in a limousine.
Over
 starving children and the church bells tolling outside my
 window.

Over
  suburban teenagers with eating disorders and the
  newscaster on the flickering screen.
Over
  the black white white black look of fast food places, banks
  and college campuses.
Over
  bombed-out buildings and crashing planes and even
  envelopes that self-destructed.

  Over.   Over.   Over.

I walked backwards and tried to discover my voiceless tracks.

A Woman Alone

FRANCA RAME *and* DARIO FO

translated by Gillian Hanna

A Woman Alone was part of a triple bill performed by Gillian Hanna in 1989.

Franca Rame and Dario Fo were highly successful in writing, directing and performing satirical comedies for the conventional theatre in the Fifties. In the Sixties they abandoned it and Fo began to write for a wider audience in factories and workers' clubs, producing political interventionist work in Italy which was internationally acclaimed. In 1970 Fo and Rame founded the theatrical collective, La Comune, in Milan. Much of their work has been performed and translated into English: *Can't Pay? Won't Pay!*, *Accidental Death of an Anarchist*, *Female Parts*, *Mistero Buffo*, *Trumpets and Raspberries*, *Archangels Don't Play Pinball*, *Elizabeth*, *An Ordinary Day*, *The Pope and the Witch*. In 1997 Dario Fo was awarded the Nobel Prize for Literature.

Gillian Hanna is an actress and translator.

When Franca Rame performs *Medea*, she does it in an idiom, a dialect that produces a woman rooted in the earth, in reality. I have tried to render this in simple plain English, but there is a danger that the play can sound like a mock epic, or that Medea can sound like a 1950s Radio 4 matron. My feeling is that each performer should use any regional accent with which she feels most comfortable and adapt the text using regional colloquialisms as necessary.

Gillian Hanna

'Come over here! Hurry up! Move yourself! Medea's locked herself in the house with the two kids! She's ranting like someone possessed. She's screaming her head off! She's gone out of her mind! She won't listen to reason! Her eyes are bulging out of her head – as though she'd been bitten by a tarantula! She's gone mad with jealousy . . . she can't believe it . . . her old man Jason's gone off with a younger woman. She's got to get out of the house and leave the kids – but she just won't face up to it. Medea just won't see sense! You talk to her. You're the oldest, you know her best . . . stop her being so stupid!'

'OK, I'm the oldest, I'll talk to her . . . I know her . . . I'll talk some sense into her . . . Medea! Medea! Come to the door! I've got to talk to you. Listen to me, girl, have a bit of sense, will you. Stop being so selfish. You should be thinking about your kids. If Jason marries again, they'll be much better off: bigger house to live in, nicer clothes to wear, there'll always be masses of food on the table: they'll be living in the lap of luxury . . . And they'll be going up in the world . . . all the nobs and big wheels'll be bowing and scraping to them . . . they might even get to live in the King's Palace! You love your kids, don't you Medea? Well then, you've got to make a sacrifice for the sake of the children! Be a good mother and not a hysterical woman! Just face it – you've got to give in with good grace for the sake of your own flesh and blood.

'No . . . no . . . no one's made you look like a fool . . . no one's insulted you. Your husband hasn't got a bad word to say about you . . . he says you're the best woman in the world . . . he says no one could have loved those children more than you have . . . or him, come to that . . . he says he'll always think fondly of you . . .

'What are you up to, Medea? Speak to me! Say something, for God's sake. Open the door, Medea. Come out and talk to us . . . we're all in the same boat as you . . . we've been through it too

. . . cried our eyes out! You're not the only one who's been dumped by a husband – it's happened to us too . . . we know what you're going through.

'Get out of the way! Medea's decided to come out! . . . Here she is! My God, she looks like a ghost! Her hands are white . . . she's as pale as a sheet . . . you'd think she hadn't a drop of blood left in her body . . .

'Hold her up . . . she's going to fall down . . . sit down here, Medea . . .

'Make some space, will you . . . let her breathe.

'We're listening.

'Shut up, will you . . . she wants to say something . . . Medea's going to speak.

'She can't speak! All that screaming's made her lose her voice! Give her a glass of water, she's parched. There, that's it . . . Now, say what you want to say, Medea. Tell us about it . . . It'll make you feel better . . . Get it off your chest . . .'

'Friends . . . my dear women friends . . . what does my husband's new girlfriend look like? I've only seen her once, and that was in the distance. I thought she looked . . . so beautiful . . . so young . . .

'You know I was fresh and beautiful once . . . when I was sixteen and my husband first set eyes on me . . . I had long black hair and white skin . . . and my breasts were so firm, they used to practically burst out of my blouse . . . no wrinkles on my neck . . . no sagging jowls . . . and my stomach was so flat you couldn't even see it under my dress . . . my hips were so slender, my whole body was so fragile, when he took me in his arms he was always petrified he was going to snap me in two or hurt me . . . and when he made love to me, his hands'd shake – he'd be shaking all over, he was so terrified – even laying a finger on me seemed like blasphemy to him.'

'We've all been through that, Medea. But it's over and done with now. Gone . . . it's just fate . . . women's destiny: men trade us in for younger flesh, younger skin, younger breasts, voices, lips . . . it's the law of nature . . . that's how it's been since the world began!'

'What law are you talking about? Who dreamed up this law? Did all you women think it up? Write it down? Did you go out into the streets and get up on your soapbox and bang your drum and say "This is the law! This is Holy Writ!!"? It was men . . . men . . . men who dreamed it up . . . they wrote it down, they signed and sealed it and said it came down from Heaven on tablets of stone . . . and then the King gave it his seal of approval . . . and they did it to use it against us – against women.'

'No Medea, it's the law of nature. It's natural. Men get older slower than us. They ripen as they get older, we wither . . . we swell up and then we fade away . . . they get wiser and more mature. We lose our power and they grow more powerful . . . that's the rule that makes the world go round.'

'What a bunch of idiots you are! Listen, I understand it all so clearly now. Of all the clever things men have done to get one over on us, this is the cleverest. They've got you believing in their law . . . they've brainwashed you . . . you repeat the lessons they teach you like parrots and then you think you're happy . . . you grovel at their feet and yet you won't rebel!'

'Rebel? Listen, Medea, listen . . . Talking like this is only going to make the King angry . . . Why do you have to set yourself against his rule? Just calm down, Medea, and ask him to forgive you and then he'll leave you alone to live your life in peace.'

'Live my life in peace? Live my life? What sort of life do you think I'll have? All alone? Shut up here in my house? Alone? Like a corpse? No voices . . . no laughter . . . no love of any kind . . . no children, no husband . . . they're celebrating already – and they haven't even buried me yet! And I'm supposed to keep my mouth shut for the sake of the children? That's just blackmail . . . downright bloody blackmail!

'Listen to me, my friends . . . The most awful thought has just occurred to me . . . I can't seem to get it out of my head . . . it's pounding in my heart: I've got to kill my children. Oh sure, I know I'll always be remembered as a wicked mother, a woman who was driven out of her mind with jealousy . . . but it's better to be remembered as a wild animal than forgotten like a pet nanny goat! Milk her, clip her, then throw her out. Send her to market and sell her . . . she won't even make a single bleat in protest! I have to kill my sons.'

'Help! Get over here quickly! Medea's gone off her head. She's not talking like a mother! She's ranting on like an old streetwalker . . . someone's put a spell on her . . . she's absolutely barking mad!'

'No sisters, I haven't gone mad . . . I've thought about it over and over again; and over and over again I've stamped the idea out of my brain . . . I've bitten my hands, I've beaten my arms with stones till they bled . . . all to stop myself using them as weapons against my own children . . . At first I thought I'd commit suicide: I couldn't bear the thought of being thrown out of my own home, banished from the country – even though I'm a foreigner and don't really belong here – I couldn't stand the thought of being carted away like some poxy old whore . . . Oh I know everyone despises me now – even you my dear friends – I'm a burden. Everyone's embarrassed by a woman who's surplus to requirements . . . especially when she kicks up a fuss. Even my kids would rather forget about me. And then when I've gone, everyone'll forget I ever existed . . . I'll be as invisible as if they'd never had a mother at all . . . As if Medea had never been born . . . never been loved . . . never been taken into bed by a man, never been caressed, kissed or made love to. Medea was dead before she was born! And if that's true, if I'm dead already, if everyone has killed and buried me, then I can't kill myself all over again, can I? I want to live! But I can't live unless my children are dead . . . I've got to kill my own children . . . flesh of my flesh . . . blood of my blood . . . life of my life . . .'

'Aargh! Run, you lot. Go and get some rope . . . We'll have to tie the poor thing up! She's completely demented . . . she's possessed by some sort of devil – it's making her say these terrible things!'

'Get away from me! You lay one finger on me and I'll stab you straight in the guts with this pitchfork!'

'Run for it! Run! She's gone berserk! Run for it! Run! . . . Stop! Wait! Jason's coming . . . her husband's coming . . . Get out of the way. He'll know how to handle his woman . . . let him through . . .

'Look Medea. You can calm down now . . . it's your husband, Jason.'

'Oh Jason, it's too kind of you to leave your sweet little bride, your delicious rosebud, just to come and see me! Oh look at his open honest face coming towards me . . . but he's walking a bit hesitantly . . . he looks a bit put out . . .

'Sit down . . . no it's all right . . . I was only pretending to be crazy . . . I was only joking . . . I wanted to put the fear of God into this lot. I just felt like seeing them all run around, weeping and wailing, and then laughing, laughing till the tears ran down their cheeks! I've got nothing else to do to pass the time these days. It's OK I'm quite lucid now. The thing is, I've been going over and over all this in my mind, and I've finally come to a conclusion: I must have been completely stupid to think I could keep you all to myself . . . for ever. I just saw red . . . I was just being a typical brainless jealous woman . . . well you know what women are like . . . weak and spiteful, quick tempered . . . we burst into tears at the slightest excuse . . . Say that you forgive me, Jason. I can't help it, it's just my own weak nature . . . You did the right thing, finding a new young bride . . . new bed, nice clean sheets . . . and you'll have a whole new set of relatives – all very important people – and they'll be my relatives too, because your family will be my family . . . That makes me happy . . . very happy . . . If you'll forgive me, I'll make all the arrangements for the wedding . . . I'll get the marriage bed ready for you and scatter the sheets with rose petals . . . I'll be better than a mother to your young bride . . . I'll teach her everything she needs to know about love . . . If that'll make you happy! . . . Now do you believe I've come to my senses?

'And to think I called you a traitor! A man isn't a traitor simply because he swaps one woman for another . . . a woman ought to be happy just being a mother. After all, that's the best reward she can possibly have. I can't think what got into me, saying this law men have made, that lets you trade in one woman for another, was a kind of blackmail! What was I thinking of when I said this cage you've got us locked up in was an unholy insult? Whatever put the thought into my head that you'd chained our children round our necks like millstones to keep us in our places – just like you chain a hard wooden yoke round a cow's neck to force her to stand docilely while she's milked and mounted . . . That's how crazy I was, Jason, I actually believed all that . . . and I still do!! And I'm going to smash this cage you've got me shut up in . . . I'm going to throw off the unbearable weight of the yoke you've laid on my neck . . . I'm going to shatter your filthy blackmail once and for all!!

You've used your laws to chain me to my children, and condemned me to a living death.

'My friends, listen to me breathing . . . with one breath, with one deep breath I could breathe in all the air in the whole wide world.

'My little boys have got to die, Jason. They've got to die so that you can be crushed to a pulp – you and all these stinking laws you've invented. My friends, give me the weapon . . . poor desperate Medea . . . plunge the knife into your children's soft flesh . . . aaah, they're bleeding . . . it's like sweet honey . . . they're bleeding . . . Oh my heart, forget these children are the flesh of my flesh . . . they're bleeding . . . Don't shudder when they scream: "Mother . . . have mercy . . . Mother!"

'And a terrible howl will echo round the world: "Monster . . . bitch . . . unnatural, cruel mother . . . she-devil!" And through my tears I'll whisper: (*almost under her breath*)

'Die, die, so your blood and bones can give birth to a new woman! (*at the top of her voice*) Die! You must give birth to a new w-o-o-ma-a-a-n!!'

The last syllable turns into a musical note which dies as the light fades.

Passion

LAURA CURINO
translated by Gabriella Giannachi and Mary Luckhurst

dedicated to Federico Negro

Laura Curino was born in Turin, Italy, in 1956. She works as an actress and since 1978 has co-written most of the plays for Teatro Settimo. She has received the following awards: The Francesca Alinovi Award (1984) for *Esercizi sulla tavola di Mendeleev* at the Festival of Santarcangelo, the Ubu Award (1985) for *Elementi di Struttura del sentimento* (from J. W. Goethe's *Elective Affinities*) at the Festival of Santarcangelo, the Waves Award (Copenhagen, 1987) for *Riso Amaro* in Milan, 1987, Edinburgh Festival Fringe Award (1989) for *Stabat Mater*, the Ubu Award (1991) and Taormina Arte for *La Storia di Romeo e Giuletta*, and Il Contemporaneo Award (Milan, 1994).

Gabriella Giannachi is a lecturer in Theatre Studies at Lancaster University.

Mary Luckhurst is a playwright, translator and lecturer in Modern Drama at York University.

With thanks to John Lennard for lay-out and design.

Laura Curino is one of Italy's leading theatre actresses. She was a founding member of *Laboratorio Teatro Settimo*, set up in 1979, now famous throughout Europe.

Passion was premiered in Turin in 1993 and directed by Roberto Tarasco. It met with immediate critical acclaim.

Passion details Laura Curino's childhood memories of the 1960s. It is a highly personal monologue, interweaving a whole range of very different voices from 'Zone Seven', otherwise known as Settimo, a satellite seven miles from the city of Turin. She discovers Settimo to be a typical example of the new wave of industrialization spreading throughout northern Italy. It is a place full of migrant workers from the south, alienated both by the surroundings and the grim working conditions in the factories.

Passion is Laura Curino's journey from her cramped flat and overcrowded classroom, and her adventures with friends, relations and acquaintances all struggling amid the devastation of Zone Seven, to her eventual discovery of and liberation by theatre. This liberation came about through the production of a part of *Mistero Buffo* by Dario Fo and Franca Rame, which was based on the story of the Passion and instilled Laura with a life-long passion of her own for performance. *Passion* comes across almost as a stream of consciousness, with voices echoing from real and fictional life. These fictional voices are some of the characters that Laura has played during her professional career, such as Carlotta, who is based on a character from J. W. Goethe's novel *Elective Affinities*. At the end all the voices are drawn together in the performance of *Passion*.

Passion presented some thorny problems in its translation, largely due to the wealth of regional Italian dialects in the original. We decided to keep the Italian location and not to try to find a British equivalent as we felt this would have destroyed the essence of the writer's narrative; as a result, not all the voices have been given a dialect, but different characters are indicated by differing fonts, and in some cases by speech-prefixes.

Gabriella Giannachi and Mary Luckhurst

I wrote *Passion* on the road, travelling through Europe when I was performing *Stabat Mater* in people's homes. The only home I had at this time was a nine-seater Mercedes which the company practically lived in while on tour: it was the only place to get any peace and quiet. I wrote it from memory, rediscovering, despite everything, a certain nostalgia for the place where I'd grown up. I was catapulted in to a ravaged city where no child had been born for twenty years, and spent a restless childhood trying to think up a means of escape.

This play is about the people whom I swore to loathe for ever, but they have come to represent a universe that I can no longer forget. It might have been more beautiful to wake up to the sound of the Arno in Florence or to the smell of the sea, but that's not how it turned out.

The voices belong to women who taught me how to grow and from whom I learned that we cannot choose where we're born, but that we are born to choose where we want to go and with whom.

I'd like to thank Roberto Tarasco who directed this play and provided a significant input to many of the stories, to Gianluca Favetto for coming up with the version which you are about to read, to Gabriele Vacis – perhaps the last child to be born in this nameless city – for having woven the threads of these characters together, and to Federico Negro whose support was very precious to me.

Finally, I would like to thank Mary Luckhurst and Gabriella Giannachi for their meticulous translation, and add my appreciation for Gabriella's support of my work in the last few years.

Laura Curino

Passion

– May I come in?

Strange how we always said this when we were in already.

– May I come in? . . . Look, look how big it is!

And there I was, not seeing – or rather seeing but not understanding – or rather understanding but not liking what I understood.

– Look, what a beautiful home!

Opposite there was an eight-storey tower block and around it four identical, though smaller, tower blocks. And holes, holes and more holes and piles of earth, cranes, foundations and bulldozers.

– Oh look, this one's even got an intercom!

A little machine with its belly ripped open and all the intestines spilling out. And they call this home.

Once I had a home – a real home.
    A real home has a sloping roof and red slates. This one had a flat roof! A real home has windows with shutters that open like secrets. This one had a blind that snapped down like a guillotine!
    Above a real home there must be a sky, a vast sky and it must be blue.
    And there must be a chimney with a trail of white smoke going as far as the horizon – but that's where the beer factory was!

– Curino, Curino, I know what beers are! They're terrible animals that roar like thunder and pull apart anyone who goes near! And there's a whole factory of them!!

– Here's the central heating system, the inside loo, and the central television aerial . . . And now we've even got gas in our own homes!

What am I supposed to do with gas in my own home? I used to live in a home with a simple country-kitchen shiny cast-iron Aga which was fuelled with wood and coal. When the coal ran out you went to the shop to buy some more and while you were there you stopped for a chat. Then you went back home, your hands all dirty from the coal.

To wash yourself you had to heat the water on the simple country-kitchen shiny cast-iron Aga. Then the coal would run out again and you had to go and buy some more, and you'd meet a friend and chat some more. When you got back home you had to start all over again and Mum would heat the water with BP gas.

BP gas; with its typical cupboard, white, pink or baby-blue and its little drawer for cheap metal cutlery that never closes properly. When you opened the door you'd see the kitchen floor: why? Because the little BP-gas-cupboard didn't have shelves, it had a gas 'bomb'.

Because the 'bomb' always finished on Sundays we'd have to eat at Auntie Alba's. At Auntie Alba's we'd catch up on all the family gossip. If I was a good girl, when the bomb-man came he'd take me for a ride in his BP van.

Of course, in the old house you'd freeze to death when you went to the loo in winter. But at least in the summer you could have a chat with your neighbour over the fence.

And here they want me to talk through an intercom!

– Curino, Curino . . . Watch it! It's F I A T who want to control everything. It's all programmed: each tower block has four white-collar workers, three section-leaders, one foreman and the rest are workers and there's maybe . . . one test-inspector.
  Have you seen the excavations?

– They're for the new tower blocks, they're going to build a few there and some more . . .

– No, they're the ditches. They fill them with water and put crocodiles in so that you can only enter or leave the F I A T village over a drawbridge!

– What crocodiles? What drawbridge? We have standards here, you know! Standards!

– May I come in? Surveyor? Where . . .?

– Come in! Come in! Sorry I'm late. Some nut on the
building site's found some Roman tombs and I 'ad to slip
him a few bob. Stitched it good and proper! Cement over
the lot and on we go!

Ah! I don't understand why you factory workers
whinge. You're getting homes, aren't you? And some
homes!

Kitchenette: length: two feet for the electrics, two
feet standing room, two feet for the enamel sink with
built-in draining board . . . Width: two feet for the
four-ring designer-oven; two feet for the fridge . . . I
can see from your face that you're used to the old
coolers, but now you can regulate the temperature! You
put the fruit at the bottom, the cheese in the middle and
the meat at the top. 'Course, that's if you can afford
meat! But if you can't, you can always put the old man's
packed lunch there. We speak the same lingo! Most of 'em
don't even know what a packed lunch is! You know, the
wife makes starter, main course side-dish and dessert –
well, pudding – she shoves it all in the box, shuts it
tight and fourteen hours later the old man bangs it over
the heat and Bob's your uncle!!

Oh, where am I? This is the lounge.

– Mum, where's the dining-room gone?

– I'm talking about the lounge!

Roomy, spacious! You can get your settee in here, your
armchairs, table, dresser, hostess trolley, standard
lamp. Over here, and you'll note no trouble has been
spared, is the central television aerial-socket . . .
TV for everyone.

– Mum, does that mean we won't go to Auntie Alba's any
more?

Auntie Alba had a beautiful television positioned high up above
us. My mum sewed a frilly skirt for it, to protect it from the dust.
It sat up there like a ballerina. We went in the evenings and took

our own stools: the women drank coffee and the men 'just a dram' . . .

– 'Don't stand on ceremony . . . Hey, kids, would you like some of Auntie Alba's rose-hip syrup? You really do have everything these days. In my day . . .'

– Ssshhh! Can't we send her on to the balcony? Then I'll show you the bedroom . . .

On the balcony? There isn't room to swing a cat! Either you throw yourself over the edge, or you lie on the floor, take a deep breath and wait for the nausea to go away. Glued to the floor you can risk movement.

A rotation of the head to the right: beyond the railings and the tangle of cranes, almost hidden by the chemical fumes, is the Basilica di Superga. Viva Turin United! Pity they're all dead! Their plane crashed into the hill on a foggy night.

Rotation of the head to the left:

CLUNK! . . . CLUNK! . . . CLUNK!

– *What's that?*

– The free-fall American-style hygienic-eliminator: the little woman peels a potato, washes a couple of courgettes, the sprog's nappy, the chicken giblets and off they go, a free-fall down into the waste-pipes!

But the free-fall American-style hygienic-eliminators didn't last longer than three months. By the end of the first month we'd already been invaded by insects, but they were small and we could defend ourselves.

At the end of the second month Auntie Alba came for a visit:

– 'Oh nice, yes, . . . very nice . . . What a beautiful little flat! Don't take me the wrong way but why are there all these little bugs around?'

Beetles and cockroaches, a whole colony of them!
By the end of the third month we weren't getting any sleep because of the rats ransacking the waste pipe.

This is how the neighbours dealt with the emergency:

– **ALDO! the buggers are coming up again!**

– Rats! Do me a favour! These buggers are fatter than cats, just like the ones at the hospital!

– This is hou ah do it: ah take a nice wee piece o' cardboard, some sellotape, and a beautiful pot o'geraniums . . .

– Those bastards will eat your petunias for lunch, do you see! Poison your meatballs, that is their way, bach! Are those barricades up yet?

– **Aldo! The Montellas are making a barricade. Bring the hose-pipe. Let's drown them!**

The second influx of tenants faced guerrilla warfare: man against rat. Luckily they were more clear-thinking than us. Though they were exhausted from the journey north they did the only thing they could: they phoned the Health Inspector.

When the pest control arrived their van got stuck in potholes because the road hadn't been finished. The workers couldn't even get into their flats because the stairs were blocked with the new tenants' furniture and the lifts still weren't working.

They blocked up the free-fall American-style hygienic-eliminator one insipid dawn . . . I was Lawrence of Arabia and I kept a constant watch on the desert combat from my watch-tower on the balcony. There were trenches, holes and more holes, piles of earth, and the flashes of light against the bulldozers, the carbon fumes of the diggers!

I ended up in the outskirts of the outskirts of the city which didn't even have a proper name: I lived in Zone Seven, seven miles from a city which *does* have a name.

In 1966 there were only hazard warnings; no-entry signs, flashing lights, cones but no pavements; not even a road or a shop-window; in fact – not even a shop.

Before coming here the stork was going to bring me a little brother. But what now? There aren't any storks here.

– Children! Children! The light! Who switched off the light! Lo Mutolo – switch the light back on or I'll take a tumble.

  Hey, children! Haven't you washed yourselves today? What was that, Lo Mutolo? The smell is external. Lo Mutolo, THE LIGHT!! Right, now all sixty-one of us can take a good look at each other! We're here for a useful morning of mutual high-intensity pedagogical collaboration!

Curino! Late again! Come in and sit down at your desk! From now on you'll take after the unimpeachable model of your brilliant teacher: you'll be in front of the educational institute at 8.30 *on the dot.* Not like my colleagues who are all *cappuccino* and *croissant* and leave me to charge around after their pupils like a blue-arsed fly!

– Now, kids, who can tell me where we're at with the Venn diagrams? . . . Hey, Blondie, zip up my dress and I'll give you a kiss! . . . Where are we?

– **Where we're at? I don't know . . . What is this new teaching method, anyway? English book, yellow cover, dictation. Remember. 'i' before 'e' except after 'v' . . . 'd' er 'c' . . .**

– The Lord is my shepherd, I shall not want . . . Help!! Not my eyes, class! Cigarettes leave a scar . . . aim at my legs!

– Curino! Curino! Stop gabbing or I'll move you!

– Stop your noise! Ah want the silence of a graveyard. Ah dinna want tae hear a pin drop! Ah've crossed the straits and travelled the whole peninsula to find . . . what? Creatures wiout manners, morals, sensitivity, culture, or emotion! Get me a transfer back home!

Poor things! They did what they could. They came, worked for a fortnight and then got their transfer.

They were all young, newly qualified, pale, thin, rootless and needless to say, they were spinsters.

But where I'd come from I had *the* teacher: Tullia Puritan! Her very name was a manifesto, a flag, a declaration:

SUFFER THE LITTLE CHILDREN TO COME UNTO ME.

Shame on those who dare to lead astray one of my little ones!

But in this place we were taught in the tower block because the schools hadn't been built! Instead of blackboards we had balconies, the girls' and boys' lavatories were bathrooms, and in the morning I had to buzz the porter to let me in. Classes were in shifts and because some of my neighbours worked from dusk 'til dawn I was terrified that one day the teacher would register me for a 'night-shift'.

– Be quiet, Curino, be quiet! Things come and go: like teachers, like fireflies . . .

That first summer swarmed with fireflies searching for the fields, the fields that had been there the year before . . . After that they never came back.

– Be quiet, Curino, be quiet! Things come and go: like teachers, like the stenches!

Oh, yes, pungent, acrid and insistent with an acidic aftertaste – like a laundrette. Today's man wears *FACIS* clothing!

Zone Seven, on the left bank of the River Po, gets the Tramontana wind from Turin and the Libeccio from Chivasso . . . the Libeccio from *FACIS*, the Tramontana from . . .

Oh, a new whiff! Subversive, radical and highly alcoholic! Or is it petrol, a Molotov cocktail? No, No, that all came later . . . Ah, now I know! Aerosols: S I V A aerosols! Very dangerous!

What about this one? Hmm . . . Oriental, nocturnal, sensual: burning rubber! **CEAT** Cables? No, that'd come with the Mistral. Tyres! That's it! *PIRELLI* tyres!

This one's penetrating . . . asphyxiating . . . toxic – like the smell of boiled cabbage on a Sunday morning. Got it! A warm broth of cephalosporin cultures! Antibiotics! What do they call them? farmitalia!

And what do we have here? *Oh là là! Un bouquet varié, quelque chose de fleuri . . . Mais oui. C'est L'OREAL de Paris! Alors, mes petits choux, mais vous croyez que L'OREAL de Paris c'est à Paris? Oh, les innocents, mais non! L'OREAL de Paris c'est pas à Paris, c'est à Zone Sept! Et ça sent pas bon!*

– *Have you heard? The wind's changed! Today it's LAVAZZA coffee . . .*

97

Rosa on the first floor had a lover who worked in coffee.

— Rosa, where did you say you're from?
— *Guess!*
— Are you from Salerno?
— *They moved all the people from Salerno to Zone One.*
— Then you're from Palermo?
— *I'm not a southerner . . . and all the Sicilians have been put in Zone Four. If at first you don't succeed . . .*
— Give me a clue! What was it like where you used to live?
— *Oh, where I come from you can keep your windows open all year round. You can smell the basil and rosemary in the sun. And in the evening when the wind turns the fresh sea air reaches you.*

— Be quiet, Curino, be quiet! Things come and go: like waves, like shift workers' shuttles that take daddies to work . . . Be quiet, the customers are on their way!

Rumours had started going round that my mum was good at sewing. So clients started to arrive from the city. This is how I met the indigenous population – and the Lady!

The Lady didn't feel sick at the stench of boiled cabbage. Only occasionally she looked a little flushed. The Lady went from looking after her irritable old mother who suffered from God knows what to looking after her young manager who suffered from God knows what. In Zone Seven people gossiped a lot about her, not only because she had a responsible position, she practically managed the factory, but also because of her ambiguous relationship with the director. Every day they went for coffee together. And on Saturdays it was a business lunch! Whatever that means . . . Anyway, he never married her claiming a severe illness which prevented him from having children.

— Appropriately!

He said to the typists.

— Dress appropriately!

He said appropriately, meaning with more dignity, and the typists would button themselves up again.

The Lady was feared.

Whenever she came with her two sisters, mum would go into nervous breakdown mode. She'd fill her mouth with pins, so as not to be rude to them.

– Take it in here . . .
– Longer here . . . a bit tighter here . . .
– Looser but not too much . . .
– Isn't it a bit tight round the hips?

The sisters had tempers. The Lady would tell them to 'get a move on' because she had 'meetings' to go to.

– 'Meetings'? – I never understood that word. I always thought that it was only rich people who had meetings.

The Lady was 'rich', and 'beautiful'. Well, she was maturing, but she was still fascinating with her gleaming hair all pinned up. Oh no, not in a bun: the Lady had a chignon! A long time after she'd left you could still smell her *Pond's* cream in our flat. I wanted to be like her.

That is, until one day . . . she'd come to order dresses for the two sisters who had an important occasion coming up: the theatre.

– The theatre, not a theatre.
–A theatre not in a theatre?
– This is theatre theatre.

The Lady knew perfectly how her sisters' dresses should look.

– Well, an important occasion . . . a shantung, a crêpe de chine, a cadi that would hang properly, demi longueur, décolleté, raglan sleeve, revers, and pinces here with sequins there, pockets and a half belt on the back . . .

But when she came to deciding on her own dress:

– Oh, I don't know . . . you decide . . . a chemise?

A chemise?!! A chemise!! A chemise is not something you wear . . . How can I put it? It's a renunciation! It's a nothing, a negation, a shapeless bag! An extension of a man's shirt!! Neck, sleeves and buttons, nothing worth remembering. A cover, little more than a dress. A makeshift solution that mum would recommend to older, stouter clients. But not for the Lady, no, she still looks so young!

> – But I don't need it! . . . I wouldn't wear it! I'm in the office Monday to Friday. Oh, factories need to be looked after, they're just like men – they get sick, God help us! And on Saturdays I have to prepare for Mondays . . . I have my business lunch – even in the afternoon . . . Security has to stay and wait for me to leave. The guard has to wait until I've finished. And in the evening the factory really does shut down. One must rest some of the time.
>
> And on Sundays? Since mama passed away there's no one to look after on Sundays any more . . .

On Sundays there wasn't that much to do, if you exclude Holy Mass which was celebrated in a basement – they still hadn't built a church – by a missionary brought in especially from Venezuela.

There wasn't much to do in the rest of the town. The main event for many years was the transformation of the old school into a Town Hall.

In the city centre they had a proper school, a listed turn of the century stone building with a half-decent façade and two separate entrances for girls and boys. One of those schools that imprints itself on the memory from the very first; wide corridors with very high ceilings, science labs and maps charting cities that no longer exist . . .

One day they boarded it up and turned it in to a building site – and all its consequences: rows at the town council; legal action against contractors; and then opinion polls . . . And the usual handful of OAPs stationed in front of the building site advising the workmen, the bricklayers getting browned off, and the OAPs wandering off, grumbling.

> – Don't knock on my door when the school falls down . . . I never saw anybody throw a plank of wood!

Two years later they took the boards away and the new Town Hall appeared: it was absolutely identical to the old school – except for a sign which said:

MUNICIPAL MANSIONS

much like putting up a sign on a primary school which says:

PALACE OF LEARNING

What shocked me most was that the Town Hall still had the old separate entrances for boys and girls – this confirmed the ultimate sterility of the place.

Anyway, in an attempt to calm the enraged detractors, the town council decided to subsidize a cultural event: a theatre production, to be precise. I say 'subsidize'; in fact they handed over a derisory sum of money!

In the meantime I'd become a frog. Fat! Well, maybe not that fat but I felt I was: round short legs, long arms! Well, maybe they weren't that short or that long but disproportionate. You know how it is at that age: too much here – not enough there, a vast forehead and protruding, goggle-eyes. The optician even played a trick on me:

– Madam, we'll do the little girl a nice cheap pair of glasses suitable for sun and eye problems . . .

In swamp-green! Add to this that I never went outdoors and my skin was a greenish colour – and the picture is complete.

To get me away from all this Cwistina stormed in to my life one Sunday morning, preceded by the most imperious ring at the door I had ever heard.

– May I use your telephone? I'm expecting some important phone calls and mine's worn out. I'll give you my place on a sewing class in exchange. Ah, you're a seamstwess! Well, what about Owiental cooking classes, you know, gwasshoppers, worms and ants . . . We don't like them but there are cultures that weally like them a lot. Mr Cuwino, you're a mechanic . . . What an interwesting life you must lead all day on the assembly line . . . have you ever wead: *Zen and the Art of Motorcycle Maintenance*? . . . Oh, you've got a daughter . . . What a beautiful daughter . . . well, sort of . . . I don't know why but I've just wemembered that book *The Fantastic Bestiawy* by Borges . . . Do you like flies? . . . Mrs Cuwino, would you let her come to the theatre with me tonight? Maybe something'll come out of this . . .

Cwistina was the prototype of a human kind that was to reach a peak a few years later and of which there are still examples: they're obsessed with evening classes. They'd go to the 'local information buweau' and ask if they held 'twaining courses, classes, workshops, or seminars', – it wouldn't matter what they were: theatre, cinema, music, bio-mechanics, origami . . .

– The weally important thing is to fall in love with the teacher and all go out for a pizza on the last night.

Cwistina didn't take classes to do something but to have something to do. And it's not that she attended them to train for this or the other job. No! Cwistina did this or the other job so that she could attend classes.

In those days she stuck up innocent little white notices in every corner shop which read:

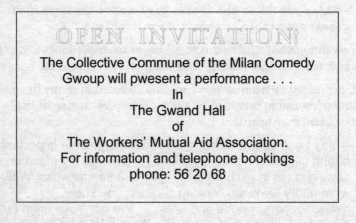

OPEN INVITATION!

The Collective Commune of the Milan Comedy
Gwoup will pwesent a performance . . .
In
The Gwand Hall
of
The Workers' Mutual Aid Association.
For information and telephone bookings
phone: 56 20 68

My phone number!
That's how Cwistina was. She loved short-cuts. And that day,

the day we went to the theatre, she insisted that we take one. I didn't want to because it went through **PARAMATTI**, the abandoned factory, and past the old ruined villa, where the madwoman lived.

Now you'd think that abandoned factories would be on the outskirts of a town but in Zone Seven they're right in the centre and they're not abandoned at all. On the contrary, they're alive with clandestine activity: craftsmen, black marketeers, discos and dodgy businesses. There were even illegal battery farms for chickens and rabbits, which is perhaps why the meat on our tables always looked so pale . . .

There was also a pack of gun dogs. They belonged to a colleague of my dad's who was employed as a hunter near Venice. When he came to work for F I A T he hadn't the heart to leave them behind. To supplement her salary Cwistina often took them for a walk. So they recognized her and all started barking and all we could do was to run away through a hole in the wall in to the garden of the abandoned villa.

The villa belonged to an estate which had been so parcelled-up and shared-out that no one knew who actually owned it. An old nanny lived there simply because everyone had forgotten about her. Her name was Magna Carlotta.

Magna in Piedmontese means 'aunt', but Cwistina said that this was impossible because Carlotta's family came from a place called Magna Grecia . . .

– It can't possibly mean 'Auntie' Gweece, it must mean 'gweat' . . .

Great Carlotta used to wander around the garden speaking incomprehensible dialect and reciting the verse of ancient and modern poets. She would stand for hours by the pond, or rather the puddle where they used to say that the little boy, whom she'd so passionately cared for, had drowned.

Cwistina loved venturing in to the gardens, overgrown with shrubs and blackberry bushes. All its exotic plants had become entangled and all the little flowers hybrids. Deep down amongst the tangle of plants there were stone seats, mutilated statues, and the remains of grotesque antiquities . . .

MAGNA CARLOTTA One, two, three, four . . . Hence! Away!
Fetch the candle! Look. What be that? Who be'st thou? Boy or
girl? A frog? Ooh! Thou has bitten me! Wench! Viper! Hence!!
Did I affright thee? Be not afraid . . .

  (*to the audience*) Oh, there thou art! Be not afraid. My bark be
worse than my bite. Why be thy hand in front of thy mouth?
Hast thou an ache? Thou should'st drink whiskey. I always drink
– whether I ache or no. Thou, thou be staring with thy big eyes.
Clean'st thou thy spectacles? Had'st I spectacles, they'd ne'er
be clean. I'd keep 'em dirty so I wouldn't be seeing nothing. But
thou'st right to clean 'em, thou'st young. Clean 'em, clean 'em
good and proper . . .Now I be seeing thee, thou seem'st like
lots of little birds on a branch, all sitting on thy little chairs. Well,
I'll come down to thee. My, but thou'rt dressed-up! All this
finery! . . . Thou look'st like the Black Madonna of Oropa! Hast
been there? Nor me . . . They do say 'tis beautiful. A beautiful
big church with a beautiful big Madonna. Outside they do sell
lots of little Madonnas – all the same, all little and hollow. There
be no holy water inside 'em. That one be in Lourdes. She has
water in 'er but no child. I once had a little Madonna with a Child
but I put it away. I felt sad looking at her. Thou look'st a bit like
her with all that gold. Wa'st costly? . . .

There were a certain number of gaps in the
rows of potted plants and a spoiled symmetry
about the treetops . . . Just as the gardener
must not let himself be distracted by other
interests, so the peaceful progress of the plant
towards lasting or transient perfection must
not be interrupted . . .

  We expend far too much on paving our way
through life . . . Instead of settling down right
away to enjoy ourselves in moderate
circumstances, we expand more and more and
make things more and more uncomfortable for
ourselves. Who now has the benefit of my lake
and my gardens? Not us, but unfamiliar

visitors, inquisitive strangers, travellers passing through.

Didst thou understand? I learned it all by heart. I never forget nothing. Archangel Gabriel . . . 'tis all his fault. I don't mind if I do scream it out. He comes and goes. Puts ideas in thy head.

Maria, you will be the mother of Christ, queen of the people.

Great – like my masters. The villa, the park . . . the puddle. . . If thou break'st a mirror . . . seven years of bad luck! The child fell and drowned . . . T'was not thy child, t'was mine . . .

Oh, 'tis a sad story! . . . So sad! Art still there? Away! To bed, there be nothing here. To bed! Be'st weary? . . . Thou be right. Thou ha'st no cause to be weary? Once upon a time I was very weary. Once upon a time there were lots of people here. I had to clean, iron, sew. Hard work it was, but satisfying. I baked cakes. Then all the men left and the women went away. We stopped planting those high trees in the park. Now the walkways be overgrown, and the flowers . . . The flowers all be wild.

Hell is not something that exists in the future: if there is one it exists here and now and is the hell that we live every day in being together. There are two ways not to suffer it. The first one is easy for many: to accept hell and become part of it until one no longer sees it. The second one is dangerous and requires constant learning and watchfulness: to look for and be able to recognize who and what in the midst of hell is not hell, make it last and give it room.

And give it breath.

ROSSANA Stop it! Switch off the music! Where do you think you are?! The worse the band the longer the warm up! . . . All we need tonight is a microphone. Cristina! Get out of here and take your frog of a friend with you! . . . Your shoes are all muddy. Have you been at the villa pestering the old woman again? Why don't you just leave her alone?

Anyway, I said: Comrade, you work in the Town Hall,

can't you make a compulsory purchase order? You could have bought the garden rather than let them build a shopping centre.

– *Comrade, do you have any idea how long it takes to get a compulsory purchase order? Three or four years. Maybe even longer. I can't even make a vague forecast. And do you know where your old woman will be in ten years? Dead and buried. It'll take too long . . .*

– Oh yes, and just because it takes such a long time they don't bother at all! It takes time! Of course it takes time! Rome wasn't built in a day! Doing anything well takes time! A child takes nine months . . . try to have a child in two months. It's not possible, it's not ready! That's why there's been a drop in the birth rate. Now they just take them ready made: children from India, Biafra, South America . . .! As for myself, I haven't any . . . not that I tried to . . . well, maybe when I was younger . . . There's no point anyway; they grow up, become potential juvenile delinquents and the council has to build a Care Centre for them. Know what that is? It's a place where delinquents learn to play the guitar from other delinquents, but because no one can play it properly, they get bored and all go and be juvenile somewhere else.

– *Rossana, if you want to risk a theatre production in the Worker's Association Hall, go ahead but you'll be the one answering to the Party.*

– Tonight's performance . . . bookings? . . . tickets? . . . I suppose I can't charge, what would the Party say?!

– *Rossana, no way! You can't charge. Theatre's a service for the proletariat and should be available to all. Anyway, you're the intellectual, you can give the introductory speech for our comrade comedians from Milan.*

– He says 'You're the intellectual' in the same way he'd say: 'You're a piece of shit!' So I've been writing the speech and burning the dinner for three days. My lover's complaining:

– *Rossana, I'm sorry to have to break this to you but I think you've reached a turning point in your life . . . Do as you wish. You're free – but the choice is politics or culture . . . You're free . . . Trade union or culture . . .*

– Yes, freedom . . .

Testing . . . testing . . . one, two, three . . . Oh, it works! Freedom is the creation of freedom, in every moment of life, with simple, fundamental words. Its deepest essence is ours.

Freedom is not non-confrontational peace or self-deceiving search.

It is not escape. It is not second-rate avant-gardism. It is with us every day, every moment.

'You surf through the Labrador's fur, as its febrile brute muscles vibrate beneath your ardent hand. In the fur of every moment.

Freedom is not to repeat the omnipresent fates of our parents; the scurrilous jests of our grandparents. It is to investigate their smiles and hugs. To transform the leopard's fur into the lion's mane; the golden skin of the snake into the mottled husk of the python. To turn this and that inside out.

Freedom is not to become lost and to become lost. For the sake of the soul, our dreams, the jaws of the God of time, the cortex of our hearts.

Freedom is so very dear to us that we never wish to lose it or desire to confront it.

Freedom is neither choice nor tyranny, neither percussion nor constraint. It is choice and tyranny. It is percussion and constraint. It is to flex your fingers on the keys of the instrument you're playing, where the most painful sounds live. Sounds of celestial penetration, desperate lovers, cherubs hovering, teasing each other in the ether and created by a wood carver, straining to complete his exquisite sculpted beauties in his portentous inlayings, scraping deeper and deeper to satisfy the connoisseur's eye.

Freedom is a man's honest heart, the kiss offered up by a woman, the never-changing smile of a child, the serene departure of the old, the hand that you felt and that you love.

Freedom is so very dear to us. We find it day by day like a bud, a plant we rediscover every evening. It grows each night in the weighty, variegated power of our dreams: those makers of freedom, signallers of the way. Our dreams: gods or god, bodies or essences, or parables, or farewells.

For you, Artist, freedom is your quivering hand, searching, dreaming, copying, writing, beating. It is the comma and the meaning. It is the sleep and the precision. It is the Zen branch, it is the Dürer face that I copy again and again. It is the beautiful face of a daughter. It is the fellowship of men, the search for truth. It is being together in the evening and telling each other stories, in the memory of time . . .'

Many years later, even in front of the staring eye of a python, Rossana would have remembered that far-away evening, during which Dolores had tried to break the ice:

– *¿Donde vás?* Stay here. They really like your speech! They only silent because they impressed. Come back! You can't leave the audience like this! I no go on the stage – I no good. You much heat up . . . me too . . . in another sense . . . Rossana is my brother . . . She help me when I arrive . . . My brother find me a house – he a priest. My brother say we are all brothers. We all in this city – we all brothers, sons of many mothers, many mothers, many families. But one big family. They come to visit. In the evening they go home. You have nice day. You very happy. I go home. I very happy!

Me – I like here. I like city. Rossana no like city. She say me stupid. *No sé* . . . They all complain. I like. Rossana complain. She say:

– There's no peace here. It never stops, not even at night. Noises in the distance . . . There isn't even the relief of darkness . . . flashes in the sky all night long.

– I know why. No is the city's fault. Is the fault of the guardian angels. They unemployed. They play cards all day, all night . . . in the sky over us. They no cannot come to earth because is no baby hospital here and so is twenty years that no children are born here. Here you die, you get married – the same . . . So the guardian angels get old. Their wings have the dandruff because they so dry. This is why some mornings the city has cover of red dust and I do washing again.

Of course, sometimes, I feel homesick for my country, where we sang and danced and fucked all night . . . Sorry! But now we have good things here too. Rossana and me organized a theatre – in the Workers' Association Hall. Extraordinary! Everyone came! All the communists . . . Today you never believe so many communists . . . but then there were priests who came because they misunderstood the title. They thought we wanted deal with the Catholic centre. There were two bishops who were much angry and came to excommunicate the priests. All the OAPs – they bought roses for the actress – they no been to the theatre for a long, long time and they no understood the customs. And all the teachers unfortunately push for the best seats – they want to make group photo with the actors. All of Fiat's Zone Seven was there. Rosa with her husband and her lover, who exchange dirty look with each other. And the Lady's sisters in long dress and the Lady in a blue chemise and a man from Venice with all his dogs. Cristina was there with little frog who talked and talked and still talk now. Then the comedians arrive, the tall one from Milan, his teeth stick out, you know the one from *Anarchist*

Death of an Accident . . . you know? He make you
laugh. He say: '*Laugh! Laugh! Laughter cures the
world. But be careful, there isn't much to laugh about.*'
And you laugh and laugh until your heart get smaller
and smaller and it fly away and you don't know where
it is. Then his wife came – the one who played the
Madonna. She spoke in ancient language – no one ever
heard it before but they all understood – It was so
primitive even I understood and I no good at this
language. They all quiet – even little frog.

What a shame! I must go now . . . you can stay
longer. I sorry that you didn't see that performance,
especially the wife, the Madonna. It late now . . . I go.
You want to know about it . . . You really do?

Well, in a few words: they kill the Christ on the
cross. And under the cross all the pious women cry
who don't want Maria to see him. No is good that a
mother should see her son dead like that on the cross.
So one want to stop her. Another want to hide Jesus
with a sheet. Another one say there is no point because
a mother will always know her son. But all the women
are always the same actress . . . she acts them all . . .
You will understand later . . .

Maria come to see him. She scream against people
who hurt him so much. Her poor Christ – he no guilty.
She curse them. Her poor little Christ want her to go
home. He say to his mummy, he say that he have to
die, that he have to go through it to the last breath but
if she there he no cannot do it and is more pain for
him. But she want to take him away. She even try to
bribe a soldier, a soldier who is so important that
actress must have had much talent to act him. She was
acting the soldier as well. I wanted to get up and throw
him out and everyone say to me shut up! what?! shut
up! So Maria want to give him her earrings so that he
can take her shawl, climb the cross and put the shawl
under the arms of her son to help him stay on cross.
The soldier who is very stupid he say something right.
Maria, do you hate your son so much that you want

110

him to live longer? Why you no kill him instead? Kill her son! Maria no can bear the truth and she faint. In her sleep she see the Archangel Gabriel, the one who start all this mess.

This Archangel Gabriel, he so vain, he so self-centred, he say things like: '*I really sympathize, I so sorry, I understand.*' When I hear him speak I finally understood all that stuff about the sex of the Angels, you know – no being man or woman.

Maria get so angry, she say he betray her. She say he told her she will be the Queen of all women. Queen? Of this beautiful throne? Queen? If she know this before she would never have wanted baby, not even if father God in person had come and not that blasphemous pigeon, the holy spirit. And she say to him: '*Go! The coloured feathers on your wings will get ruined here. Go! Your eyes will wear out seeing all this mud, this blood, this gangrene and the worms. Go! You will ruin your ears listening to all these screams and shouts and the crying. Go because you no are used to this. Because in paradise there no is famine, no war, no prison, no drought, no raped women, no hanged men, no children without a smile, no lost and desperate mothers. Go! You no are the one who had to keep the little one in your swollen belly. You no screamed at his birth. You no give him your breast. You no cry when he was sick. You no wake up at night to try to lull him back to sleep when his teeth came. Go! Gabriel! Go!*' And so she curse him and curse him again! And the mortified Archangel lost all his vanity and say:

– Maria, Maria, forgive me! I thought I was suffering like you but now I know that is impossible. But I came to say that it will be your sacrifice and your son's sacrifice to open the doors of paradise so that all men and women can enter for the first time.

(Dolores/Maria raises her eyes to the sky, bows in an act of submission but an instant before the stage darkens, she shakes her head slowly as if she's not convinced. Then she bows again and shakes her head. She's still not convinced. She bows again, and yet, no, she still isn't convinced . . .)

Theresa

JULIA PASCAL

Julia Pascal is a playwright and theatre director. She was the first woman director at the National Theatre. *Theresa* was adapted for BBC Radio and broadcast as *The Road to Paradise* in 1996 and 1997. As the first play in her Holocaust Trilogy, *Theresa* is followed by *A Dead Woman on Holiday* and *The Dybbuk*. All have been seen in Britain and Europe. Further produced plays include *Year Zero/L'Année Zero, St Joan, The Yiddish Queen Lear* and *Charlotte Brontë Goes to Europe*. Her BBC television play *Charlotte & Jane* won BAFTA and Royal Television Society Prizes.

Characters

Theresa Steiner
French Student
Narrators
Cassandra
Herschel Grynszpan
Josef Steiner, Theresa's son
Man at Vienna Station
Jewish Woman at Vienna Station
English Official
English Ladies
Lydia Askew
Boy and Girl, Lydia's children
Mathilde
Franz Schön
W. R. Schulpher, a policeman
Guernsey Women
Nurse
Gestapo Officer
German Soldier
Guernsey Girl, a nurse
Nurse Spitz
Matron

The production can be performed by five actors.

Theresa was premièred at the Gulbenkian Studio Theatre, Newcastle, on 9 April 1990.

Prologue

Theresa Steiner dances/moves to Strauss's The Blue Danube. *This action to suggest Jews being made to dance. Memories of a first ball in Vienna. Being in a concentration camp and observing horror, reaching out to fellow camp inmates; it is a foretaste of the play itself. It also suggests the end of an empire. The dance should be expressed jaggedly against the sweetness of the Strauss.*

COFFEE HOUSE IN VIENNA, 1938

This is to be spoken in English as below and echoed by the same text paralleled in German.

Theresa I walk towards the Café de la Bourse on Taborstrasse with its huge windows and sparkling crystal . . . Does the emperor live there?
   A man stands in front of the café. It's a cold winter morning. The man is well dressed. He gazes at the window for a minute then strides away. Nonchalantly. He returns casually and looks at the shiny chocolate gateaux, the sweet white sponge cakes laced with thick cream. He makes my mouth turn to water; I almost taste the sweetness of the chocolate, the rush of pleasure in my mouth, the gust of life and happiness of black chocolate.

Theresa speaks Polish. This is translated in English by the actors in following passage.

Nachwileracam do swojego dziecinstawa Warsawie. Napoleonka. Tak sie to ciastko nazywa. Ja tez tak paczylam przes szyby, ale ten sklep nie mial krysztalow to byl maly sklep sprzedajocy zwykle ciasteczka, ale nie dla mnie. Moja matka

powiedzíata nie mozemy sobie na to pozwolic. Wybij to sobie
z glowy.

*Actors run on stage and divide these lines. They mime the child
in Warsaw.*

For a moment I am back in the Warsaw of my childhood.
Napoleon. A Napoleon cake. It was called. I stared at the shop
window; this shop had no crystal or highly polished glass; it
was a small cake shop selling everyday cakes. But not for me.
No Napoleon for me. My mother said, 'No we can't afford it.
Forget Napoleon.'

This man standing outside the Café de la Bourse on
Taborstrasse is too old to have a mother saying no. She lies
beneath marble. He visits her once a week. Or did until
recently. He suddenly stands to attention as if in memory of a
duel or the war. I imagine medals on his chest under his thick
coat. Mine is threadbare. He stands to attention and walks
casually into the café. As the doors open a gust of sweetness
and warmth mixed with tobacco and perfume clouds out into
the street. I follow. He sits at a marble table and a thin girl in
waitress black and white comes to him. He is presented with a
gilded menu on thick cream paper. I can feel its ribbed texture,
thicker than the soles of my shoes. Women fill the room with
gaiety; their low murmurings betray pleasure as their
chocolate-filled mouths move in well-painted bows. A dark red
lipstick is in fashion this winter of 1938. The waitress arrives
with a Schwarzwalderkirchertorte.

How far is it to the Black Forest?

She gives him the plate and he spreads a well-starched white
white napkin over his knee.

She returns with steaming coffee on a silver tray. The thick
whipped cream almost flows out of the cup. The carpet is thick
pile. I don't notice my thin shoes now. Silk curtains adorn the
walls, draping them like at the theatre. Most of the well-
dressed men and women are sipping chocolate and delicately
pushing small portions of petit fours through their rouged lips
or beneath well-trimmed moustaches.

He pushes aside half of the Black Forest cherry cake. I
examine it from across the café. I can almost taste the thick

cream, the soft dark sponge, the red kirsch and the kick of the alcohol.

He pushes it aside as if he has had enough; it is the studied effect of a man playing the millionaire. He takes out a newspaper, crosses his legs and casually lights a cigarette, inhaling it deeply into the base of his lungs.

As he does, he looks out of the highly polished crystal glass window. SA men are beating Jews in the cold morning.

They are having great fun with an elderly couple of Jewish workers pushed on to their hands and knees, forced to scrub the street. A group of pretty prostitutes are screaming with laughter at the pair old enough to be their grandparents.

'Give them some fresh water.'

And a bucket of piss and shit is hurled at the Jews.

The man in the café turns his face away.

He is white.

He eats his cake quickly. Too quickly. It was meant to last all morning. Now it's gone. The waitress is standing beside the marble-topped table with the bill.

He puts his hand in his pocket for the three thousand.

His last few schillings change are for her tip. She smiles.

His last banknote on a cake and a coffee. He leaves the crystal-glass, marble-tabled, thick-pile carpet, silk-curtained Café de la Bourse and walks out from the perfumed, sweet, chocolate-filled air into the cold winter morning. Turning away from the raucous laughter of the prostitutes and away from the men in uniforms, he looks down on to the heads of the old couple; their veined hands scrubbing the street. He stares in frozen fascination while the well-dressed men and women in the café continue sipping their chocolate and ordering another cake.

VIENNA MUSIC CONSERVATORY, 1938. THE LESSON

Theresa gives her final lecture to her students in Vienna Conservatory.

Theresa Today we were to continue our discussion on Schoenberg. We will not be doing that because today is my last day as Professor of Music in this Conservatory. The Nazis have forbidden Jews to teach gentiles. We Jewish teachers must disappear.

As undergraduates you have the right to expect the broadest education. We are all the inheritors of those who question our bourgeois, conservative society. New forms are being expressed. James Joyce, Sigmund Freud, Alban Berg, Stravinsky, Schoenberg, Weill, Eisler are a few who challenge the old order. These men are despised by the Nazis. Hitler sees them as 'degenerate'. But what is 'degenerate'? To him all Jews are degenerate. To him Bolsheviks, Communists and Socialists are degenerate. They are taking these so-called degenerates to Dachau.

When I was a young woman I used to stare in fascination at my own hair. Sometimes a strand of black, coarse frizzy hair would appear. My hair always had to be tamed when I was a child and there were hours spent by Mother brushing it in some kind of order. I used to cry because it wasn't smooth and fair like other girls'. It was like a Gypsy's, they would say. Or an African's.

The Nazi ideal is to make people with hair and features which conform to the Aryan stereotype. In this new world there will be no room for our differences. Our quirky individual differences. Beauty will be made to order.

They are already killing their own old people and they want to kill all Jews, Gypsies, Communists and homosexuals – anyone who doesn't fit into the myth of the Super Race.

Up to now you've been lucky enough to taste the flavour of these new languages. You've listened to Schoenberg, read Sigmund Freud, seen the works of Erwin Piscator and Georg Grosz. Whether you accept the Nazi art is up to you. But you will have tasted the forbidden.

Whatever happens to me, you must go on. Remember our discussions and whisper them to your friends. Seal them in your brain cells until this order is over.

Pause.

I wish you long life.

Note: in the following, the French Student should be the same performer who plays Cassandra.

French Student May I speak to you, Frau Doktor Steiner?

Theresa Yes, of course.

French Student My name is Esther Jacobson. I am from Paris. I heard your talk.

Theresa You are not one of my students, are you?

French Student No. I am studying Fine Art. Or rather, I was studying.

Theresa You are a Jew?

French Student I have a Jewish grandmother.

Theresa You could go back to France.

French Student And if the Nazis invade France there will be plenty of 'righteous Christians' who will be delighted to talk about my grandmother.

Theresa What will you do?

French Student I have to go to Palestine. It's the only place we can be safe.

Theresa And if the British don't allow you in?

French Student I'll get in illegally. Come with us?

Theresa I can't do that.

French Student Why not?

Theresa I don't speak Hebrew.

French Student You'll learn.

Theresa There is more to it than the language. I am a European. I am not a Zionist. Europe is my home. We are Austrians. My husband fought in the last war. My parents came from Poland. I speak Polish, German, French and English. These are my languages. I am a European. Why should I be pushed off this continent because one man says so? I have the right to live here. Why should I be forced to live in the Middle East?

French Student How will you survive?

Theresa I will go to London. I have made arrangements. I will go to London with my son. We will wait until this is over. We will start again.

French Student Excuse me, but aren't you being a little naïve?

Theresa Naïve? (*Beat.*) Maybe you are right. I have become a

Christian Jew. I've got used to a little bit of anti-Semitism every day. A remark about a large nose, a dark appearance, love of money, killer of Jesus.

French Student Maybe I'll see you next year? In Jerusalem?

Theresa Maybe.

KRISTALLNACHT/THE NIGHT OF THE BROKEN GLASS. 9 NOVEMBER 1938

Scene opens with Theresa and Josef moving to Krysztof Penderezcki's 'To the Memory of the Victims of Hiroshima/zu Gesdachtnis der Opfer von Hiroshima'.

Both are in isolated spot. The mood is of terror and isolation as if to express the experience of Kristallnacht.

Lights up on whole stage.

Narrator Kristallnacht. November 1938. In Paris a young Jew kills a Nazi diplomat.

Herschel The Nazis. They killed my parents. Now it's your turn.

Cassandra The little Austrian with a moustache who failed as a painter was delighted. It was the perfect excuse.

Theresa Kristallnacht.

Narrator The Night of the Broken Glass.

Theresa Kristallnacht.

Cassandra Listen, Jews, you have the warnings. Go. Get away from the little man with the moustache. He wants to break your bones like glass. He wants to burn your flesh. And take the gold from your teeth. And if you have no gold, he will take your teeth. He will take your skin and make lampshades. He will make a mountain of hair. A mountain of hair. A mountain of hair. And teeth and glasses and shoes and dresses and jackets and trousers. And one day, in the future, a young woman will go into a second-hand shop in Heidelberg and she will look at the shirts hanging on the rail and she will see names like *Goldberg*, like *Freidmann*, like *Jacobson*, like *Steiner*.

Theresa Like *Steiner*?

Cassandra *Josef Steiner.*

Theresa I sewed the name in his shirts.

Cassandra *Josef Steiner* sewed into the collar of a shirt made for dancing in . . . But who will remember these men? These women? Murdered by the little man with the moustache?

Herschel You killed my parents.

Cassandra Today they'll say it never happened. How could it happen? Who would do such a thing? (*becoming a French anti-Semite*) *C'est une invention juive!*

Herschel (*actor playing Herschel becoming a neo-Nazi*) *Es ist eine judische Erfindung.*

Theresa (*actor playing Theresa momentarily breaking character to express Polish anti-Semitic view*) *Wynalazek zydowski!*

THE DEPARTURE

Spotlight on Theresa only. She sings a childhood Polish song.

Theresa
  Cherwone jabtuszko
  przekrojone ma krzyz

  Czemu ty dziewczyno
  Krzywo ma mnie patszysz
  gesi za woda
  kaczki za woda uciekaj dziewuyno
  bo cic poboda
  ja ci buzi dam
  ty mi buzi dasz
  ja cic mic wydam i ty mnic nic wydasz
  ja za woda, ty za woda
  Jakzi ja ci buzi podam
  podam ci jz, na lystczku
  czekaj, czekaj kochaneczku!

As the music gets lighter and jollier, other actors throw a case, a hat and a coat at Theresa to break the mood. Train sounds.
  Lights up on Theresa and Josef.
  Production note: this scene is done as the two stylize packing. Theresa folds and unfolds a long 1930s coat

continuously. Josef tries to button his shirt but it always comes out wrong.
    Train sounds.

We've got to go. Can't you see what's happening?

Josef Yes, I'll follow. I can't go yet. I've got too many people to see. I've got to finish everything. The newspaper . . .

Theresa You've no job. You've no family apart from me. What is there to stay for?

Josef It'll soon pass. It's just a temporary situation. It won't last. I can't speak English.

Theresa You'll learn quickly. I've got visas for both of us.

Josef Give me mine, Mother. I'll follow. Go find somewhere comfortable for us. You can be a cook and I'll be an English butler. I'll look good in a butler's uniform.

Theresa Don't make me go alone.

THE JOURNEY TO ENGLAND FROM VIENNA

Train sounds. Vienna station.

Theresa They put a J in my passport. For Jew.

Man Jude.

Theresa If Jesus wanted a passport –

Man They would stamp a J in his.

Viennese Jewish Woman (*to unseeing crowds on platform*) Take my baby. Take her with you. I can't get a visa. I can't get a job in England. 'No maids. No cooks. No nannies. No cleaners.'

Man (*English Official*) No German teachers, definitely no German teachers.

Woman Take my baby. Let her live. There's an address. An agency. Good people will take her. Will find her new parents. I beg you let her live.

Theresa opens her arms and takes the baby.
    Male actor sings 'Wiedele Wedele'.
    By now everyone has placards around their necks with 'Wien nach London' for the Kindertransport – except, of course, Theresa.

Train sounds continue.

Theresa Holland! People shouting, giving us sandwiches and chocolates. London.

Train sounds stop.

Men in bowlers. Umbrellas. I register as an alien.

Man Alien.

Theresa I have only ten marks. It's all they allowed me to take.

Lady 1 (*English accent*) You can work for me. You can't use the hoover. Use the brush and pan. Servants only break the hoover. Believe you me.

Male Foreign Office Official Now you have to register with me every week. Remember you are an alien. If you move towns you have to register. If you move districts, even districts here in London, you have to register. You have to register.

Lady 1 If you want to eat in the house then you have to eat in the scullery.

Time passes, stylize movement.

What are these crumbs? You've been eating your breakfast in my kitchen haven't you?

Theresa Please, I have to go out Friday. My day off. I have to go to the station. To see if my son is arriving. From Vienna. I must meet the train.

Lady 1 No, you've been eating in my kitchen. No more days off for a month. Subject closed.

Theresa Excuse me, madam –

Lady 1 Don't!

Scene cuts to Liverpool Street Station, London.

Announcer (*voice-over*) The train arriving at Platform Four is the connection from Vienna via The Hook of Holland and Harwich.

Theresa sees someone she thinks is Josef. As she reaches out to him he moves away, singing 'Hanschen Klein'.
Scene cuts back.

Lady 1 I want to talk to you, Steiner. You deliberately went against my orders and went to the station. You're sacked.

Theresa (*as if to police*) Change of address. Theresa Steiner.
Domestic. Leaving London. Going to Wiltshire. To work. As a
domestic.

Lady 2 Theresa Steiner? I know we spoke about your coming
here. I had a phone call from your previous employer this
morning, Mrs Powell. A very respectable lady. She said you are
unreliable and disobedient. She said you went out directly
against her wishes.

Theresa My son. I had to see if he was coming. From Vienna.
My day off.

Lady 2 I don't know why they just don't intern the whole bloody
lot of you.

THE INTERVIEW

*This scene starts with Theresa walking from door to door in
search of work. Each door is slammed in her face. Finally she
comes to the house of Lydia Askew, set against Noël Coward's
'Don't Let's Be Beastly to the Germans'.*

Theresa Mrs Askew?

Lydia Yes?

Theresa It's about the advertisement in *The Lady*.

Lydia Oh. I was expecting a younger woman. (*Pause.*) Oh,
excuse me. How rude. Do come in.

Theresa Thank you.

Lydia Tea?

Theresa Thank you.

Lydia With milk?

Theresa Yes, please.

Lydia How long have you been in this country?

Theresa Three weeks.

Lydia I see. Not long is it?

Theresa No, not long.

Lydia And how do you find the English?

Theresa (*pause*) Very polite.

Lydia But cold?

Theresa Yes, how did you know?

Lydia I didn't know I was going to say that.

Theresa I think you read my mind.

Lydia Have something to eat. A cake? It's a good Battenburg.

Theresa Battenburg? A royal cake?

Lydia (*awkward*) Yes, I suppose you could say that.

Theresa It's very colourful.

Lydia Now where were we?

Theresa The job.

Lydia Yes, well as I said, I really was looking for a younger woman. I can't pay much.

Theresa That doesn't matter.

Lydia Have you any experience as a nanny?

Theresa I'm a Professor of Music at Vienna Conservatory.

Lydia I could tell that you were something else, something higher in the world.

Theresa I have experience with children.

Lydia Oh?

Theresa I have a son.

Lydia A son. I hadn't realized you were married.

Theresa I am a widow. My husband died in the First War.

Lydia So did my father. (*Pause.*) But on the other side, of course.

Theresa Of course.

Lydia And you are a German.

Theresa An Austrian.

Lydia I'm sorry, an Austrian . . .

Theresa I am also a Jew . . . that's why I had to leave. My family came to Vienna when I was a child. From Warsaw. From Poland.

Lydia Poor Poland.

Theresa Yes, poor Poland.

Lydia Was your father rich?

Theresa Not all Jews are rich.

Lydia I'm sorry, that's very crass.

Theresa They were musicians. They were not rich.

Lydia And you have a son, you say?

Theresa Yes.

Lydia And where is he now?

Theresa He's still in Vienna.

Lydia Would you like to meet my little girl?

Theresa Oh, yes, please.

Cut to children. Boy sings 'Ring-a-Ring a Reihe' (Ring-a-Ring a Roses in German) – a clapping game with the little girl. Theresa joins in. Boy disappears. Little Girl is left. Theresa brings the Girl centre stage to have her hair brushed by Lydia. Little Girl carries a bald Victorian doll.

LYDIA'S STORY

Although this is a monologue the action includes everyone. Halfway through the male actor plays Edward Askew. He lifts Lydia and flirts with the other woman. Chopin's Opus 27 No.2 in D flat is used against the first half.

Lydia I can talk to you. I don't know why I feel this but I know I can talk to you. Maybe it's because you're not from this country. You know nothing about me or where I come from. I liked you instinctively. *Simpatico*. Isn't that what they call it? Or maybe because you're older. You could almost be my mother. Hardly. My mother's not like you. She's not one for talking. Not about anything serious. Not that I ever saw much of my mother when I was a child. They sent me away. My sister Joy and I were both sent away to boarding school. Different boarding schools. We were both without friends. That was the idea. To make us independent. To make us 'nicely behaved young women'. Make nicely behaved young women out of us. Is that what I am? (*Pause.*) Yes, I suppose it is.

And then after school came the dances, the presentations, the long dresses and the correct shoes. Everything had to be so correct. I hated it. And all those young men who kept calling at the house. Pale-faced men with stammers and 'good prospects'. How I hated them. Was this all life had to offer? 'Yes,' Mother said. 'Yes,' Father said and disappeared into a bottle of whisky. We had maids. They were fun. Irish girls with stories about fairies who stole babies. I liked those. They were always fun. But Mother wanted to get rid of them. They used to take me to church with them. Incense. I remember. When Mother found out she gave them the sack. So there was never anyone to talk to. Not really talk. There was only

Mother and Father and Silence Is Golden and Little Girls Should Be Seen And Not Heard.

Daughter gets up with doll and leaves space. Actress now becomes the other woman.

And then I met *Him*. Edward. Edward Askew. His father and my father were great friends. Edward had always been away at school and I'd played with him occasionally in the holidays. But I never thought he'd want to marry me. He was too tall. Too good looking. Too everything. I heard he'd been with lots of women; he told jokes, laughed a lot. But he came and took me out. To the cinema. To the seaside. We walked on Brighton Pier and the wind was so high my skirt flew up. He laughed and said I had good legs. I blushed. Then he said he wanted to marry me. I laughed. I thought he was mocking me.

We got married. Five years ago. That first night I was scared. He was sweet with me. Very sweet. And then the babies came quickly. He seemed to get bored. Stayed out late. And if we did go out together I saw his eyes follow others. I felt small and insignificant, as if I didn't matter any more. He wanted to be with others. I knew that. And at night, when he came in late, he turned away from me in the bed and I felt such a pain in my stomach, it was more than the pain of a child's birth. For hours I lay awake beside him, wanting him to touch me but knowing that somehow everything had changed. What was it? Was it the babies? I didn't know. And when the war came, he volunteered immediately.

With relief, I thought. Relief to get away from me and back to a life of his own. Like school with the boys. I sometimes think maybe he'll die and then I won't have to watch him watching all those others. It's a terrible thought but I can't help it and then I just long for him, long for how it was before the babies, when we walked on the pier and he held my hand. And every time the post comes I wonder if it'll be a letter, a letter telling me the worst, or is it the best?

His death would free me!

I wouldn't have to put up with the thought of other women any more; his eyes on their breasts, their hips, their legs.

Are all men like that? Do they all make us feel so small?

Theresa My father worked in a toy factory. I had wonderful toys for Christmas. In school we all wore aprons. My mother made me special aprons. Every night my mother darned our stockings. And Father's socks. She darned the socks and supervised us in our homework.

There was always music in the house. Mother sang songs. We had gas light. We sat around the stove to keep warm and sang songs. My grandfather came from Bavaria. He told us stories of Hansel and Gretel.

Theresa and the actor playing Josef – as a child – sing 'Hansel and Gretel' in German.

He read us fairy-tales. Hans Christian Andersen. The Brothers Grimm. I hated dolls. They were so cold. They sent me to the hospital because of the measles. It was so lonely. Grandmother came and brought me dolls. But I didn't want them. Where was my mother? They put us in high beds because there weren't enough cots. And then they made me go on the potty. Sister said, 'I'll put the potty in the bed and then you can "go" in the bed.' I said, 'No, I'll wait till I go home.'

When the war came I was always so hungry. By then I was married. Like you, I was only a short time married. He was killed in 1917.

When I was a little girl I taught myself to read. When I went to school it was a shock. I sat in the second place. The first in the class was Mathilde Liebich. She was the daughter of the headmaster. She was supposed to sit next to me. First was the first and the second was me. But she wouldn't.

Mathilde I don't want to sit next to you because you're a Jew. I don't like Jews.

Theresa Then I didn't want to be second to her. I wanted to be third. (*Pause.*)

My son. He promised to follow me. I got a visa each. I got invitations. He could be a butler in Kensington. I was to be the maid.

Music for the Savoy Hotel links into next scene.

THE SAVOY HOTEL, LONDON, 1938

The Savoy lounge where German émigrés go to hear the music.
  Two maids get ready and then set up chairs. The scene should
have elements of absurdism. Theresa enters and sees a young
man standing with his back to her.

Theresa Josef?

Young man turns.

Franz Sit, please. Franz.
Theresa Franz?
Franz Franz Schön. Berlin.
Theresa Theresa. Steiner. Wien. Vienna.

  Franz extends his hand and becomes very English.

Franz How do you do?
Theresa Thank you very much.
Franz Nice weather.
Theresa How long did you take to learn English?
Franz From going to the cinema.
Theresa Ah.
Franz Coffee? Tea?
Theresa Coffee. Yes, coffee.
Franz Coffee in England is awful.

  Franz beckons to Waitresses, they ignore him. This happens
  several times.

They never see me.
Theresa People must be going to the opera. In Vienna.

  Waitresses bring coffee.

Franz The coffee. So thin. Cake?
Theresa No, thank you.
Franz I understand. It's not Sachertorte.
Theresa What did you do in Berlin?
Franz Professor. Architecture. Berlin University. You?
Theresa Professor of Music. Vienna Conservatory.
Franz *Erste Stock. Zweiter Stock. Dritter Stock. Vierter Stock.*

Ja, Madam. Nein, Madam. Bitte schön, danke schön. I work
the lift here. This is my tea break. I come for the music. The
memories of home.

Theresa You like England.

Franz Yes. Yes. Yes. You?

Theresa I'm getting used to it. How old are you?

Franz Thirty-one.

Theresa I have a son in Vienna.

Franz How old is he?

Theresa Also thirty-one.

Franz A Professor of Architecture?

Theresa No. (*Pause.*) Franz.

Franz Herr Professor Franz Schön.

Theresa Nice name, Franz.

Franz What's your son's name?

Pause.

Theresa Do you have a cigarette?

Franz Bad for health. Your son?

Theresa Let's listen to the music, shall we?

Franz I come here every day to listen to the music.

Theresa I have to go soon. I've got a job. Nanny.

Franz Between five and five-thirty every day. My tea break. In
this place.

Theresa Between five and five-thirty.

Franz Or in the lift. Number Seven. It's the best lift.

Theresa gets up. Franz kisses her hand.

Theresa Goodbye, Herr Professor.

Franz *Auf Wiedersehen.* Don't forget. Lift Number Seven.

*Theresa exits. Franz is thrown the bell boy's hat by a Waitress.
He dusts it and places it on his head. Hold his humiliation for a
moment then scene changes.*

LYDIA'S HOUSE

Voices over. Chamberlain's declaration of the beginning of the war.

Theresa has stylized movement during the voice-over. Lydia is preparing the Little Girl's clothes.

Lydia Go. We've got to go.

Theresa Go? Go where? Where can we go?

Lydia I can't risk it. The children. What happens when they start bombing London?

Theresa But where can we go? I'm a Jew. I can't just go anywhere. I'm an 'enemy alien'. I have to report, don't forget.

Lydia We'll go to the Channel Islands. My brother's wife lives there.

Theresa Where are the Channel Islands?

Lydia Near France.

Theresa Near France. Is that safe?

Lydia Don't worry, they're safe. They're British. We'll all be safe there.

Sound of ship's horn.

GUERNSEY, SEPTEMBER 1939

Two Guernsey Women and one British Policeman. Policeman is W. R. Schulpher, same character throughout the rest of play.

Narrator Guernsey.

Policeman Theresa Steiner. Registration. Now you are on the island of Guernsey you must report to me. And surrender your passport.

Guernsey Woman 1 Who is that woman?

Policeman An outsider.

Guernsey Woman 2 A Jew.

Guernsey Woman 1 They say the Germans are getting closer to Paris.

Policeman They've occupied Paris.

Guernsey Woman 1 Paris! Will we have to evacuate?

Guernsey Woman 2 No. I'm staying here.

Guernsey Woman 1 The army will save us.

Policeman Don't be silly. The army's all left.

Guernsey Woman 2 We don't have to go, do we?

Guernsey Woman 1 I don't want to go to England.

Policeman The Guernsey authorities have said we'll be safe with the Germans. They won't hurt us.

STRANDED

Stylized movement from Theresa and Lydia during this voice-over.

Announcer (*voice-over*) People of Guernsey. Evacuation boats will be ready for boarding immediately. The Germans are expected any day. British military personnel have been evacuated from the island. No danger is expected to the local community but anyone wishing to leave the island for Southampton must register immediately.

THE BETRAYAL

Lydia I've got to go. I need tickets for two adults and two children.

Policeman You can go, madam. This lady stays.

Lydia You don't seem to understand, Inspector. She is my nanny. She's been living with me in London for over a year. She's my responsibility.

Policeman Theresa Steiner was born in Vienna. She has a 'J' stamped in her passport. That means she's a Jew.

Theresa Yes. I am a Jew.

Policeman Austria has been annexed by the Germans. So this woman belongs to the Germans. They'll decide what to do with her. In the meantime she can work as a nurse. She'll be useful here.

Lydia But the Germans haven't invaded.

Policeman Yet.

Lydia You can let her go.
Policeman She stays with me. Subject closed.

Ship's horn sound.

Lydia Theresa. Please forgive me. I have to get back. For the children's sake.

Theresa hugs Lydia. Lydia accepts the moment then pushes Theresa away.
   Scene then shifts to surreal and repeats with different lighting states.

THERESA'S NIGHTMARE

Lydia I need tickets.
Policeman This lady stays.
Lydia My responsibility.
Policeman Vienna. J. Jew.
Theresa Yes. I am a Jew. I am a Jew. I am a Jew.
Policeman Belongs to Germans.
Lydia Haven't invaded.
Policeman She stays with me.
Lydia Forgive.

REPLAY 2

Lydia I need tickets.
Policeman This lady stays.
Lydia My responsibility.
Policeman Vienna. J. Jew.
Theresa Yes. I am a Jew. I am a Jew. I am a Jew.
Policeman Belongs to Germans.
Lydia Haven't invaded.
Policeman She stays with me.
Lydia Forgive.

REPLAY 3

Lydia I need tickets.
Policeman This lady stays.
Lydia My responsibility.
Policeman Vienna. J. Jew.
Theresa Yes. I am a Jew. I am a Jew. I am a Jew.
Policeman Belongs to Germans.
Lydia Haven't invaded.
Policeman She stays with me.
Lydia Forgive.

REPLAY 4

Lydia I need tickets.
Policeman This lady stays.
Lydia My responsibility.
Policeman Vienna. J. Jew.
Theresa Yes. I am a Jew. I am a Jew. I am a Jew.
Policeman Belongs to Germans.
Lydia Haven't invaded.
Policeman She stays with me.
Lydia Forgive.

REPLAY 5

Lydia I need tickets.
Policeman This lady stays.
Lydia My responsibility.
Policeman Vienna. J. Jew.
Theresa Yes. I am a Jew. I am a Jew. I am a Jew.
Policeman Belongs to Germans.
Lydia Haven't invaded.
Policeman She stays with me.
Lydia Forgive.

REPLAY 6

Lydia I need tickets.
Policeman This lady stays.
Lydia My responsibility.
Policeman Vienna. J. Jew.
Theresa Yes. I am a Jew. I am a Jew. I am a Jew.
Policeman Belongs to Germans.
Lydia Haven't invaded.
Policeman She stays with me.
Lydia Forgive. Forgive. Forgive.

THE COLLABORATION

French-speaking actor plays the Narrator.

Narrator The swastika flies from the Arc de Triomphe. France continues to sleep.

She sings the following song to Eric Satie's music. Lyrics by Henry Pacory. She dances with a Gestapo hat. The song symbolized France's collaboration with the Nazis. Title 'Je te Veux' to be performed with irony.

1	2
J'ai compris	Je n'ai pas de regrets
Ta détresse	Et je n'a qu'une envie
Cher amoureux	Près de toi
Et je cède	Là tout près
A tes voeux	Vivre toute ma vie
Fais de moi	Que mon coeur
Ta maîtresse	Soit le tien
Loin de nous	Et ta lèvre la mienne
La sagesse	Que ton corps
Plus de tristesse	Soit le mien
J'aspire	Et que toute ma chair
A l'instant précieux	Soit tienne.
Ou nous serons heureux	
Je te veux.	

Repeat verse 1.

THE OCCUPATION OF FRANCE

'Frère Jacques' to be performed by the German and the French actors.

German performer takes a simple movement of being stroked on the back of the neck as a child. He sings 'Frère Jacques' in French. Gradually the movement becomes repeated. The stroking turns out to be a beating by an oppressor. He gradually changes from joyful child to victim of Nazis. His movement and sound gradually becomes more and more anguished. His 'Frère Jacques' changes into 'Bruder Jakob'.

Frère Jacques	Bruder Jakob
Frère Jacques	Bruder Jakob
Dormez vous?	Schläfst du noch?
Dormez vous?	Schläfst du noch?
Sonnez les matines	Hörst du nicht die Glocke?
Sonnez les matines	Hörst du nicht die Glocke?
Ding dang dong	Ding dang dong
Ding dang dong	Ding dang dong

French performer starts as a little girl at a concert. Gradually her French verse becomes German as she is forced to sing in German. Her movement gradually changes. The little girl is kicked in the leg, forcing her into a can-can step which becomes a goosestep.

THE INFORMER SCENE

Guernsey.

Nurse I'll see you at the end of the war. In 1943. In London. Under Big Ben. The War's bound to be over in a year.

Theresa (*also in nurse's hat*) Come on, let's make the beds. Let's have a race, see who can make the beds quickest. I can do one in three minutes.

Policeman We're making a list of Jewish people on the island.

Narrator Do you know who the Jews are?

Nurse Yes, they're people from Palestine like Theresa here.

Narrator Do you like Theresa?

Nurse Yes, she's pretty. But it's a pity her appearance is spoilt by her big Jewish nose.

Policeman Theresa Steiner. You have to report to us every week.

Theresa My son. In Vienna. I was waiting for him to come. Do you know what happened to my son?

Nurse It'll soon be Budelot Night. Where will I get fireworks now?

Theresa What's that?

Narrator The end of the year. *Bout de l'an.*

Nurse When we burn the Guy.

Theresa Burn the Guy?

Narrator 1 In the Nazi concentration camp on the British island of Alderney the prisoners arrive in the uniforms of 1941.

Narrator 2 They still wear them in 1942.

Narrator 1 When a man dies because he is beaten to death in Alderney others cluster around him to inherit his tatters. A carrot is thrown from a window by a cook.

Narrator 2 A Russian slave worker sees it and runs for it.

Narrator 1 A Nazi watching him takes out his whip and lashes the Russian on the face, on the head, on the body, until he is nothing but a red thing, a hideous thing, a poor, starving dead thing.

Narrator 2 *Ils prennent les combattants juifs français de la résistance et les enferment dans un tunnel. Ils les enfermerons dans un tunnel pour les priver d'air. Au dessus du tunnel les prostitués françaises prennent un bain de soleil à Alderney.*

Narrator 1 They take the Jewish French Resistance fighters and lock them in a tunnel. They will lock them in a tunnel to starve them of air. Above the tunnel the French prostitutes sunbathe. In Alderney.

Narrator 2 Some Guernsey women share their beds and open their legs to the Nazis.

Narrator 1 'Jerrybags', the locals call them.

Sound of marching songs.

Nurse I hear their marching songs. So many good-looking Germans. So tall, so young, so handsome.

Narrator 1 Who can blame the women for falling for them?

Nurse Who can blame them for wanting a little bit extra?

Nurse (*to Gestapo Officer*) Herr Kommandant. My brother is breaking the law. He's got a radio.

Narrator That woman eats well tonight.

Theresa What about my son. Have you any news of my son? He was to come and find me. I've no letters, no message, no nothing.

Gestapo Jews are forbidden to go to the cafés, cinemas, museums, weekly markets.

Policeman Libraries, sports places, family bathing places.

Theresa The *Guernsey Evening Express*, 19 June 1941.

Narrator 2 A number of French prisoners of war returned and were welcomed by the Mayor of Lyon on behalf of Marshall Pétain. (*She sings 'Marechal Nous Voila', the song of the Pétainists.*)

Nurse Mr Roosevelt's dilemma.

Narrator 2 Whether to join the European War –

Narrator 1 – or not.

Gestapo A trade and clearing agreement has been concluded at Agram between Hungry and Croatia.

Narrator 2 The British mail steamer *St Patrick* of 2,000 tons engaged on the service between England and Ireland –

Narrator 1 – was sunk as a result of an attack by a German plane on 13 June 1941.

Gestapo Great success in assuring the nation's food supplies has been achieved in Germany.

Narrator 1 While cycling down Les Baisseries last evening Miss A. Falla, an employee of the telephone exchange, came into contact with another cycle ridden by Miss Amy of Monument Gardens. As a result Miss Falla is suffering from a dislocated shoulder.

Gestapo Blackout dusk to dawn.

Narrator 2 Couvrefeu – Curfew.

Gestapo Nine p.m. to six a.m.

Narrator 1 *La Gazette Officielle*. (*She gives everyone a newspaper.*)

Nurse *The Evening Press*.

Narrator 1 Second Order relating to Measures against Jews.

Gestapo Zweite Verordnung über Massnahmen gegen Juden.

Narrator 2 All Jewish economic enterprises, or any enterprises which have been Jewish since 23 May 1940, are to be declared by 31 October 1940 to the competent local authorities.

Gestapo *Judische wirtschaftliche Unternehmen oder solche wirtschaftlichen Unternehmen, die nach dem 23 Mai 1940 noch judisch gewesen sind, sind bis zum 31 Oktober 1940 bei dem zustandigen Unterpraefekten anzumelden. Jews cannot take part in –*

Policeman – wholesale and retail trade.

Gestapo Hotel and catering industry.

Policeman Navigation.

Gestapo Banking and money exchange.

Narrator 1 Dealing in automatic machines.

Gestapo Third Order.

Policeman Relating to Measures against Jews 26 April 1941.

Gestapo Jews.

Nurse Any person having at least three grandparents of pure Jewish blood.

Narrator 2 A Jewish grandparent.

Policeman A person married to a Jew –

Nurse – or who subsequently marries a Jew –

Theresa – shall be deemed to be a Jew.

Policeman In doubtful cases –

Nurse – a person shall be deemed to be a Jew.

Narrator 1 We are informed by Essential Commodities that there will be half a ration of meat issued this weekend.

Nurse Beef or veal.

Narrator 2 F. Beckford, funeral undertaker. Motor hearse and cars supplied. The trade supplied.

Nurse St George's Hall open for roller-skating every Tuesday, Thursday and Saturday, seven till ten p.m.

Narrator 1 Gaumont Cinema this week. *Ein Leben Lang.*

Nurse *Her whole life.*

Narrator 2 Fascinating German film.

Theresa English subtitles.

Gestapo Jews are forbidden to go to the cinema, cafés.

Theresa They talk of slave workers here on Guernsey.

Narrator 1 I see them all. The Spanish Republican digging with his hands into the sides of the hill, digging to make the military hospital.

Gestapo Operation Todt.

Narrator 2 Operation Death.

Narrator 1 They beat and beat him till he hit back. They didn't kill him.

Gestapo This time.

Nurse The Jews? Where are they? They just seemed to disappear . . .

Narrator 2 The Germans didn't weed out the Jews.

Theresa They didn't need to.

Policeman List of Jews resident in Guernsey –

Gestapo One: Dumequin.

Narrator 1 (*as character*) Née Fink.

Policeman Religion?

Narrator 1 (*as character*) Church of England.

Gestapo Two: Brouard.

Narrator 2 (*as character*) Née Bauer.

Policeman Religion?

Narrator 2 (*as character*) Church of England.

Policeman Three: Spitz.

Narrator 3 (*as character*) Auguste. Born Vienna.

Policeman Occupation?

Narrator 3 (*as character*) Domestic.

Policeman Religion?

Narrator 3 (*as character*) Jewish.

Policeman Four: Steiner. Theresa.

Nurse Yes. Theresa Steiner, that's her.

Policeman Born?

Theresa Vienna.

Policeman Occupation?

Theresa Nurse.

Policeman Religion?

Theresa Jewish.

Gestapo Jude.

Cassandra Pauvre Juive.

Policeman From the Island Police to the Gestapo. Sir. I have the *honour to report* that the Jews resident in the Bailiwick of Guernsey are of the following nationalities: British, Dumequin Elizabeth née Fink; British, Brouard Elda née Bauer, 109 Victoria Road; German, Steiner Theresa, Castel Hospital; German, Spitz

Auguste, Castel Hospital; Czech, Wranowsky Annie, Clos de Ville, Sark. I have the honour to be, Sir, your obedient servant.

Narrator 2 I have the honour to be.

Theresa Sir.

Policeman Your obedient servant.

Theresa Guernsey Police Inspector.

Narrator 1 W. R. Schulpher.

Narrator 2 Letter from A. J. Roussel Esq., His Majesty's Greffier, Royal Court Guernsey.

Narrator 1 Dear Sir –

Theresa Re-relating to Measures against Jews.

Narrator 2 I have to report that this office has taken charge of the stock of a small wholesale ladies' underclothing business which was abandoned at the time of the evacuation.

Narrator 2 I understand it was conducted by a –

Narrator 1 – Mrs W. Middlewick at her private residence at 36 High Street –

Narrator 2 – whom I believe was of the Jewish faith. The business has not been carried on since the stock was taken over.

Narrator 1 The stock consists of –

Narrator 2 – 143 pairs of ladies' artificial silk stockings.

Narrator 1 186 ladies' vests.

Narrator 2 992 pairs of knickers.

Narrator 1 Twenty combinations.

Narrator 2 378 slips.

Narrator 1 Four coats, summer weight.

Narrator 2 Twelve coats, winter weight.

Narrator 1 Six costumes.

Narrator 2 Nine cotton frocks.

Narrator 1 Five wool frocks.

Narrator 2 Sixty-four nightdresses.

Narrator 1 Twenty-one suits pyjamas.

Policeman Letter to the Gestapo. Sir.

Woman 1 Julia Brichta.

Woman 2 Hungarian.

Policeman I beg to report that I have seen the above-named woman. As far as she is concerned.

Woman 1 My parents aren't Jews. I'm not a Jew. (*Crosses herself frantically.*)

Woman 2 Annie Wranowsky.

Narrator 1 German.

Policeman Enquiries have been made by the Senechal of Sark within the Bailiwick of Guernsey concerning the above-named woman.

Woman Neither my parents nor my grandparents were Jews.

Policeman Her passport, Number 558, issued in London –

Woman On 13 February 1939.

Policeman – is stamped with a 'J'.

Narrator 1 I am your –

Policeman – obedient servant.

Narrator 1 W. R. Schulpher.

Narrator 2 Inspector, Guernsey.

Theresa Letter to the Gestapo.

Narrator 1 Dear sir, I have the honour to be your obedient servant.

Theresa Order Relating to Measures against the Jews.

Narrator 2 Regarding the registration of Jews.

Narrator 1 I have the honour to report that the order –

Narrator 2 – which accompanied your letter –

Narrator 1 – was communicated –

Narrator 2 – to the Royal Court of Guernsey.

Narrator 1 I can assure you that there will be no delay in so far as I am concerned in furnishing you with the information you require. I have the honour to be –

Narrator 2 – your obedient servant.

Narrator 1 Your obedient servant.

Theresa Signed –

Narrator 1 Victor G. Carey. Bailiff.

Blackout.

JOSEF'S LETTER

Josef Dear Mother
 I write this because I know you'll never receive it. I made a mistake not coming with you. Now I'll never be an English butler. Strange to think this is my last day of life. It's brave to take your own life, don't you think? Better that it happens this way. I saw the Nazis beating an old Jew and dragging him into the

public lavatory in the Opera House. They made him clean the lavatory with his bare hands. Then they made him smear the shit on his face. After they'd finished laughing they crushed his head on the ground until the blood spilt all over the marble floor. Why did I watch? Why didn't I stop them? And if I'd tried, my head would now be crushed. They are taking us to Dachau. So far I've escaped but time runs short. I don't want to go to Dachau. They'd send you a parcel of my ashes and ask you to pay the postage. It's better this way. Better to be a Stoic in the old Roman fashion, don't you think, Mother?

Many of my old schoolfriends have disappeared. Vicki, my first girlfriend. Do you remember her, Mother? You were quite jealous. Vicki went to Dachau. (*Sings phrases from 'The Blue Danube' and speaks at the same time.*) They shoot Jews on the banks of the River Danube and in the ballrooms people still waltz.

Vienna still looks the same. The opera houses and cafés are still full. And when we disappear nobody notices.

They say the war will mean a Third Reich that lasts for a thousand years. Reich means Rich. The National Socialists are interested in money. And you in London, Mother? Maybe it'll work out better for you. Are you a maid to some rich English lady? They say the English are good people, good to foreigners and that they don't hate the Jews too much. But, when the Nazis get to England, where will you hide?

There's so much I haven't done, so much I haven't seen, Mother. Nobody will ever know my name. Nobody will ever remember me. Only you. In the last moments before I die I will think of you.

(*Wryly*) Don't worry. I've already forgotten Vicki. (*Crushes paper defiantly.*)

THE GUERNSEY GIRL

Cross fade to St Peter's Port, Guernsey.

German Soldier Your bike, Fraulein, is there something wrong?
Girl Yes. The tyre's gone.
Soldier May I help you?

Girl I don't know.

Soldier Does your father have a car?

Girl He did have. Before . . . the Germans took it.

Soldier Where do you live?

Girl Not far. Street number fifteen.

Soldier What was the name of the street before?

Girl Before?

Soldier Before we came?

Girl Margaret Street.

Soldier And now the names are all changed to numbers.

Girl I think I prefer that.

Soldier Do you?

Girl Where are you from?

Soldier München.

Girl München. Where is that?

Soldier In the south of Germany.

Girl München.

Soldier Have you been to Germany?

Girl I've never been out of Guernsey. Except for a day trip to Jersey. But we don't like Jersey people.

Soldier You'd like Germany.

Girl Why?

Soldier There's more fun there than here. In camp we call this the arsehole of the world. Oh, excuse me.

Girl Why do you call it that?

Soldier It's so dull here. We have theatres, café, opera. There's nothing to do here. But wait.

Girl Wait for what?

Soldier For the war to end.

Girl And you'll win?

Soldier *Heute Frankreich. Morgen England.* Today France. Tomorrow England.

Girl You're right. It is dull here. The blackout. The curfew.

Soldier There is the cinema.

Girl German films.

Soldier With subtitles.

Girl Yes.

Soldier I'd love to take you but we can't sit with you. (*Pause.*) You're very pretty.

Girl Am I?

Soldier Yes. Very pretty.

Girl You speak English well. Where did you learn?

Soldier In school. I like Shakespeare. *Julius Caesar*. 'The fault, dear Brutus, lies not in our stars but in ourselves that we are underlings.'

Girl I don't know any quotations.

Soldier I could bring you some coffee. Do you like coffee? Or new clothes. A silk blouse, perhaps? They sell them in our shops. They are brought over from Paris. For the officers to buy for their wives. I'll get you one if you'll see me again. Tomorrow?

Girl A silk blouse. Yes, I'd like that.

Soldier Tomorrow then. Same time. Here on road nineteen.

Girl I'll be here.

Soldier Heil Hitler.

Girl Heil Hitler.

Hold the girl in spot. She's giving the Hitler salute. The actress plays the role of the Nurse in the next scene, which suggests she's the same character. The Radetsky March links the scenes.

CASTEL HOSPITAL GUERNSEY

Three nurses shaking sheets to the Radetsky March. British Policeman looks on. The scene opens in mid-conversation.

Nurse No, no, no, he's not a doctor.

Nurse Spitz Really?

Theresa A doctor can be a doctor without being a medical doctor, you know.

Nurse (*to audience*) They know everything, these 'continentals'.

Theresa (*beckons Spitz*) Vienna?

Spitz nods.

I remember you. One day in the park. I was walking with my son. I saw you on the bench. The bench where Jews were forbidden to sit.

Policeman No Jews –

Gestapo – are allowed –

Theresa – to sit.

Spitz To sit.

Theresa I heard you were a Communist.

Policeman A Jew *and* a Communist.

Theresa Your father repaired shoes. Spitz?

Spitz Auguste. From Vienna.

Policeman Spitz.

Theresa I heard someone say there's another woman on the island.

Policeman Another Jewess on the island. Theresa Steiner *and* Auguste Spitz *and* –

Nurse Marianne Grünfeld from Silesia.

Light change.
Gestapo Officer clicks his fingers. The British Policeman stands behind him. Both are in spotlight.

GESTAPO

The Guernsey Police have been most helpful. In fact the Island authorities – although they consider themselves British – have behaved like true servants of the Reich. We shall certainly have no trouble here. If the British are going to be so helpful then there's no need to worry about any trouble once we take the mainland. I don't know why we are at war with England at all. As you can see, a spirit of cooperation and willingness to help us root out these Jews means we can quickly clean up the Island. These three women can be shipped to Auschwitz as soon as we are ready for the transport. Order to Paris. Three Yellow Stars. *Sofort!*

THERESA'S DORMITORY

Blackout. Gestapo Officer with torch.

Gestapo Where is she? Where's Theresa Steiner? You, Matron, you're in charge, tell me where she is.

Matron Of course, Herr Kommandant. Theresa Steiner is one of my nurses. She's upstairs in the nurses' dormitory. Nurse Oldman will take you.

He shines torch on nurse who points to Theresa sleeping.

Gestapo Theresa Steiner. You have three minutes to pack one suitcase before you leave with me.

Theresa Leave with you? Why? What's happening?

Gestapo All Jews are being taken off the island.

Theresa Why?

Gestapo Pack immediately. Unless you want the rest of the nurses to suffer.

Nurses throw case, coat and hat at Theresa. Final image of Gestapo Officer standing behind Theresa. Hold in spot. Bring up sound of trains. Mix with 'The Blue Danube' echo. Return to high-volume trains going to Auschwitz and slow blackout. End.

Trace of Arc

ALI SMITH

Ali Smith was born in Inverness in 1962. She has published fiction, poetry and criticism, *Free Love*, a book of short stories (Virago, 1995), *Like*, a novel (Virago, 1997), and, most recently, *Other Stories and other stories* (Granta, 1999). Other plays include *Stalemate*, *The Dance*, *Comic* (all produced in Cambridge and the Edinburgh Fringe) and *Fifteen Minutes* (Traverse Theatre, Edinburgh).

Trace of Arc was first produced by Smug Cat Theatre at the Canongate Theatre, Edinburgh, in 1989 with the following cast:

Conscience Rebecca Evans
Trace Jane Tonge
Jackie Gina Clarke
Mrs Lord Victoria Combe

All other parts were played by Catriona Grey.

Directed by Sarah Wood

Set lighting is dim, showing a pantomime supermarket set, one checkout, a display stall, a trolley, pantomime display food stacked and presented. Enter Conscience, comes in front of the set, one arm raised as if to catch people's attention at a social affair.

Conscience Um. Can everybody hear me? Are you all listening? Can you all – this lighting isn't exactly the kind of thing I want . . . well, it'll have to do I suppose. I just want a quick word with you before the play begins. It won't take long, if you can all hear me at the back . . .? If you could just listen. I don't mean to barge in on you or anything. I know you've all come to see a play, not listen to me recite a moral diatribe at you. I know you've come to enjoy yourselves really. After all, enjoyment is very important, isn't it? So. I'll keep it short. I've just written down a few things I want to – (*Searches in pockets.*) Oh dear, I, um – (*Looks again.*) I seem to have, um, I must have left – (*Checks all possible places.*) No. Well, I'll just have to remember. Oh, I never get it right. I'm always forgetting something. I'll never get my wings. Well, when I say 'wings' – don't get me wrong. It's just, you know, a saying. Actually there are no such things as actual wings. There's no flying involved. I'm glad about that, to tell you the truth. Haven't the head for heights. And as for haloes. Well, whoever heard such nonsense. Haloes, they're only a useful device for indicating who's important in paintings. Can you imagine having a halo? I'd always be leaving mine in Marks and Spencer's; some shop assistant would find it, I can hear her now, 'What's this halo doing in the jumpers?' And while we're talking about such matters I'd just like to make one thing clear. I am not an angel. Or a saint. Yet. (*Looks at her watch suddenly.*) Oh, but we'd better get on. The Unities, you see. If you know anything about the stage, you'll know about the Unities. That's unity of time, place and action. For those of you who don't know, it means that things happen on the stage as they would in real life. At the same rate of time, all in the one place, and one thing after another logically. Consequence, you see. I'll spoil it if I'm not careful. Not Supposed To Be Here, and all that. Oh dear, that makes me sound rather inconsequential, doesn't it? But I'm a great lover of the theatre, a great lover of the stage. I like a good play. I certainly wouldn't miss a play about a saint. I go to all the saint plays. (*Looks suspiciously at the set over her shoulder.*) I *did* hear this was supposed to be a version of *Joan of Arc* . . . (*Examines the set doubtfully, wanders round it poking at it.*) Well, it had better be, I don't want to waste my evening. As long as it's a good play. (*Suddenly remembers.*) Oh, but my announcement! Heavens, I forgot. (*Composes herself, back into official stance.*) Now. I just want you all to listen. I just wanted to say. Um, just to say save the whale. And that there are a lot of things that we should be thinking about and, um, doing something about. Like seals. And Nicaraguan coffee. And homeless people. This is international year of the homeless, you know! Oh no, that was last year. Nevertheless, a lot of people don't have homes. So we should all be doing something about it. I mean, what is the point if we don't?

Um . . . there were some other things I had to tell you. There was, now let me see. My memory, I tell you. I remember, once I forgot something very important. It was when I'd gone to see a stage version of the life of St Teresa of Avila . . . or was it the other Teresa . . . No, no, I mustn't digress, I mustn't. I was telling you about, now let me see. I had to tell you something about hamburgers and trees. I think. But the important thing is. You should all send money anyway. That's all I wanted to say. Money should be sent right now. And there was something about people dying because they don't have enough to eat. And something about a disease. And I think I had to remember something about the ozone layer. And could you possibly put something aside, some little thing for the pensioners? They do need it. It's a shame.

Have you got all that, now? I just wanted to appeal to your better natures. Captive audience, you see. I don't like to have to do it, but it's what I have to do. Even when you're enjoying yourself at a play, you have to remember the serious things in life. (*Goes to sit down in the front row, half there, stops and comes back.*) I nearly forgot. Do think about pollution. Did you know that, because of terrible pollution, female whelks are developing penises? You may laugh, but it's not very funny for them. And do be careful what fruits you buy at the supermarket. A little thing, a small purchase, can mean a great deal of suffering for some person somewhere else. Always check the –

Noise behind her as people scuffle, about to move on to the stage.

Oh dear, the play. I've overrun. Many thanks for listening, you've been very patient.

Behind her, as she moves to take her seat, Jackie and Tracy, both late teens, bowl on to the stage, chasing each other round the set, laughing, late for work.

Jackie We're late, we're late, we're late – Tracy, we're late –
Tracy (*looks round stage*) It's all right, she's not here, she won't know –
Jackie She'll be upstairs, today's money day.
Tracy So it is. Blast. That means –
Jackie Oh bloody hell. (*Puts on voice.*) Late again, girls? You know what I think of lateness, girls. Lateness is a disease, Jackie. A social disease, Tracy. And what do we do with diseases, girls? What do we do with inefficient workers, Tracy?
Tracy Fire them, Jackie, eh, I mean, Mrs Lord.
Jackie Nothing as simple as that, my girl. The loss of a limb in forfeit at least. You will be asked to hand in one leg at the end of the week. Entrails and guts are acceptable in exchange. And be on time in future, Jacqueline. Punctual, Tracy. (*Comes out of voice.*) You get the lights, I'll sort the tillroll – (*She fumbles with the checkout.*)
Tracy Right . . .

She switches on lights. Stage lights up, extremely bright after the dim beginning. The set is coloured pastel, clashing pinks and yellows and oranges, and somewhat overcrowded in the way small supermarkets tend to be cluttered. Big signs hanging from the ceiling and plastered on the displays: LOWEST EVER! EVER WONDERED WHAT'S IN STORE? COME

*AND VISIT WONDERSTORE!! PRICES FALL
FURTHEST AT WONDERSTORE!!! VALUE FOR
MONEY AT WONDERSTORE!!!! WE'RE NOT
BLUFFING – YOU PAY NEXT TO NOTHING!!!
BARGAINS GALORE AT WONDERSTORE!!! The two
girls charge round the stage putting things where they should
be, making sure everything's in place. They meet centre stage.*

Jackie The doors!
Tracy The doors!

*They dash off in opposite directions, offstage momentarily.
They meet again, centre stage, catching their breath, just as
Mrs Lord enters, impressive, queenly, in charge.*

Mrs Lord Good morning, girls.
Girls Good morning, Mrs Lord.
Mrs Lord You were late this morning, girls. Weren't you?
Girls (*chastised*) Yes, Mrs Lord.
Mrs Lord Now that's hardly the spirit, is it girls? You know
what I think of lateness. What is lateness, Jacqueline?
Jackie A disease, Mrs Lord.
Mrs Lord What kind of a disease, Tracy?
Tracy A . . . (*She genuinely can't remember.*)
Mrs Lord Can't you remember, Tracy?
Tracy I think it begins with . . . or maybe . . .
Mrs Lord Don't you ever listen, Tracy? What kind of a disease,
Jacqueline?
Jackie A social disease, Mrs Lord.
Mrs Lord A *social* disease, Tracy. I've told you often enough.
Where's the spirit? *Mmm?* Will we ever keep the ball rolling
without the right spirit? Come along, come along! Tracy, the
foodstuffs.
Tracy Yes, Mrs Lord. (*Goes to side of stage to sort display.*)
Mrs Lord Jacqueline, the checkout. Here's the money, sort it. Put
that brain of yours to some use, girl, then perhaps you'll prove
to me that you have one.
Jackie Yes, Mrs Lord. (*Goes to sort checkout.*)
Mrs Lord Neither of you are irreplaceable. All I have to do is
lift the receiver and call the agency. Plenty of people looking

for work in our prosperous area. As I stand here in this small but bustling town, where unemployment was high and a true flowing economy hard to come by before the Plant was set up, I want to be proud of my supermarket. What do I want, girls?

Girls To be proud of your supermarket, Mrs Lord.

Conscience shifts irritably in her chair, and begins to take notes, shaking her head, maybe making little noises of disapproval.

Mrs Lord (*strolling round her supermarket, admiring it*) I *know* how I like a supermarket to be run. I know how I like *my* supermarket run. Shop-shape, everything where it belongs. We all have to pull together. Now where would we be if we didn't all pull together? We'd be all over the place, wouldn't we, and nothing would ever get done. Because, let's face it, people *need* supermarkets. I need them, you need them, everybody needs them. They provide us with a cost-effective, time-effective means of living, speedy access to the necessary foods and goods. A humane way to eat, a proof of our civilization. Jacqueline?

Jackie Yes, Mrs Lord?

Mrs Lord Help Tracy with the stacking.

Jackie Yes, Mrs Lord.

Mrs Lord I mean, think of it this way. Every single one of us working here in this little supermarket – I don't deceive myself, I know this is only a little supermarket. But in a small town, we serve our purpose, and that, I think, is what life is all about, don't you, girls?

Girls Yes, Mrs Lord.

Mrs Lord Every single one of us working in this little supermarket is a part of the great family, the Great Chain of Supermarkets. From the littlest tin in the pyramid to the manager, the arranger, the one at the top of the pile. And we are all part. Never forget that, girls. Think how far we have come. In stone-age times, a caveman would have to go out in all sorts of savage weather, with bows and arrows, or, goodness, bits of stick and rock even, to have to run after savage animals and kill them for food, bring them home to his wife – and then there was no time left to do anything else with the day. Supermarkets have taken the 'savage' out of survival. Now we can simply call in at the supermarket, pick up exactly what we want, and Hey Presto, or Hey Co-op, Hey Sainsbury – Hey Wonderstore (*she gesticulates around her, ham actress.*), we can use the rest of the day to do all those other things; look after the children, clean the house, relax and watch television – or simply earn more money for more food. (*Inspired*) Oh, girls –

Girls Yes, Mrs Lord.

Mrs Lord In my own lifetime I have seen such changes for the better. From corner-shop to superstore, small to big business. Much more room for so many more things to sell. And so many more people to buy them. Especially since the Plant was installed, work has come to this town on a scale there never was before. And money. So many more people, so much more money. We all ought to be thankful to the Plant, girls.

Girls (*not quite in unison*) Yes, Mrs Lord.

Mrs Lord (*menacing*) A little more efficient, please, girls.

Girls (*immediately*) Yes, Mrs Lord.

Mrs Lord Now, where was I . . .?

Jackie Being thankful to the Plant, Mrs Lord.

Mrs Lord Yes, that's right. We've all got the Plant to thank for the success of Wonderstore – for our wages, girls. What more could one want from life? Everything in its order, everything in its place, at your convenience. And what happens, Jacqueline, if one tin is out of place?

Jackie If one tin is out of place, Mrs Lord, the whole pyramid will fall.

Mrs Lord And what does that teach us, Tracy?

Tracy (*confused*) Not to stand too close to the tins, Mrs Lord?

Mrs Lord Foolish girl. It teaches us that place and purpose are of the utmost importance, and that we must keep our place in the pyramid or all order will be destroyed.

Tracy (*to Jackie, whisper*) What pyramid? Whose order? Are we making an order up?

Jackie Shh!

Mrs Lord I can safely promise all clients that at Wonderstore we will cater for their every need. Won't we, girls?

Girls Yes, Mrs Lord.

Mrs Lord Provided they have the money. That's only fair.
Commodity is the best policy. Commodity for commodity,
that's my motto. On with it girls. In the best spirit. Are the
doors unlocked?

Girls Yes, Mrs Lord.

Mrs Lord Right then. Sell sell sell. Good morning, girls.

Girls Good morning, Mrs Lord.

*Exit Mrs Lord. Tracy and Jackie carry on with their stacking
and sorting and pricing. On Mrs Lord's exit, Conscience
stands up and comes to the front again, first to speak to Tracy
and Jackie.*

Conscience I hope you two won't mind if I just have a little word
with the audience about what they're watching. You should
probably listen too. I've made some notes about it, and I've a
couple of things to say.

*Turns to audience, unaware of the fact that Tracy and Jackie
don't acknowledge her at all, and they don't; it's as if she's not
there.*

Right ho. First things first. I'm actually not very satisfied with this
play. In the first place (*consults her notes*) it doesn't have
anything to do with saints. That's just a personal quibble, but I
think it can be taken further. If a play's going to advertise itself
as something, well, then it ought to at least oblige its own
description. Don't you think? Second, I don't think it's a very
classy play. You always know a play lacks class, don't you
think, when characters say things like – wait a minute, I wrote
it down – like 'As I stand here in this small but bustling town
where unemployment was high and a true flowing economy
hard to come by before the plant was set up.' I mean honestly.
When information is passed on so cheaply, well, where's the
hope? And something else I feel I have to mention. A lot of that
last scene struck me as propaganda. Really it did. But the thing
that worried me the most, the thing I'm determined to find out
about, is this P-L-A-N-T. Plant. I do think there's something a
little suspicious sounding about it. Don't you? I've been
content in other plays just to watch. But something intrigues

me about the structures here. Sometimes you just have to be involved. If you'll excuse me, I'll just ask these girls a few questions.

Goes across to Tracy and Jackie, who remain completely oblivious of her throughout the following.

Jackie (*mimicking*) And what happens, Jacqueline, if one tin is out of place?

Tracy I still don't get it. What does she mean, pyramids?

Jackie She means stacks of tins, Trace.

Tracy Oh I *see*. Are we getting Egyptian goods in?

Jackie (*patient*) No, nothing like that. She was just using her usual rhetoric.

Tracy Her what?

Jackie It's just the way she says things. Never simple.

Tracy I thought Rhetoric was the capital of Iceland. I'm sure it is. I've got an uncle who lives in Rhetoric.

Jackie Sometimes, Trace, I think you're not all there.

Tracy Where? (*Looks.*)

Jackie Sometimes I can't believe you're serious. Can't believe you're really as daft as you seem.

Conscience Excuse me.

Tracy Well, I am.

Jackie Yes, I know.

Conscience I don't mean to interrupt.

Jackie Sometimes I think if I have to spend another week in this bloody place I'm going to scream and shout and bloody create –

Conscience What swearing!

Jackie Pull the bloody display down on top of me, what a way to go!

Conscience Um. Excuse me, but if I could –

Tracy You'd hurt yourself.

Jackie Would you blame me, Trace?

Tracy Absolutely not. I'd blame whoever you told me to blame.

Jackie Oh well. I've no one to blame but myself. Mustn't get worked up, we've a long day ahead. It's a job, eh?

Conscience These girls are so *rude*!

Tracy We're lucky to have jobs, my dad says.

Jackie I know, I know. But honestly, Trace, it'd try the patience of a saint. Don't you think?

Conscience A saint?

Tracy (*shrugs*) Didn't know they had patience. I'd have thought they were the ones who lost their patience and got things done.

Conscience At last. A saint.

Jackie I didn't mean it quite so literally.

Tracy Quite so what?

Conscience Now here I can help you. Saints are my passion. Not that I am one, or anything. But I know all about saints. Glorious details about them. Like Saint Blandina. One of my favourites. She was a slave girl, tortured relentlessly by tormentors for her being a Christian, and they accused her of cannibalism and incest and all sorts of unsociable vices. And all she would say under torture was, 'I am a Christian and we do nothing vile.' Wasn't she brave! Wasn't she good! And – (*Realizes they haven't paid any attention to her at all.*) Um, excuse me, are you listening to me?

Both girls absorbed in different tasks round the stage, completely ignoring her.

Hello? Hello – o? (*Claps her hands.*) Hello there?

Jackie (*looking out to the side right through Conscience*) Here comes Mrs Jones, Trace. Whose turn is it at checkout?

Tracy I don't mind. You can choose.

Jackie You do it then.

Tracy Right.

She nearly walks into Conscience, who swivels round.

Conscience Didn't you hear? (*Follows Tracy to checkout and calls into her ear as if she's deaf.*) I was telling you about Saint Blandina, whose tormentors had never known a woman show such endurance as she did. (*Runs across to shout at Jackie similarly*.) Her tormentors tied her in a net and threw her to a bull, she was gored to death but was brave enough to –

Enter Mrs Jones. She goes straight to Jackie, who smiles and welcomes her.

Jackie Good morning, Mrs Jones. And how are you today then?

Mrs Jones Everything simply tastes better with Tip Top!

Jackie And how's Mr Jones?

Mrs Jones (*sadly*) Only a third of the fat of single cream. (*Takes the trolley and moves towards the display stand and stacks of food with it, sadly.*) Two of my dogs have delicate tummies – I wouldn't feed them anything else.

Jackie Oh, I am sorry to hear that, Mrs Jones. But I'm sure everything will work out just fine.

Mrs Jones (*speculative*) Success on a plate.

Jackie Yes, I know. See you tomorrow, now. Take care.

Conscience has been standing listening to this, trying to make sense out of it, completely confused. Turns to audience. On stage, Jackie prices goods and pares her fingernails, Mrs Jones does her shopping. Tracy waits for Mrs Jones to come to the checkout, staring into mid-air, in a dream.

Conscience (*to audience*) Am I mad? Is this stage overrun with mad people? I don't know what to think! They can't hear me even when I'm standing next to them, I don't think they can see me either. Am I here? This is very confusing. And as for that lady. Am I mad? Or is she talking in a different language? I recognize the words, but they make no sense. These girls seem to understand her. They had a conversation with her. (*Calls to Mrs Jones, Jackie, Tracy in turn.*) Hello? Excuse me? (*to audience*) See? (*Sinks to floor, defeated but thoughtful.*) I really don't quite know what to do. How am I going to find out anything about this suspicious Plant thing?

She sits, broods, watches. Mrs Jones reaches the checkout.

Tracy Hello Mrs Jones, what've you got today, then?

Mrs Jones I can't afford this washing powder *and* this fabric conditioner.

Tracy And how's Mr Jones keeping?

Mrs Jones There's no taste like Heinz.

Tracy Well, you tell him we're all asking for him. Bye-bye now. Manage your bags? Bye.

Exit Mrs Jones. Girls exchange glances and look up.

Jackie We'd better stay where we are, she'll be down any second.

Tracy I know.

Jackie Nothing changes.

Enter Mrs Lord.

Mrs Lord Everything going fine, girls?

Girls Yes, Mrs Lord.

Mrs Lord Was somebody just paying us a visit?

Jackie Mrs Jones, Mrs Lord.

Mrs Lord And what did she buy?

Tracy Well, she bought some coffee, and some, was it sweetcorn, and um –

Mrs Lord What did she buy, please, Jacqueline?

Jackie (*monotone, a practised answer*) Pork chops, broccoli, potatoes, catfood, coffee, sweetcorn, eggs, milk, Mrs Lord.

Mrs Lord Good, good, that's the spirit. Now. Tracy, could you clean out the cold trays at the back? An order of lamb is coming.

Tracy Yes, Mrs Lord.

Mrs Lord And Jacqueline, on checkout, please.

Jackie Yes, Mrs Lord.

Mrs Lord Good. Fine. On we go, girls, on we go. (*Exits.*)

Conscience (*to audience, as Mrs Lord exits, nearly tripping over her*) I don't think she can see me either. This is truly a strange and disconnected play. Something strange is happening. Something . . . (*She realizes as she thinks.*) . . . something is being covered up. That's it! This is a cover-up! A huge, organized cover-up! And *I've* been sent to solve it! (*Proud, stands up.*) Me. At last. This is my chance. My project. (*Looks up.*) Thank you. I'll do my best in the face of all adversity. (*Looks across at Tracy and Jackie, as usual, oblivious; calls to them.*) Do you hear? I'm going to do my best to get to the bottom of this. (*Begins to survey them, and stage, closely; examines bits of set, picks things up and puts them down, detective style.*)

Tracy Did she say lamb?

Jackie (*nearly asleep on checkout*) What?

Tracy Did she say lamb was coming?

Jackie Yes.

Tracy How do you manage to remember all those things to tell her?

Jackie I just know the right responses.

Tracy What do you mean?

Jackie It's too complicated to explain.

Tracy Oh. You're very good at this job.

Jackie (*dozing*) Mm.

Tracy And I'm not.

Jackie Mm.

Tracy So how come I'm quite happy but you're bored silly?

Jackie Mm.

Tracy Lamb. I think it's a shame for lambs.

Jackie You would.

Tracy I mean, they don't know anything about it, and suddenly they're eaten.

Jackie Well, if they don't know anything about it, then it's all right.

Tracy No it isn't! It's a shame for sheep, too. I always think it's a shame for animals.

Jackie Nobody makes you eat them.

Tracy I suppose. Doesn't stop me liking what they taste of. My mum says vegetarians get diseases because they don't eat meat.

Jackie (*looks at the clock on the wall*) Mm.

Tracy It's a shame.

Jackie (*looks at her watch*) Uh huh.

Conscience This is what we need. Compassion for living things. I think I'll try again. (*Goes to Tracy.*) Hello again. I do agree with you. It's a terrible –

Tracy I mean, you can see the shape things really are, like chickens and pigs and cows, when you take off the feathers and the skin, like they are when the butcher brings them in for the packer. But they have to be dead. Do you think people look like that underneath the top covering?

Jackie Don't think about it, Trace, you'll only make yourself miserable.

Conscience (*running across to Jackie*) But you *must* think about things like that, it's terribly important!

Tracy Well, I know, but it's a shame.

Conscience Yes! It's a shame!

Tracy I mean, sheep aren't daft, you know.

Jackie Mm.

Tracy People say they're daft, but they're not. People just talk a lot of rubbish sometimes.

Jackie Don't they just.

Conscience There's no need for sarcasm.

Tracy Yes, don't be sarcastic.

During this speech Conscience realizes to her surprise that Tracy must somehow have heard her.

My uncle, the one who lives in Australia –

Jackie Not Rhetoric?

Tracy No, Australia. My mum's brother. He has a sheep farm.

Conscience You *heard* me . . .

Tracy And he had a little intelligent sheep once. A really clever sheep.

Jackie I'll bet.

Tracy It was.

Conscience You heard me. I know you did.

Tracy He sent us photographs of it. I'd like to go to Australia, wouldn't you?

Jackie Not really.

Tracy Imagine it. Like on *Crocodile Dundee*!

Jackie Exactly.

Conscience (*appeals to audience*) She heard me. Don't you think?

Tracy All that open space. And sun, and deserts and sand and mountains and the most amazing colours in the flowers . . . and those bears with the funny noses . . .

Jackie Koalas.

Tracy Yes, and big huge rocks, like the one where those girls in white got lost.

Jackie What girls?

Tracy The ones on the picnic, remember, in the film. The beautiful girls, with long flowing hair and a kind of haze round them. One of the actresses who got lost up that rock was the lady who plays Mrs Mangel in *Neighbours*.

Jackie I wish she'd stayed lost.

Conscience Maybe she didn't hear me . . .

Tracy That's the thing about people on films or acting in things. They never look like real people. They never look like you or

me. They never have spots. They're a special colour, like there's
a special land they live in. They always look a different colour
to us.

Jackie From us.

Tracy They never get colds and have frayed bits round their
noses.

Jackie Colds aren't relevant.

Tracy Aren't what?

Jackie They don't mean anything. They exist on a different
mundane level from the things that are meaningful that we see
on TV or in the plots of stories or films.

Tracy You've lost me.

Jackie It's too difficult to explain.

Tracy Oh.

Conscience I'm so inefficient. Why am I so inefficient?

Tracy But that sheep I was telling you about.

Jackie What sheep?

Tracy The one my uncle taught to do a trick. He once saw this
horse do a trick at a circus.

Jackie A horse now.

Conscience It's all so inconsequential. I can't see what to do.
Can't see what's happening . . .

Tracy The horse tapped out numbers with its hoof. I mean, the
audience would call out numbers and the horse would tap
them out with its hoof.

Conscience Or . . . maybe she *did* hear me.

Jackie And your uncle taught this sheep to ride a horse?

Tracy No no *no*, he taught the sheep to count!

Jackie Oh.

Conscience Maybe I have to find my way in . . . as if it were a
maze . . .

Jackie So people could call out numbers and your uncle's sheep
would count them out?

Tracy Yes. He sent us photographs. The sheep's name was Snowy.

Conscience Maybe I've got to get through all the meaningless
corridors to reach the centre . . .

Jackie I'd have called out, 'Two thousand, three hundred and
forty four!' But that's because I'm – what am I, Trace? I'm Too
Clever For My –

Tracy Own Good!
Conscience Perhaps if I concentrate all my being, really psyche
myself to cosmic proportions, home in as keenly as I can –
Tracy Can we do the story? Can we do the story?
Jackie The Too Clever Story?
Conscience Perhaps if I meditate, close my eyes, concentrate,
concentrate my soul, my self –
Tracy Yes, the Too Clever Story!
Jackie Right, we'll do it.

> *She gets up out of checkout, passes across the stage by
> Conscience, who's just about to begin clenching her body and
> self in concentration. Jackie unwittingly says to Conscience as
> she passes:*

Excuse me.
Conscience (*aghast, amazed*) *She saw me!*
Jackie What am I, Trace?
Tracy You begin, you begin –
Jackie Too clever for my –
Tracy Own good!
Conscience She did! She definitely did . . . I think . . . (*Can't
understand why her presence seems to have no effect at all.
Stands confused through the following.*)
Jackie Who tells me, Trace?
Tracy Your father.
Jackie And?
Tracy Your mother.
Jackie And?
Tracy Your boyfriend.
Jackie And?
Tracy The man at the careers office, and me, and Mrs Lord –
Jackie And birds on the trees tell me when I walk to work. What
do they say, Trace?
Tracy You're too clever for your own sweet tweet good!
Jackie And chickens wrapped in Cellophane in the freezer
counter tell me. What do they say?
Tracy Too clever! You're too clever! You ought to be headless
like us.
Jackie What do I do all day?

Tracy You watch the clock.

Jackie All day. My prime *raison d'être*. What is it, Trace?

Tracy Your prime something.

Jackie *Raison d'être*.

Tracy Raising deckchair.

Jackie All day. From when the hands on my clock by my bed meet in a ticking conspiracy –

Conscience (*to audience, getting involved with what's being said*) That's really rather well put, isn't it?

Jackie Out to get me. To get me out of bed, down the stair, up the street into here, where that clock on the wall and I, we sit, eye to eye, all day, tick, tick. What does it say, Tracy?

Tracy You're too clever.

Conscience I'd better not interrupt. This is getting rather heartfelt, don't you think?

Jackie And when I told the man at the careers office I wanted to go to college to study English and drama, what did he do?

Tracy He laughed.

Jackie And what did he say?

Tracy You'll never get a job if you do that.

Jackie And when my father sent me back to the careers man to ask for a job, what did he say?

Tracy You were trying to be too clever for your own good, weren't you? Well, there's a job going at Wonderstore, they could use someone clever. You passed your maths, didn't you?

Jackie That's right. And what does my boyfriend say?

Tracy You've no ambition, love.

Jackie And whenever I look in the paper for jobs and talk about moving away, what does he say?

Tracy You're too bloody clever for your own good, girl.

Jackie (*suddenly pondering*) Tracy?

Tracy What?

Jackie How come, you know, how come you can play this game with me, remember all these answers and things to say, but when it comes to having to remember things for Mrs Lord, other things like that, you just can't? How come?

Conscience Yes, I was wondering that too.

Tracy Oh. Don't know. Haven't a clue. Never thought about it.

They drift back to original positions, Jackie at checkout, Tracy other side of the stage.

Maybe because it's more important. Those other things, they don't matter. This is important.

Jackie (*who's drifted away inside her own head, not hearing her*) And my mother, she says, you shouldn't complain, Jackie love, a job's a job, hard enough to come by these days, and Mrs Lord says you're a good efficient worker. And it's not exactly hard work, look at your father and your brothers, working all those hours at that Plant, coming home exhausted, so tired sometimes they can't eat their supper. And my father comes home from work and eats his supper, and says, look, girl. You've had your education. You've had your fun. But now it's time to stop being so clever and get into the real world. What do you want? It's no picnic, girl! It's no easy ride! There are things you've got to do. You're too clever for – what does he say?

Conscience (*moved*) Too clever for your own good.

Jackie Trace? Eh? What am I?

Tracy Here's Mrs Brown coming, Jackie. Who's on checkout?

Jackie (*sighs*) My turn.

They position themselves as before, vice versa. Conscience comes to centre stage to speak to audience.

Conscience This is terrible! These two poor sensitive and intelligent girls trapped in this trivial and inconsequent play! I'll *have* to do something about it. And I still haven't discovered the secret of the Plant. How can I attract their attention?

Enter Mrs Brown, the same woman as before, wearing a different coat.

Tracy Good morning, Mrs Brown. And how are you today, then?

Mrs Brown For people who lead an active life, Sure deodorant won't let you down.

Tracy And how's your son?

Mrs Brown (*sadly*) Now Whiskas is even tastier. (*Takes the* *trolley exactly as before, sadly.*) How do I know? My cat told me.

Tracy Oh, I am sorry to hear that, Mrs Brown. But I'm sure everything will work out just fine.

Mrs Brown The taste of paradise.

Tracy Yes, I know. See you tomorrow now. Take care.

Tracy prices goods, Mrs Brown does her shopping, Jackie waits, watching, for Mrs Brown to reach the checkout. Conscience comes forward to speak to audience.

Conscience I don't understand these interludes at all. But I'm not giving up easily. I'll solve it. I'll find my way through. I don't mean to boast but I'm well known in high-up circles for my sticking power. I'm like St Agatha. My favourite third-century martyr. Do you know, she was tortured and tried for her beliefs – they say they even cut off her breasts. That's how all the pictures show her. Now she's the patron saint of bellringers. Because apparently her cut-off breasts resembled bells. And in some countries, you know, because her cut-off breasts also looked like bread, they bless bread in churches on her feast day. Fifth of February. So it's important to stick to your beliefs. To endure in the face of torture or confusion. You might end up with a feast day. Not that I'm opportunist, or anything. (*confidential*) But this *is* my chance. My time has come. I know it has. In here. (*Clasps her heart.*) Now. (*Surveys scene on stage.*) Firstly, I *know* they know I'm here. Even if it's only subconscious. My task is to make it conscious. Secondly. They're saying exactly the same things. That woman is the same woman simply pretending to be another woman. Talking the same sort of nonsense. My task is to find out why. Right. Thirdly. I've still got to find out about that sinister Plant.

Mrs Brown has reached the checkout.

Jackie Hello, Mrs Brown, what've you got today then?

Mrs Brown Once bitten, forever smitten.

Jackie And how's your son keeping?

Mrs Brown I could do with a D.

Jackie Well, you tell him we're all asking for him. Bye-bye now. Manage your bags? Bye.

Exit Mrs Brown, walks unseeingly past Conscience and treads heavily on her foot. Conscience cries out in pain, hops about holding her foot.

Tracy What was that?

Jackie What was what?

Tracy That noise.

Jackie What noise?

Tracy I thought I heard a cry.

Conscience (*clutching foot*) It was me.

Jackie A what?

Tracy Like something in pain.

Conscience I am. It's *very* sore. She stood on my foot.

Jackie Perhaps it was one of the chickens. Mourning its lack of a head. One of the tins of beans? A bean crying from the depths of the sauce, mourning its loss of individuality. 'I am a forsaken bean! Pity, oh pity me!'

Conscience It was *me*.

Jackie A cry from the subconscious of my trapped and bored soul?

Tracy I was sure I . . .

Enter Mrs Lord, stands on Conscience's other foot. She yells in pain again.

There it is *again*!

Jackie There what is again?

Mrs Lord Everything going fine, girls?

Girls Yes, Mrs Lord,

Mrs Lord Was somebody just paying us a visit?

Jackie Mrs Brown, Mrs Lord.

Mrs Lord And what did she buy?

Jackie Pork chops, broccoli, potatoes, catfood, coffee, sweetcorn, eggs, milk, Mrs Lord.

Mrs Lord Good, good, that's the spirit. Now. Jacqueline, could you restack at the back, please. Leaving a large space for the eggs, there are more coming in a large order.

Jackie Certainly, Mrs Lord.

Mrs Lord What was that, Jacqueline? Do I detect a hint of sarcasm, my girl?

Jackie No, Mrs Lord.

Mrs Lord Because, let's put it this way, Jacqueline. Clever or no clever, whether you can read big books or not, whether you know the meanings of big words like philanthropist or misanthropist, a job is still a job, and you're extremely lucky, mark my words, to have a job at all, young lady. Extremely lucky. What are you?

Jackie Extremely lucky, Mrs Lord.

Mrs Lord When you answer me, it's '*Yes*, Mrs Lord', or '*No*, Mrs Lord.' Do you understand?

Jackie Yes, Mrs Lord.

Mrs Lord Yes. And Tracy, on checkout, please.

Tracy Yes, Mrs Lord.

Mrs Lord Good. Fine. On we go, girls, on we go. (*Exits.*)

Conscience (*sitting holding both her feet*) That awful woman. Dreadful woman.

Jackie Yes, Mrs Lord. No, Mrs Lord. Three bags full, Mrs Lord. What happened to that sheep that your uncle had, Tracy?

Tracy The clever sheep?

Jackie Yes.

Tracy Snowy? The one that could count with its feet?

Jackie That's the one.

Tracy It went mad, and they ate it.

Jackie Oh. Figures.

> *It's evidently lunchtime; they take out sandwiches and eat them. Relapse into inconsequent mode, waiting for the next thing to happen, bored, static.*

Tracy I saw a programme on the television once about this woman who kept sheep like dogs.

Conscience This awful play . . . Dreadful play . . .

Tracy This woman, her husband left her. He said the sheep got more attention than he did.

Jackie Figures.

Conscience I cannot stand much more of the inconsequence of this . . .

Tracy She used to keep them in her front room.

Jackie Did she?

Tracy One sheep jumped right up and sat on her lap.

Jackie Really?

Conscience I can feel it. I am going slowly mad . . . slowly insane . . .

Tracy But I like eggs. Eggs, they're beautiful really.

Jackie Tell that to the people who got ill.

Tracy I know. It's a shame. But they're still beautiful to look at, still, oh I don't know, proof of something.

Jackie What do you mean?

Tracy Oh, I don't know. I mean, like, the fact that it's so beautiful. Someone made it so beautiful. Or something. And someone or something made it tough. I mean, imagine, Jackie Imagine you've got one in your hand right now.

Jackie goes back to reshelving and pricing, shaking her head.

Jackie No, Trace, you're the one who does the imagining. You do it.

Tracy Feel it. Smooth, hard, cool, round and cold. And fragile. Feel how fragile it is – but tough. Squeeze it and it won't break. Drop it, though, and that's a different story.

Jackie Sometimes, Trace, I think there's something ever so slightly feeble-minded about you, I really do.

Tracy I'll have to get a real one, just to feel it, feel it cool. It's like proof. Like a sort of hope.

Jackie If you're lucky. Beware of bad eggs, Trace. Egg Russian roulette.

Tracy (*coming back with an egg box, taking out an egg to examine*) I don't understand you sometimes.

Jackie And I don't understand you. The way of the world.

Conscience has been slowly boiling up, listening, growing more and more frustrated, suddenly springs to her feet and stands in front of Tracy.

Conscience AAAAARGH! Can you hear me?

She runs across and does the same to Jackie; both girls remain oblivious.

AAARGH! Will you listen? Now *listen*! You. And you. Listen to me. Something's going on. I don't know what it is, but it's going on. *A terrible play* is going on, and you're part of it. You're helping it! Letting it! An inconsequent play. Yet something so important is happening outside this hopeless inconsequence! Sheep! Eggs! What you've seen on television! Triviality! And there's such a lack of communication between you all. You don't seem to see! Look around you! A woman, the same woman, comes in, talks nonsense, and leaves. Another woman cracks the whip and you do what she says. No questioning. What is this Wonderstore? And what is this Plant? What is it all about? Why do you nearly hear me sometimes yet never other times? Why can't you hear me now! It's so important! What has it got to do with Joan of Arc? Why is this play pretending to be something it's not? What's happening? If you'd only listen to me . . . you'd maybe ask yourselves what's happening. Can you hear me? Will you listen? Can you see me? I know you can. I know you both can. Listen to me!

She takes Tracy's arm and shakes it; she's been completely wrapped up in her egg-wonder, and is surprised. The carton of eggs flies up into the air and falls to smash.

Tracy Don't break the – you've broken the eggs! Oh, Jackie, she's broken the eggs!

Jackie Well, she'll have to pay for them.

Conscience You *can* hear me . . . you *can* see . . .

Tracy (*looks at her as if for the first time, picking up bits of egg*) Never mind, it's just eggs. But they are beautiful. Well, they were. You shouldn't break things, though. I hate to see things broken.

Conscience Yes, yes, I do too.

Tracy I'll clear it up.

Conscience No, no, I'll do it, it was my fault, I'll, um, I'll get a cloth.

She goes to her seat in the front row, takes a cloth out of her bag. Tracy goes to Jackie.

Tracy Who's that lady?

Jackie Nothing to do with me.

Tracy But who is she?

Jackie What lady. I can't see any lady.

Tracy I can. Over there.

Jackie Tracy, be careful. Don't get involved. It'll only mean trouble. Listen to me. There's *no one there.*

Tracy But there *is.*

Jackie Imagining things. You'll get into trouble. You know what'll happen. You'll lose your job. And then where will you be? We're lucky to have jobs.

Tracy Jackie, what *are* you talking about?

Jackie I *know* Trace. I know. There's no one there. Now leave it at that. Take my word for it. (*Looks at her watch.*) Mrs Smith'll be in, any moment, we've had Mrs Jones and Mrs Brown, it's Mrs Smith next.

Tracy (*approaching Conscience*) Yes, but –

Jackie Come back, Trace. Any second, it'll be –

Tracy (*to Conscience*) Um, excuse me, I –

Jackie (*hiss*) Tracy!

Tracy I – I mean, I would have done that. I dropped them, after all. I'm sorry I made such a fuss. Just that I'm fond of eggs.

Conscience I'm only sorry I scared you with my ranting.

Tracy Was that you? All those voices?

Conscience Well, I –

Tracy Saying all those things I couldn't understand? Was that you? And I thought it was my head. And was that you who made that noise back then?

Conscience Yes, when the tiresome woman stood on my –

Enter Mrs Smith, same woman, first coat on again, takes trolley and runs over Conscience's foot again.

AUGH!

Tracy Oh, oh, your poor foot!

Conscience No, no, it's all right really, really it is.

Jackie Em, good afternoon, Mrs Smith. (*hiss*) Tracy! Your *lines!*

Tracy (*to Conscience*) You'll have to excuse me, just for a moment. (*Runs across to take up position for speaking to Mrs Smith.*) Good afternoon Mrs Smith. And how are you today, then?

Mrs Smith Cats make haste for the munchies taste.

Tracy And how's your son?

Mrs Smith (*sadly*) Vorsprung durch Technik.

Tracy Oh, I am sorry to hear that, Mrs Smith. But I'm sure everything will work out just fine.

Mrs Smith It's the family soap that never stops caring.
Tracy Yes, I know. See you tomorrow now. Take care.

> *Mrs Smith goes to do her shopping. Jackie, on checkout, hisses at Tracy.*

Jackie It's not my turn on checkout. It's *your* turn. You'll foul the whole day up, Trace, for everybody. Come on! Get a grip!
Tracy Oh, Jackie, I am sorry. I know. But you'll manage. It's just the once.
Conscience Yes, yes, at moments like this it's often imperative that you bend the rules a little. It's not always the people who keep to rules who do best, you know, Jackie.

> *Jackie is ignoring her, pretending to be oblivious.*

Take Saint Pelagia the Penitent. Now she was a notorious dancing girl in Antioch, well known for her sensual dances of desire. One day the Bishop of Edessa came past and saw her performing one of her most provocative dances, and he went back to all the other bishops, and said to them, 'This girl is a lesson to us who think we're holy men. Look at her. She takes more trouble over every little movement and spasm of her body than we do over our prayers, or with our souls, or with our flocks of the faithful.' And then one day Pelagia overheard a sermon by him, was moved to repent, was baptized, went to Jerusalem, disguised herself as a man, became a hermit on the Mount of Olives and spent the rest of her days there as a solitary.
Tracy Oh, what a beautiful story!
Jackie Beautiful? Bloody irrelevant.
Conscience Nothing irrelevant about it! It's a very important story. In fact, it's not a story, it's a fact. That girl gave up what she was doing and went to live in a cave!
Tracy In a cave! Really? How thrilling!
Jackie Well, what's that got to do with bending the rules? Mmm?
Conscience Well, um, well – (*at a loss*)
Jackie See! You were just using it as an example for your own benefit. Like most people of your type. You use things as examples just to fit your topic of preaching, not to fit real relevant situations.
Conscience Not at all. Um, um, the, um, it was the bishop who

bent the rules. That's what I meant. It was the bishop. He recognized the, um, the possibility for saintliness in the most unexpected place. Yes, That's it.

Tracy And she lived in a cave, in a cave as a solitary, all by herself for the rest of her days!

Jackie Amen.

Conscience Well there's no need to be rude though.

Mrs Smith (*who's been waiting now for some time at the checkout*) The dirt said hot, the label said not –

Jackie There's every reason to be rude. All that rubbish about Blandina who endured torment and was tied in a net and gored to death. I mean, what's that got to do with us? Really? What's it got to do with life now?

Tracy (*thrilled*) Gored to death? Oh, how horrible!

Conscience Yes, but for her *beliefs* –

Tracy (*even more thrilled*) For her beliefs? Oh, how brave!

Mrs Smith The dirt said hot –

Jackie And that stuff about Agatha –

Conscience *Saint* Agatha. *Saint* Blandina.

Jackie All that stuff about breasts cut off. I mean, who are you trying to scare? We're not children. And we're not stupid. That sort of thing just doesn't happen. Nobody's tortured and tried for beliefs nowadays. Nobody's breasts are cut off. There's no such savagery.

Conscience Don't you read newspapers? Don't you keep up to date with what's happening in the world? Haven't you heard of Amnesty International? Haven't you heard of Nicaragua? In May 1984 the Contras attacked a farming community in the north, a place called Castillo Norte, castrating and cutting tongues out of the boys there, raping and cutting the breasts off a four-months pregnant girl while she was still alive. They left these people naked, then burned them.

Jackie (*visibly shaken*) But . . . but in any case. That couldn't happen here. Nothing to do with us.

Conscience Of course. I see. Nothing so savage could happen to us. Not here in this small but bustling town. Nothing could tear our bodies apart, could it? I can't think of anything. Can you?

Jackie (*determinedly not listening*) And there's no such thing as

sainthood now. We don't have it. We don't need endurance the
way they did then. Or the courage of our convictions. Not the
way people do in other places, other countries. There's no
place for it. In fact it's dangerous. You've just got to get on
with it. Live life.

Conscience Oh dear. Oh dear, dear, dear. What happened to
your sense of idealism? Everybody's born with one, what
happened to yours?

Mrs Smith The dirt said *hot*!

Jackie Dangerous!

Conscience How? In what way? Exactly what is it that's
dangerous? And how?

Jackie That sort of idealism's dangerous!

Conscience This sort of idealism's indispensable!

Jackie Leave us alone!

*They stand, locked in opposition created by these last
exclamations. Tracy is sitting on the floor staring into space,
dreaming about the stories she's heard. Mrs Smith is in
despair, confused, lost. Enter Mrs Lord, angrily and suddenly,
on the echo of Jackie's last exclamation. Silence, fear on
Jackie's face, relief on Mrs Smith's, determination on
Conscience's, who watches every move, and Tracy jumps up
to do as she's supposed to but it's clear that she's thinking of
other things. Note: neither Mrs Smith or Mrs Lord seems in
the least bit aware of Conscience's presence at any point.*

Mrs Lord What's going on here?

Mrs Smith marches up to her, whispers triumphantly in her ear.

The dirt said what? Really? The label said who? Is that a fact?
Don't worry, Mrs Smith. New Ariel will get it clean.

Mrs Smith smiles, relieved, comforted.

And who (*Turns to girls.*) was supposed to be on checkout duty?

Tracy comes forward to take the blame, but Jackie interrupts.

Jackie Um. It was me, Mrs Lord.

Mrs Lord Right, Jacqueline. If you would kindly serve Mrs
Smith, who appears to have been waiting some time . . .

Jackie Yes, Mrs Lord. (*She does so, under scrutiny.*) Hello, Mrs Smith, what've, um, what've you got today, then?

Mrs Smith The dirt said hot, the label said not, but new Ariel got it clean.

Jackie And how's your, oh, what was it, how's your son keeping?

Mrs Smith A washing that's white at a price that's right.

Jackie Well, you tell him we're all asking for him. Bye-bye now. Manage your bags? Bye.

Exit Mrs Smith.

Conscience (*to audience, proud*) Imagine me remembering all those facts about Nicaragua. I'm really on the ball tonight.

Mrs Lord (*surveying the calm*) That's better. Much better. Now. I don't know what was happening here before I came down to stop it. But let me tell you it had better not happen again. There are plenty of people looking for employment. I just have to lift the receiver of my telephone. Plenty of people who could use a decent salary. We all have to pull together. We all have to keep the faith. And don't you girls realize the importance of the everyday ritual of shopping at Wonderstore? Don't you realize that the general public derive a truly necessary comfort from this ritual? A sense of security? Safety? A promise, girls, that things are in place. And you are the guardians of that promise. You are the keepers of that security.

Girls (*with Conscience standing alongside, mimicking*) Yes, Mrs Lord.

Mrs Lord You mustn't disrupt it. You mustn't abuse it.

Girls (*and Conscience*) No, Mrs Lord.

Mrs Lord Good, good. Now. Everything going fine, girls?

Girls Yes, Mrs Lord.

Mrs Lord Was somebody just paying us a visit?

Jackie Mrs Smith, Mrs Lord.

Mrs Lord And what did she buy?

Jackie Pork chops, broccoli, potatoes, catfood, coffee, sweetcorn, eggs, milk, Mrs Lord.

Mrs Lord Good, good. Back to work, girls. We may only be a little shop, but you know what they say, a chain is only as strong as its weakest link. We must be strong, girls.

Girls Yes, Mrs Lord.

Mrs Lord That's the spirit (*Exit.*)

Tracy (*turning immediately to Conscience*) Tell us more stories about those saints, please tell us.

Jackie Trace, don't you think we're in enough trouble as it is?

Conscience (*turning to Jackie*) You heard me tell the stories in the first place, (*turning to Tracy*) but you didn't. (*to Jackie*) You could hear me all along, but you chose not to. Is that right? And Tracy couldn't hear me. Could you?

Tracy I heard voices. I didn't understand. And I heard some pain cries.

Conscience But you could hear it all. Could you?

Jackie I can't hear a thing.

Tracy Tell me about Agatha and Blandina.

Jackie *Saint* Agatha. *Saint* Blandina.

Tracy Yes, yes, tell me.

Conscience Well, I think we could probably set up a little arrangement . . .

Jackie What sort of arrangement?

Conscience I'll tell you more about the saints . . . if you tell me what's going on here.

Tracy What's going on where?

Jackie She doesn't know.

Conscience In this play.

Tracy What play?

Jackie She doesn't know, I tell you. She doesn't know what's happening.

Conscience This play. This one. On this stage. With those two women who keep coming in and out. With those people watching out there.

Tracy (*to Jackie*) What does she mean?

Jackie Nothing to do with me. Trace, you chose to hear her.

Tracy But you can hear her too.

Jackie I can't hear a thing.

Conscience Look. This is getting tiresome.

Jackie Well said.

Tracy See! You heard her.

Jackie I think there's something in my ear.

Conscience And I do have rather a lot of work to do. I have several other plays to visit, you know. So. If one of you could just tell me – If you could just tell me, Tracy –

Tracy (*keen*) Yes –

Conscience Why does that lady keep coming in and out?

Tracy You mean Mrs Lord.

Conscience Yes, the one who tells you what to do.

Tracy That's Mrs Lord. She's the manageress. She keeps the supermarket running.

Jackie Shop-shape, everything in its place, one can out of the pyramid and the whole thing topples, commodity is next to godliness, come along now, sell, sell, sell.

Conscience Well, if you're so cynical, why stay here?

Jackie It's a job.

Conscience But it's a terrible job. It's a trivial play.

Jackie I know.

Conscience Why do it then?

Tracy There aren't any other jobs.

Conscience But there are other ways to live without having a job.

Tracy Are there?

Jackie No.

Conscience Yes!

Jackie Berries on bushes. Herb stems boiling into soup over a campfire. The pure life. A romantic rabbit or two if you can catch one . . .

Conscience Now that's unfair –

Jackie Or there's always shoplifting.

Conscience Those aren't the main things, the salient points, you know. You don't live by bread alone –

Jackie That's right, you eat words instead. Watch out, Trace. You leave your job, your pay, you'll end up eating your words. Or her words.

Conscience I've no time for this quibbling. Mrs Lord is the lady who tells you what to do and gives you money for it. Right? What about you, Tracy, are you happy here?

Tracy Oh, I'm perfectly happy, I'm *not* clever enough for my own good. At least, I mean –

Conscience Yes, yes. And who's that other lady?

Tracy What other lady?

Conscience The one who talks as if she's mad.

Tracy What lady?

Conscience The one who keeps coming in and talking nonsense, you saw her –

Jackie She means Mrs Brown, Mrs Jones and Mrs Smith.

Tracy But that's three ladies. They come in every day. They live here.

Conscience Yes, but they're all the one lady really. All the one actress.

Tracy All the one what?

Jackie She won't understand. She doesn't know.

Tracy Tell me about the saints.

Conscience Yes, in a minute. Why is that – why are those ladies so sad all the time?

Tracy Well. It's very sad. Very unfortunate. Mrs Jones's husband, Mr Jones, he used to work up at the Plant, and he's very sick now. A lot of people are in the town. It's really unfortunate. And Mrs Brown's son, he was born with a disease, there's a lot of it round here and they think he's going to die soon. And, well, it's a shame for Mrs Smith's son.

Conscience Is he ill too?

Tracy No, his wife, see, she had a perfectly good job, didn't she, Jackie?

Jackie Yes, perfect.

Tracy She worked at the shoe shop. And then she joined the protest group and the shoe shop fired her.

Conscience (*eyes lighting up*) What protest group?

Tracy The one that sits at the gates of the Plant.

Conscience Yes, tell me about the Plant.

Tracy Well, they make energy there, or something. It's all to do with security. And Mrs Smith's son's wife, she lost her job when she joined the protest group, she said it was something to do with the water and with what they were putting into the ground. And she split up with Mrs Smith's son because he works at the Plant, and now her father won't talk to her either because he works there too and it got them into trouble with the management. And her mother has to meet her secretly and she's an outcast, and she sits in the cold round a fire with the protest group. It's a shame. She lost her job and her friends and everything.

Conscience A protest group! I didn't know there was a protest group . . . and what was that about water and things in the ground?

Jackie Tracy, that's enough. (*to Conscience*) Leave her alone. You'll just get her into trouble. She doesn't know.

Tracy Do they have haloes, the saints? Has there ever been a Saint Tracy? Was she brave?

Conscience Well, em – Saint Tracy . . . now let me think – . . . I don't think there has – yet. But that lady's daughter, the brave, brave girl who went to join the protesters, how right she was. *She* could be a saint, Tracy, don't you think? She reminds me of Saint Euphrasia, you know.

Jackie Stop it. Leave her alone.

Tracy (*Wonderment*) Saint Euphrasia?

Conscience Yes, she was so brave. Do you know what she did? She broke off her engagement to a senator's son, gave all of her property to the poor, and simply avoided temptations to return to her former way of life by forcing herself to do very hard domestic tasks for the community, and by giving herself terrible penances to do, like going without food for a whole week!

Tracy A whole week!

Jackie That's right. Pack her head with nonsense. Just when she's got her life into some order. What's in it for you? Promotion for every life you change? What's the rate per convert? Or is it just job satisfaction that propels your particular ambition, particular manipulation?

Conscience You really are highly articulate, you know.

Jackie Listen, Trace, there's only one thing you've to learn about sainthood. Saints are usually dead. And they've usually been dead for a long time. And often they die pretty horribly.

Conscience Irrelevance.

Jackie (*to Conscience*) Look, she earns a decent wage. She eats and watches television and goes to the pub with her friends. She sits by the fireside in the winter evenings and in the sun in the garden on her days off in the summer. It's all right, this life. It's quite adequate.

Conscience But who wants an adequate life? Who wants life simply to be adequate?

Jackie Me! *I* do!

Conscience Don't you want to do your best? Don't you want to try your hardest?

Jackie I do! I am!

Conscience Don't you want to change the things that have to be changed before it's too late?

Jackie Ha! As simply as that! I don't believe it's possible to change things.

Tracy (*quietly*) I do.

Conscience Yes! You do. *You* know that terrible things are happening.

Tracy Em . . . yes.

Conscience That the eggs are being poisoned by people trying to make money out of them –

Tracy Yes, Jackie, the eggs –

Jackie Yes, I *know*.

Conscience That the water's being poisoned by what's being emptied into it –

Tracy Yes –

Conscience That they don't know what to do with the poisonous things that come out of plants like the one in this town –

Tracy Yes –

Conscience That maybe they're making weapons as well as energy up at the Plant –

Tracy Making what?

Jackie You don't know that!

Conscience I wouldn't put it past them –

Jackie You're completely unscrupulous.

Conscience It's possible.

Tracy It's terrible!

Jackie We'd know.

Conscience Would we?

Jackie And even if they are. It's for security. It's so that there won't be a war. That's the point of having that sort of Plant.

Conscience That's not the point at all. And what if a plane crashed into it?

Tracy Yes, what if a plane?

Conscience Or what if there were to be an accident? It has happened!

Jackie I *know*.

Conscience And what about leukaemia statistics?

Tracy Yes, what about statistics?

Conscience It's terrible.

Tracy It's horrible!

Conscience Yes!

Tracy Yes!

Conscience Terrible things are happening!

Tracy Yes!

Conscience People are exploited and tortured! People have no homes! People are dying of starvation! People are dying of diseases! Our world is being contaminated by the gallon, dug to the core and filled with poison! Forests are being cut down killing all the wildlife and endangering the ozone layer! Whales are being killed in cold blood in cold seas! Seals are culled, *baby* seals!

Tracy Yes! Yes! Yes!

Jackie Keep it down, she'll *hear* you! We'll get into trouble!

Tracy (*in a whisper*) Yes.

Conscience What are you afraid of? Shout it as loud as you can! Terrible things are happening!

Jackie You make it all sound so simple, don't you?

Conscience It *is* simple.

Jackie It's never simple.

Conscience (*to Tracy*) What are we going to do about it?

Jackie Nothing. What *can* you do?

Tracy Everything!

Jackie Like what? Where are you going to start?

Tracy Well . . . well, I'm – (*Looks at Conscience.*) Well, we're going to –

Jackie See? There isn't anything to do.

Tracy Yes there is – I can – write some letters. I can . . . I can collect money . . . I –

Jackie Mmm?

Tracy I can, I can stand outside the supermarket on a Saturday with a collecting tin.

Jackie You can't.

Tracy Why not?

Jackie You're working on Saturday.

Tracy Oh, yes. Oh, well, I can –

Conscience (*to Jackie*) Aren't you going to help at all?

Jackie I can't hear a thing.

Conscience You're too clever for your own good.

Jackie I know.

Conscience (*to Tracy*) Well, you need to make a plan.

Tracy *Me*, make a plan? By myself?

Jackie You'll have to make it after Mrs Evans has done her shopping.

Tracy It's never time for Mrs Evans already?

Jackie Here she comes – I can see her in the wings.

Tracy In the what?

Conscience I have it! Tracy, I've solved it. You can go and join the protesters!

Tracy Oh, yes! – Oh, no, I can't. I could come after work.

Conscience You don't need to work! Real idealists give up all that!

Tracy Do they?

Jackie That's right. Real idealists get all fired up by their ideals and end up burned out and placeless in society.

Conscience Real saints *know* this is just a play. And a trivial one at that, one not worth bothering about.

Tracy Real saints know that this is just a what?

Conscience A *play*! A fiction. A narrative pretence. Look. (*Takes a pantomime chicken off a hook on the display stand.*) It's not a real chicken. It's not *real*.

Tracy (*wide-eyed*) Jackie! Jackie! This chicken isn't *real*!

Jackie (*tired*) Really? You surprise me.

Conscience Never laid an egg in its life! And look at this (*Kicks one of the flats.*) See? Not exactly trustworthy, is it? Not very steady place to live or work, is it? There must be other ways to live. Other values to cultivate. Believe me, this isn't exactly Shakespeare.

Tracy (*wide-eyed*) I – I don't believe –

Conscience You've only just started believing.

Enter Mrs Evans, same lady as before. Jackie runs to the right position.

Jackie Come on, Trace, you're on checkout. Come on, there's work to do.

Conscience Yes, yes, work to do. I'll help you a bit, but you'll soon get the hang of it. Now. (*Whispers in her ear.*)

Tracy Right . . . right . . . good..

Conscience Good girl.

Jackie Good afternoon, Mrs Evans. And how are you today, then?

Mrs Evans Issue one with free binder at your newsagent's now.

Jackie And how's Mr Evans?

Mrs Evans In tests, eight out of ten cat owners who expressed a preference said their cats preferred it.

Jackie Oh, I am sorry to hear that, Mrs Evans. But I'm sure everything will work out just fine.

Mrs Evans Whenever there's a snack gap, Twix fits.

Jackie Yes, I know. See you tomorrow now. Take care.

Mrs Evans travels round with the trolley.

Conscience (*to Tracy*) See? It's the same woman – they can't even manage to get different actresses to play the different parts! Not much of a play, is it?

Tracy But that's Mrs Evans.

Conscience And is her poor husband sick as well?

Tracy He's not very well, no.

Conscience It's a shame. Has he been made ill by the Plant too?

Jackie Not exactly. He runs the Plant. He's the manager.

Tracy He had a bit of a cold yesterday when Mrs Evans came in.

Conscience Oh, honestly. This trivial, trivial play. Don't you see, Tracy? That woman is the same woman as all the other women. It's all a pretence.

Tracy Is she not real as well as the chicken?

Conscience Well, she's real all right. But she's only pretending. Don't you see, the whole structure is a pretence –

Tracy I don't understand you half the time. But I'll take your word for it.

Jackie (*hissing*) Tracy! Concentrate, will you! (*to Conscience*) I don't think you realize what you're doing.

Conscience Wait and see.

Jackie I can't see a thing.

Conscience That's for sure.

Tracy Stop squabbling.

Jackie Here she comes. Now *behave.*

Conscience Be like Saint Febriona, who was tortured, mutilated and battered to death – and lots of spectators (*She indicates the audience.*) were converted on the spot and baptized.

Tracy (*no idea what Conscience is talking about*) Well, all right . . .

Conscience We're about to sacrifice your job, Tracy. We're about to make all the difference.

Tracy If you say so.

Mrs Evans comes to the checkout.

Conscience (*to Tracy*) Say, 'Hello, Mrs Evans, what nonsense are you going to talk today, then?'

Tracy Hello, Mrs Evans, what nonsense are you going to talk today then?

Mrs Evans (*looking twice at Tracy*) Top breeders recommend it.

Conscience What do you usually say next?

Tracy I ask for *Mr* Evans now.

Conscience Well, say this – (*Whispers.*)

Jackie Tracy – take *care* – (*Covers her ears and eyes.*)

Tracy And how far has Mr Evans gone in poisoning our natural resources today? And – what was the next bit? – Oh yes . . . And would we all be safe if an aeroplane were to crash into the Plant?

Conscience whispers, Tracy adds.

Would we, Mrs Evans?

Mrs Evans (*looking distinctly ruffled*) G-go to work on an egg.

Conscience That's an old one, Mrs Evans!

Tracy That's an old one, Mrs Evans!

More whispers.

Is there any chance, Mrs Evans, that I could get you to say something that isn't just meaningless? That isn't completely out of context? (*Tracy gradually getting the hang of the rhetoric without help from Conscience.*) That isn't just any old safe cliché to hide behind and pretend the world's a wonderful normal place, Mrs Evans? Because it's not, is it, Mrs Evans? Let's face it, Mrs Evans (*picking pantomime chicken out of her trolley*) – this chicken can't lay eggs! It's not a real chicken, is it? This is just a, what was it, just a trivial structure set on top of what's really happening to us. Isn't it, Mrs Evans? Isn't it? Can't you see what's happening here? Can't you?

Enter Mrs Lord during this speech – listens – and, surveying the scene, interrupts.

Mrs Lord Tell us, Tracy. What's happening here?

Tracy turns round, not afraid, to face her.

Jackie Oh, Mrs Lord, Tracy isn't feeling very well, she said she had a fever. I think she needs to lie down, Mrs Lord, she's not herself . . .

Tracy (*shining*) This plot is a cover-up. It's all a plot! Something very frightening is happening, hidden beneath the ordinary cover-up of everyday life, and I have to do something about it!

Mrs Lord *How* inspired.

Tracy Commodity feeds commodity and we all suffer in the end! Can't you see? (*Waves the chicken in the air.*) We've got to get to the reality! We mustn't be fooled any longer! We must listen! Really hear! Really see!

Conscience That's my girl!

Mrs Lord (*determined to regain control of the situation*) Tracy, I think you should apologize to Mrs Evans. And I think you should check out her goods. We'll forget this unfortunate little interlude. Remember your position. Your acting like this is stupid, and possibly harmful. Where's your compassion? Poor Mrs Evans, she's shaking. Her husband isn't well, you know. This just isn't the spirit, girl.

Tracy (*swayed*) Oh dear, I . . .

Conscience Remember Saint Blandina. And Saint Agatha. And Saint Febriona.

Jackie And Saint Felicity.

Conscience Who?

Tracy What happened to Saint Felicity?

Jackie Her story's lost except for this one detail: on the twenty-third of November, and they don't even know what year it was, she was put to death.

Tracy Is that it?

Jackie Nothing else is known about her.

Conscience She's still a saint.

Mrs Lord I have had quite enough of this irrelevant nonsense. Mrs Evans, are you all right?

Mrs Evans The dirt said hot –

Mrs Lord Yes, yes, the label said not. Tracy. For the last time. Will you do as I ask?

Conscience Tell her no.

Tracy No. Absolutely not. Never. Never ever in a million years. I will never –

Conscience Don't overdo it.

Tracy Sorry.

Mrs Lord Tracy, you're fired.

Tracy I wouldn't be anything else in the world.

Conscience Right. Sacrifice made. Now we can leave the battle scene triumphantly.

Tracy But what do we do now?

Conscience You go and join the protesters, knowing we've revealed the sham world as it is, and I watch the play come to an end and move on to the next.

Tracy Aren't you coming with me?

Conscience Only in spirit. I have to watch the play to the end. It's my job, I'm afraid. Must be done. Much as I'd love to come and sing songs round the campfire.

Tracy Oh. Oh, well. (*Goes to get her coat and collect her things.*)

Jackie That's right, take her out into the middle of the ocean and drop her in. Never mind asking if she can swim.

Conscience As for you. It's time we did some straight talking. (*matter of fact*) I don't mean to be Old Testament about things, but that's what it comes down to. An energy well outside the limits of our power and knowledge. Fire or flood, either way, full-scale annihilation for us all. Whether we want it or not. In the face of that, it does seem silly to me to be in the pay of self-made annihilation. Irresponsible, even.

Jackie (*tired, stubborn*) Take your sainthood away, *I've* no need for it.

Conscience Forget saints, I'm talking about simply saving your skin. A huge world fire with us at stake. Us at the stake. Us.

You. Me. Them out there. We'll all burn in one red terrifying heat. Limb wrenched from limb, lungs filling with poison as we breathe. Black, black rains. And this time no ark, no rainbow, no angels descending. Not a chance. I mean, I'm really sorry, but that's the way it is. We're playing with fire. It doesn't do to do nothing about it while you can. While you have the possibility. You have to do the right thing. Saints have nothing to do with it. But we have.

Tracy comes with her coat and bag.

Tracy I'm ready. Is the last word mine?
Conscience All yours.
Tracy (*marches up to Mrs Lord*) This chicken, Mrs Lord. It isn't real. (*Turns to Jackie.*) This chicken isn't real, Jackie.
Jackie (*sighing*) I know, I know.
Tracy Will you come too?

Jackie shakes her head.

It isn't real.

Jackie turns away.

(*to Conscience*) Triumphant exit?
Conscience Come on then. (*Looks upwards, spreads her arms out.*) Will that do? I hope so. I did my best. (*Looks at audience.*) All part of the job, I'm afraid. Hope it didn't ruin the play for you. Couldn't be helped. I'm sure you understand.

Tracy leaves the stage; Conscience returns to her seat in the audience. Moment of calm on stage. Mrs Lord, who has been checking Mrs Evans' goods out through the last speeches, approaches Jackie, who's visibly drained.

Mrs Lord I trust that's all dealt with and stacked away now, Jacqueline?
Jackie Yes, Mrs Lord.
Mrs Lord What a trial. But good riddance to bad rubbish. That's what I say.
Mrs Evans The sweet you *can* eat between meals without ruining your appetite.
Mrs Lord Yes, Mrs Evans, exactly what I was thinking. I do

apologize for the treatment you've received, and hope it hasn't put you off shopping at Wonderstore.

Mrs Evans Only the crumbliest flakiest chocolate tastes like chocolate never tasted before.

Mrs Lord Quite. We'll see you tomorrow, then. Bye-bye now. Manage your bags? Bye.

Exit Mrs Evans.

Now. Of course, you'll be able to hold the fort on your own until I employ someone else?

Jackie Yes, Mrs Lord.

Mrs Lord Good, good. That's the spirit. We're not a big organization. Not a big store. But no matter the size of the shop, I won't have insurrection. It doesn't do any of us any good. And – the main thing to remember, of course, is that it makes absolutely no difference at all.

Jackie Yes, Mrs Lord. I mean, no, Mrs Lord.

Mrs Lord And when one can is removed and the pyramid falls down, what do we do, Jacqueline? We rebuild the pyramid, don't we?

Jackie Yes, Mrs Lord.

Mrs Lord I'll telephone the agency immediately. (*Turns to go, turns back again.*) Strange. I would have thought that you would have been the one to cause trouble. To do some damaging action like that.

Jackie No, Mrs Lord.

Mrs Lord No, you're too clever for that.

Jackie Yes, Mrs Lord.

Mrs Lord Good girl. Clear up this mess, now.

Jackie Yes, Mrs Lord.

Exit Mrs Lord. Jackie looks round stage somewhat dolefully. Shrugs her shoulders. Picks things up, puts them where they should be, hangs chicken up again.

(*to audience*) It doesn't do to act like that. It doesn't help. You won't catch me going off the rails like that. I know what's happening. I know you're there. But it doesn't help to admit it, doesn't do any good for people to know it's not real.

All that stuff about saints. You can't change things. You just get yourself into trouble. And bring grief to other people too. See, I *know* about saints. I had books and books about them. I used to read them over and over. And one day one of my books fell open at this picture of a woman. I mean, I'd seen the picture before. But it was like I was really seeing it, for the first time. The woman, she was tied to a log, and flames were all round her, tasting her. Like whips, like she was being whipped. The first spat round her feet, reached up and licked her, ready to eat her, swallow her whole. But she was looking upwards, with this blank look on her face as if she wasn't there, as if the flames were nothing to do with her, as if it was quite nice really. 'That's not right,' I thought. 'That's not real.' Then I thought, 'Stupid fool. Imagine letting yourself get caught like that. Imagine letting that happen to yourself.' But, well, then, well, I threw the book in the dustbin. And after that I threw out all of my books about saints.

I still remember about the saints. I knew a lot by heart. Saint Euphemia, who was hurled to wild beasts. Saint Lucy, she got a sword through the throat. Saint Pelagia of Tarsus, roasted to death. Saint Pelagia of Antioch, threw herself off the top of a house when the soldiers came to get her. Saint Eugenia had her head cut off. Saint Margaret, she survived being swallowed by a dragon and *then* had her head cut off. Saint Catherine, the famous one, tortured on the wheel. Yes, Saint Catherine of Alexandria. That's what I mean about saints – take Saint Catherine. She went to complain to the emperor about the worship of idols, or something or other that she thought wasn't right. And he made her face these fifty philosophers, and when she argued them all into the ground, the emperor was so angry he burned them all alive. Then the emperor decided he wanted to marry her, and asked her to deny her faith. But she wouldn't, so he had her imprisoned, flogged, and then publicly tied to the wheel. But the wheel broke apart suddenly, and she was left unhurt, though some of the spectators were killed by flying splinters of wood. The spectacle of her sticking to what she believed made two hundred soldiers convert on the spot – and the emperor had them all beheaded. Just think. All those people killed and hurt, because of her. Innocent bystanders. I mean, that's brave. And that's dangerous. (*Pause.*)

I know what's going on. I know the plot. Bloody hell, I'm not stupid. It's just that sometimes it does more harm to go along lines that you shouldn't. This whole community thrives on the Plant. We need it. It brings in business, money, jobs, people. It's an industry. What the hell, it's there now. (*Pause.*)

I always think of that place in Germany they bombed in the Second World War, where they bombed so hard that the pavements were molten, so that if you were standing on the pavement you would burn from the feet up . . . (*Pause. Suddenly self-righteous*) And that's why we need plants. Stands to reason. No point in being stupid about it. It's security. (*Pause.*) My father and both of my brothers work there. (*Pause.*) That Saint Catherine, when she eventually had her head cut off, it was milk, not blood, that came out of her neck. This saint business is for people who aren't human. (*Pause.*)

What'll I tell them about Trace going daft? The neighbours'll know already. Dad'll know. He'll see her at the gates on his way home. I won't be supposed to speak to her. Her own dad'll see her. What'll she do? Folk don't know what's good for them sometimes. (*Pause. Looks at her watch.*) Nearly time to go home. Last customer due, then closing time.

Enter Mrs MacDonald, same woman. Jackie moves efficiently to position one.

Good afternoon, Mrs MacDonald. And how are you today, then?

Mrs MacDonald The taste of the country without the fat of the land.

Jackie And how's Mr MacDonald? And your son? And your daughter?

Mrs MacDonald (*sadly*) Not just nearly clean, but really clean.

Jackie Oh, I *am* sorry to hear that, Mrs MacDonald. But I'm sure everything will work out just fine.

Mrs MacDonald You'll never put a better bit of butter on your knife.

Jackie Yes, I know. See you tomorrow now. Take care.

Mrs MacDonald takes the trolley as usual. Jackie moves to position two to wait silently and motionlessly for her to come with her shopping.

Hello, Mrs MacDonald, what've you got today, then?

Mrs MacDonald It's like ground coffee taste without the grind.

Jackie And how's your family keeping?

Mrs MacDonald Why can't everything be as simple as Kellogg's Cornflakes?

Jackie Well, you tell them we were asking for them. Bye-bye now. Manage your bags? Bye.

Exit Mrs MacDonald. Jackie looks at her watch.

Starving. Wonder what's for tea. Tuesday . . . omelettes, I think. Good.

Enter Mrs Lord with overcoat on, goes to the till and takes the money out.

Mrs Lord Everything going fine, Jacqueline?

Jackie Yes, Mrs Lord.

Mrs Lord Was somebody just paying us a visit?

Jackie Mrs MacDonald, Mrs Lord.

Mrs Lord And what did she buy?

Jackie Pork chops, broccoli, potatoes, catfood, coffee, sweetcorn, eggs, milk, Mrs Lord.

Mrs Lord Good, good, that's the spirit. I think we're back to normal, Jacqueline.

Jackie Yes, Mrs Lord.

Mrs Lord We can close up for the night. That can be your responsibility.

Jackie Yes, Mrs Lord.

Mrs Lord Remember to switch off the lights. I'll see you in the morning.

Jackie Yes, Mrs Lord.

Mrs Lord Don't be late tomorrow, Jacqueline. Lateness is a disease. A social disease.

Jackie No, Mrs Lord. Yes, Mrs Lord.

Exit Mrs Lord. Jackie left on stage. Switches off music. Music stops. Switches off lights. Lights dim to the level they were at the beginning of the play. Pulls her coat round her. Comes forward confidentially to the audience.

Goodnight. See you tomorrow. (*Goes to door. Door won't open in or out. Stops. Thinks. Comes back across stage. Goes to other door. Locked. Back on to centre stage.*) I can't, um. (*Laughs, comic explanation.*) I'm stuck. I can't get out. (*Tries the doors again. Tries them harder. Comes back, centre stage. Not so funny. A little panic.*) I'm . . . we're . . . um (*Trapped, not knowing which way to move. Panic builds.*) Bloody hell. Bloody, bloody hell. Right. Think. Think logically. Locked in? You can't be locked in in a play! What's happening? Right. Stuck. That's what's happening. Caught. (*to audience*) Stop looking at me like that! It's not helping. (*Backs into a flat, which shakes, and gives her a fright – the stage feels too small, she's beginning to feel hemmed in.*) Bloody hell. (*Sees audience again, turns her back on them.*) Come on. What's happening. Get it right. The day's over. The play's over. I should be able to get out. Stands to reason. I should at least be able to come out of character. (*Tries. Strains. Doesn't work.*) Bloody hell. (*Goes to the first door. Knocks hard at it.*) Hello? Hello, is anybody there? (*Runs to the other door, knocks hard.*) Hello? Hello? Can you hear me?

Conscience, in front row of audience, becomes the echo.

Conscience Can you hear me?

Jackie runs across to the other door.

Jackie Will you listen?
Conscience Will you listen?
Jackie HELLO?
Conscience Can you hear me?
Jackie No one there.
Conscience Will you listen?
Jackie (*shakes the door handle one last time*) What am I going to do?
Conscience Can you hear me?
Jackie (*sinks down on stage, defeated*) Bloody hell.
Conscience Will you listen?
Jackie What am I? Too clever for my –? (*Listens for answer.*)
Conscience Can you hear me?
Jackie No answer. Trace? Mrs Lord?
Conscience Will you listen?

Jackie Nobody.

Conscience Can you hear me?

Jackie What'll I do?

Conscience Will you listen?

Jackie Bloody hell. What'll I do?

Conscience Can you hear me?

Jackie Trapped. Stuck.

Conscience Will you listen?

Jackie No way out.

Conscience Can you hear me?

Jackie Too late.

Conscience Will you listen?

Jackie Bloody hell. (*Scrunches up, head in hands, resigned.*)

Conscience Can you hear me? Will you listen? Can you hear me? Will you listen? Can you hear me?

Black.

Purple Side Coasters

SARAH DANIELS

Sarah Daniels's plays include *Ripen Our Darkness*, *The Devil's Gateway*, *Masterpieces*, *Neaptide*, *Byrthrite*, *The Gut Girls*, *Beside Herself*, *Head-rot Holiday*, *The Madness of Esme and Shaz* and *Blow Your House Down* (based on the novel by Pat Barker).

Purple Side Coasters was commissioned by BBC Radio and broadcast on 16 November 1995 with the following cast:

Susannah Harriet Walter
Debbie Pauline Quirke
Harry Scott Charles
Kevin Matt Bardock
Ben Roger May
Nurse Tracy Wiles
Dr Daintith/Security Officer 2 John Turner
Assistant 1 Sandra James-Young
Emma/Waitress Becky Hindley
Janice/Health Visitor/Woman 2 Jane Whittenshaw
G. P./Man Stephen Critchlow
Assistant 2 Paul Jenkins
Security Officer 1 Geoffrey Whitehead

Directed by Roanna Benn

SCENE ONE

The week before Christmas. A large department store. Deb and Harry (aged 3) are walking through the busy food hall on their way out of the shop.

   Sounds of noisy shopping hall. 'On the First Day of Christmas' is playing in the background.

Announcement (*on top of the music; incoherent but enough to establish that it's the food hall*) . . . And our food hall is giving away a complimentary bottle of port to every customer who purchases a whole cheese before Christmas. (*Ding-dong to signal end of message.*)

Harry (*agitated*) Go home now –

Deb (*excited*) Hang on a sec, Harry. I've just seen someone I know –

Harry Mummy, come on!

Deb I must just go and say hello –

Harry No! (*whining*) Don't want to.

   They make their way towards the till.

Deb You've seen Father Christmas and I'm –

Harry Not the real one –

Deb He gave you some felt-tips –

Harry Don't want them.

Deb The real one's still coming on Christmas Day with Power Rangers, OK? But only if you're a good boy. You don't want that. Put it back.

Harry (*cries*) Yes, thirsty.

Deb I'm not paying that for it. We'll get you a drink on the way home.

   She grabs his hand and they go through the shoppers towards Susannah.

Hold my hand. There's a good boy –

Harry (*shouts*) Drink. Drink.

Deb In a minute – Stop shouting. (*shouting herself*) Susannah? Hey, Susannah?

Pause. Susannah doesn't respond until Deb is practically in her face.

Susannah, it's me.

Susannah (*has recognized her but wishing Deb hadn't seen her; cool*) Oh, hi –

Deb It's me, Debbie. Didn't you recognize me? Not with my clothes on, eh? (*Laughs.*)

Susannah No. Hello. I didn't expect to see –

Harry Drink . . . drink (*and underneath Deb's next line; more frustrated*) Mummy, Mummy . . . I'm thirsty . . . drink.

Deb Be quiet, Harry. (*to Susannah*) No, me neither. I ain't been in this shop since I was a kid – to see Father Christmas – so I thought I'd bring him.

Susannah And so you must be Harry?

Harry Mind your own business.

Deb Harry! It's a phrase he picked up at nursery. What are they like? Mind, bet your Thomas has more manners.

Susannah I'm sure he's picked up far worse.

Deb Bit of a change from those colicky babies.

Harry Drink, Mummy –

Deb Well, perhaps not that much of a change. Just that they can talk now. Shush, Harry. (*to Susannah*) I can't believe – Do you – How are –

Harry Yes, for me. Now.

Susannah Hectic. This has to be the most hateful week of the year . . .

Harry Mummy!?

Deb I'll just get him a drink and –

Susannah Oh, don't worry. It was nice to see you. Don't let me hold you up.

SCENE TWO

Past. Deb's room in the unit. Deb and Susannah are very high.
They are naked and dancing. Susannah is banging out the tune to
Abba's 'Dancing Queen' on the bottom of a metal waste bin.
Deb accompanies her on a comb with toilet paper over it. Then
they both sing very loudly: '– Having the time of your life. See
that girl . . . Watch that scene . . . Digging the Dancing Queen.'

Susannah (*laughing and screaming as she nearly falls off the*
bed) Hold me up – I'm falling off –
Deb Here hold the comb. Don't stop dancing.
Susannah (*trying out the comb*) I never thought I'd find myself
kissing hard toilet paper.
Deb Feels better on your mouth than it does your bum don't it?

They start singing again, laughing and dancing. It is as though
they were drunk.

They're watching. They're watching.
Susannah Dance faster then they won't be able to see us. The
answer is to keep dancing, dancing and dancing and dancing –

Nurse comes in. She closes the door behind her.

Nurse Susannah, please would you go back to your own room?
Deb She can't. We've got to keep dancing.
Susannah (*to Nurse*) Why do you try and spoil everything?
Can't you understand we're having the time of our lives?
Nurse Now. And put some clothes on, please.
Deb She can't, I'm holding her up.
Susannah Don't make me. I have to stay here and sing with
Deb.
Nurse The only thing you have to do is get some sleep, as does
everyone else.

SCENE THREE

Present. Food hall. The queue. 'Ding-dong Merrily on High'
playing in the background. Deb and Harry have got a drink and

*gone back to Susannah, who is now putting her shopping on the
conveyor belt.*

Deb Excuse me. No, I ain't pushing in. I'm with my friend. (*to
Susannah*) I thought I'd never get back. Have you seen the
jewellery on her? Here, can you put this with yours? Took us
ages to find one with a straw. Here, let me give you the –

Harry Mine, mine.

Susannah It's OK. It's nothing.

Deb In a minute. We've got to pay for it. (*to Susannah*) Please
take it.

Susannah No, no. (*giving Harry the drink*) Here, Harry.

Deb But?

Susannah Don't worry, I often eat stuff as I go around. As long
as you give them the empty packet it's OK –

Deb Oh. What do you say, Harry?

Harry Straw. Straw.

Deb Give us it here. (*She puts in the straw.*) There you go.

*He immediately starts to drink it. Susannah continues to put
her food on the conveyor belt.*

D'you always do yer food shopping in here, then?

Susannah It is Christmas.

Deb Let me give yer a hand with it –

Susannah I can manage, thanks.

Bleeps as Susannah's shopping goes over the light.

Deb Give us yer other bags, then –

Susannah It's all right, really –

Deb – So as you can get yer purse out. Harry, what d'you think
you're doing?

Harry (*looking in one of Susannah's bags*) Look, Mum. Look!

Deb Harry, don't be so fricking nosey. Get out of Susannah's
shopping.

Harry (*more politely to Susannah*) What is it?

Susannah It's a Christmas present for my little boy.

Harry I want one. Mum? I want it.

Susannah You can have it.

Deb (*to Harry*) No, you don't. (*to Susannah*) Sorry about this.
   Oi. Harry. Stop showing me up.

Harry For me?

Deb Behave.

Susannah Would he really like it?

Harry Yes. Please. Thank you.

Deb No, it's for her little boy. He won't have anything at
   Christmas.

Susannah I can easily get him another. Do take it. I'm sorry but
   I'm in such a rush. I'd like to –

Assistant 1 Forty-seven pounds, ninety-four pence, please,
   madam.

Deb Just for that? Blimey, it soon adds up don't it.

Susannah (*hands over the cash*) Here. Thank you.

Harry For me? Is it mine?

Deb No, it's not. You don't want it anyway. It's a little house. We
   haven't got room, Harry.

Harry Please.

Assistant 1 Two pounds, three pee change, thank you

Harry My present. Yes, she said for me . . . for me . . . mine.

Susannah (*to Assistant*) Thanks very much. (*Puts change in her
   purse. To Deb*) I'm sorry I should never have opened my
   mouth. Umm, why don't you take this and he can choose
   something from the toy department.

Deb I don't want to take no money off of you. No, he's fine.

Harry Toy for me, Mum . . . Mum . . .

Assistant 1 Madam, if you wouldn't mind packing your
   groceries. There's a bit of a log jam –

Susannah Debs. I didn't mean . . . It's just –

Deb Na, you're all right. I'm not so thick that I don't know when
   I'm being fobbed off. Come on Harry – (*She starts to walk off.*)

Assistant 1 (*calls after her*) Excuse me, madam.

Deb (*turns, embarrassed*) They ain't my groceries, they're hers.

Assistant 1 What about the drink? That hasn't been paid for.

Deb Oh, shit.

Susannah (*to Assistant*) I'm sorry, that was my fault. I gave it to
   her little boy and I forgot to show it to you.

Assistant 1 Actually you're not supposed to consume anything
   before it's gone on a bill.

Susannah There was no intent to defraud –

Assistant 1 Technically speaking, it's stealing.

Susannah Please just take the money and we'll be out of the way.

Deb Don't take hers. Take mine. God, just as I thought I'd got outta of this place without embarrassing meself –

Assistant 1 (*tuts, but takes the money and rings it up*) Thank you, madam. Next.

Sound of bleeps as next person's shopping goes through.

Susannah (*to Deb*) I'm sorry. Really, I feel dreadful. Don't go. Debbie?

Deb Here, hold that bag open for me – Bloody hell. What is all this stuff? I ain't never seen most of these things before – (*excitedly*) But this, now don't tell me, let me guess. (*triumphant*) It's only a fricking artichoke, enit?

Susannah Yes.

Deb You are well and truly over it then.

SCENE FOUR

Past. Three years earlier. Susannah's kitchen. Susannah is holding Thomas. Both of them are crying. Her partner, Ben, is doing his best to console them gently.

Ben Susannah, darling, it's all right.

Susannah It's not, Ben. It's ruined. Everything's ruined.

Ben Come on, it's only a mistake. It doesn't matter. I'll go and get us a takeaway.

Susannah You can't. You can't. You've only just got home. Take him. Take him. I can't breathe.

Ben OK. It's OK.

He takes Thomas. The crying continues but decreases to a whimper.

There, I've got him. (*to Thomas*) There you are. Yes, Daddy's got you.

Susannah I can't breathe. I can't breathe.

Ben Sit down. Take it easy. You can breathe, you are breathing.

Susannah I'm choking. I'm choking. Don't you understand?

Ben You're panicking. Here, hold my hand. It's OK. We're all
here. We're all safe.

Susannah Let go. Let me go. You're suffocating me.

Ben Susannah, look, why don't you lie down. I'll take care of
Tom.

Susannah If I lie down I'll drown in my sleep –

Ben You won't. Trust me. You won't. Remember how important
sleep is – what the midwife said.

Susannah I'd never wake up. I wouldn't be there when I woke
up.

Ben Stop it, sweetheart. This is nonsense.

Susannah That's what you want, isn't it? That's why you're
trying to trick me.

Ben I love you. I'm trying to help.

Susannah Then why can't you see that I'm not breathing?

SCENE FIVE

Past. Mother and baby unit. Group discussion/experience
sharing, rather than therapy.

Nurse There's only ten minutes left –

Deb Thank God fer that. I can't take much more of this de-
bloody-pressing chattering on.

Nurse Debbie, sit down, please. Now, would someone who's not
had a chance like to say something?

Deb Hells bells, it's like being at school –

Emma (*very soft whisper, but agitated*) Nurse? Nurse?

Nurse It's all right, Emma.

Janice I'm all right. I'm alright. Most of the time. What I want to
know is why I can't go home

Deb You did go home, Janice. Then you had to come back
again.

Janice Only because I had a panic attack –

Deb Yeah but it lasted all weekend, didn't it?

Nurse Debbie, why don't you go for a walk in the grounds with
Harry?

Deb No thanks. Have you seen it out there. The sun's shining.

Emma (*frightened whisper*) See, she doesn't like light. See . . . See . . .

Nurse As long as you cover up.

Deb You know them drugs we're all on is radioactive.

Nurse Debbie.

Deb 'Cos if you go out in the sun you frizzle and fry. No wonder they all have panic attacks.

Emma Beelzebub. She is the devil. She is trying to convert us all to the fires of Hades.

Deb Shut your face, you mad cow.

Emma Evil . . . evil . . .

Nurse There's no need to be frightened, Emma. Debbie is here like you. She's not the devil. Debbie, would you please not be abusive and try and concentrate?

Deb And become as miserable as this lot? What you trying to do? Finish us off? We should be dancing, dancing the night and day away.

Nurse What did it feel like, Janice?

Janice What?

Nurse The panic attack.

Janice I can't remember.

Susannah (*talks slower because of the medication*) It's like – you can't see or breathe and you're having a heart attack and you're going to die . . . it's inexplicable, despicable.

Nurse (*interrupting her*) The symptoms are real enough because you start to hyperventilate. Do you know what it's related to?

Susannah Terror. Unadulterated. Hyperventilated. Masticated, asphyxiated, unrelated.

Deb She just said a rude word. Susannah just said a rude word.

Janice It's just choking. Gagging and gagging.

Susannah Having things rammed down your throat.

Nurse What sort of things, Susannah?

Susannah The hairy bits of artichokes.

Deb What the hell are they when they're at home?

Emma She is the devil. Listen to her. She's trying to tell you hell is her home.

Nurse Debbie, please. Emma, please.

Deb Oh, I get it. It's high-society slang for bollocks.

Nurse Debbie, if you don't pipe down, Doctor Daintith will regret his decision to reduce your medication.

SCENE SIX

Toy department. Susannah, Debbie and Harry.

'Jingle Bells' and 'Ho, ho ho' Santa noises designed to attract attention to the Christmas grotto. And a cacophony of Nintendo bleeps and buzzer sounds.

Harry Me choose. Me choose . . .

Deb I don't think he can believe it. I bundled him straight into the lift after we'd seen Father Christmas. (*to Harry*) Something small.

Susannah Nothing that's too big for your room. Nothing that Mummy will trip over.

Deb Or that will make a terrible racket and drive Mummy demented. Again. (*Laughs.*)

Harry Me. Myself?

Deb Yes, you choose.

Susannah Debbie. Don't misunderstand me, but for the last couple of years I've tried –

Deb We'd better keep up with him. (*Calls to Harry.*) Harry?

Harry Me choose. On my own!

Deb Yes, but make sure you can still see me. (*to Susannah*) Sorry, what was you saying?

Susannah I don't want to talk about it. Any of it. I've put it behind me.

Deb Yeah, me too.

Susannah There are very few people who know now. Certainly nobody where I work now has any idea. If they did I wouldn't have got the job and –

Deb What d'you take me for? I'd never tell anyone. You must be joking. Surely, after everything . . . you know . . . it's not as if I've not been sunk in the same boat an' all.

Harry Mummy? This?

Deb It's too expensive, Harry. Choose something else. (*to*

Susannah) Don't worry. He might not be able to count yet, but he knows what inexpensive means.

Susannah He can have whatever he wants.

Deb Na, listen, I can't –

Susannah Honestly, Debbie, let me. Apart from my salary, I've actually inherited a lot of money this year.

Deb Oh. Oh, Susannah. I'm sorry.

Susannah Why?

Deb My mum dying was the worst thing that happened to me. Even worse than (*Stops herself.*) – you know what.

Susannah (*warmly*) Not my parents. No, my aunt. She was in her nineties. No children. She left her whole estate to me.

Deb Blimey, what you still working for, then?

Susannah I don't know where I'd be without it or who.

Harry These?

Deb You can have an Action Man if you like, but not half a dozen.

Susannah He can have something else.

Deb Na, he's got to learn to choose.

SCENE SEVEN

Susannah and Ben in their flat. Susannah is crying.

Ben It's alright, I can take time off but you're not going to get better worrying about going back to work. One thing at a time. No one's asking you to be just a mother and nothing else. What is so important about a job? I'd jump at the chance to have a year off. Frankly, I'd love to be just a father. Who you are isn't dependent on what you do.

Susannah I know . . . (*Sniffs.*) I know you're right. It's just . . . it's just that it somehow feels all wrong.

Ben Because, like the GP and midwife said, your hormones are all over the place –

Susannah I wish it was just my hormones.

Ben Give it a little while. We've both just got to readjust to us being three instead of two.

Susannah Where are you going?

Ben I've got a meeting.

Susannah Please don't go –
Ben I'll come straight back.
Susannah Don't go. I can't cope.
Ben You're OK. Thomas is asleep. I won't be late. (*Kisses her.*) I won't be long, honest.
Susannah Ben? Please?
Ben I have to. I'm sorry.

He goes and closes the door quietly behind him. However, the noise wakes up Thomas and he immediately starts crying.

Susannah (*putting her fingers in her ears*) I can't hear you. I can't hear you. I can't hear you!

SCENE EIGHT

The toy department. Sounds as before.

Harry Action Man and Action Man . . .
Deb I said one. Not two, one.
Harry (*to Susannah*) One for your little boy?
Susannah Thank you, that's very kind, Harry, but no.
Deb Susannah probably don't approve of them toys. I ain't compromised you, have I? Give us it here, I'm not going to let you pay for it anyhow.
Susannah It's quite OK. And this is on me.
Deb All right, then we'll be outta yer way.
Susannah I really didn't . . . Deb . . . How about we all go and have a cup of tea?
Harry Cake, cake –
Deb I thought you were busy.
Susannah There's still two more shopping days before Christmas. (*to Harry*) Yes and a cake. (*to Deb*) Do you still take your camera everywhere with you?
Deb Oh, don't.
Susannah Don't what?
Deb Remind me. I'm so embarrassed.
Susannah Why? (*Opens her purse.*) Look, I've still got that one, the one you took of Ben and I.

Deb I was mad –

Susannah Rubbish.

Deb Yeah, they were.

Harry Mine now.

Susannah (*to Harry*) I'm just going to pay for him then he's all yours. (*to Deb*) Have you still got the same camera?

Deb Na. We sold it when Kev lost his job.

Susannah Oh, I'm sorry.

Deb Don't worry, he's got another one. It's only one of them hourly contracts type jobs, but most people are on them now.

Susannah I'm glad he's found something else. I'm sorry about the camera, though.

Deb Don't be. I couldn't bear to look at it after I got home. That photography lark was one of me biggest symptoms, weren't it.

SCENE NINE

Past. Debbie's flat. She has just come back from a manic shopping spree. She is bottle-feeding Harry and talking to her friend, Tracy, on a mobile phone.

Deb (*very fast*) Hi ya, Trace. No, I'm talking to you on a mobile. Yeah. It's a present for Kev. Oh, he'll be over the moon, won't he. It's difficult for him see, to ring home from work. Harry's doing just brilliant. No sweat. He's just here. Can't you hear him racing to get to the end of his bottle? No wonder I'm talking fast. I won't get no peace when he's finished. (*to Harry*) No, I won't, will I, boy? Wait till Daddy sees what we've got here. (*to Tracy*) So listen, Trace, if you want any photos done. I've just bought one of them backcloth thingies and two new lenses. Yeah, tell everyone you know. (*to Harry*) Had enough? Sure? Good boy. (*She puts him over her shoulder and starts patting him on the back.*) You're joking, I'll earn the money back in no –

Harry is sick.

Oh, whoops. Shit. I got to go. No, he's just been sick. Though I s'pose I better brace meself to look in his nappy an all. Speak ter yer soon, Trace. Bye. (*She switches off the phone.*)

Harry starts to grizzle.

(*affectionately*) What you go and do that for? Now we'll have to get you cleaned up and me. No, don't go and put your hands in it.

Sound of front door opening and shutting. Kevin comes in.

Kevin What the –

Deb It's OK, Kev. He's just been sick again.

Kevin Never mind him. What's all this?

Deb Don't look like that, we got something for you, an' all. Here. I was going to wrap it up but I thought I'd better try it out first, just to check that it works. It does.

Kevin Where did you get the money from?

Deb It was on offer. D'you know they're almost as cheap as a travel card?

Kevin The line rental isn't. Nor are the calls. We can't afford this –

Deb I've still got me Visa.

Kevin Are you out of your tree? What's all this other junk?

Deb (*enthusiastically*) That's an investment, that is. I've got it all worked out. Goodbye money worries. I'm going to set up me own business.

Kevin You've got more film here than Hollywood.

Deb Yeah. Right. I'm going to do studio portraits of people's babies. Everyone wants them and before you can say cheesy grin we'll be rolling it in.

Kevin (*shouting*) Don't be so stupid. You've only got a poxy camera. You can't even focus properly. Come on, get him cleaned up and we're taking it all back to the shop.

Harry starts crying. Deb and Kevin raise their voices to be heard over him.

Deb We can't. You've not heard me. This is a mega venture. This will solve everything. You ain't got no vision, you.

Kevin Just shut it, you stupid little – It's only me earning now. They're about to kick me out any day. We're behind with the rent. We ain't paid the electricity or even the water rates. If we get cut off, they'll take him into care. We'll end up in some crap, infested hostel. God, girl, for Christsakes get a fricking grip.

Deb (*starts to cry*) Don't . . . Kev . . .

Kevin Yeah, go on cry. Cry, that's right. That's the most sensible thing you've done for ages.

Deb You don't understand –

Kevin Too bloody right – Jesus, all this stuff. What . . . what the hell's got into you?

Deb (*calmer*) I dunno. I dunno what's happening.

Kevin (*softer*) Look, I know you're excited, right? About having him. I am. I am, meself. When things are really bad at work. I just think, 'I've got a son.' And it don't matter what's going down there, I just feel cheered up.

Deb It's not like – I just can't do that –

Kevin I know. I know. I know it's hard. I wish we could have what we wanted. Who doesn't? Everyone does. But we aren't kids no more. We can't spend in the way we used to and not think about the consequences 'cos we got him now, ain't we?

Deb You don't understand.

Kevin I do. (*Pause.*) Well, what is it I don't understand, then?

Deb I dunno.

Kevin If you don't know, then –

Deb (*quietly*) Kev, I think I'm going mental.

Kevin (*affectionately*) No, you're not, you daft cow. Look, you just want to buy stuff we can't afford. If that was mental then there'd be more loony bins than shops, wouldn't there, eh?

Deb I dunno.

Kevin Yes, you do. Come here, c'mon. (*He gives her a hug.*) Give us a hug. There's nothing wrong with yer head. (*Pause.*) No, there ain't.

Still no response.

I'll prove it. Right. There was this health inspector and one day he had to go to the local nuthouse and he gets to meet all the nutters. Right? And they're all going berserk and dribbling and complete head-the-balls except this one bloke who's working quietly in a corner and the inspector is truly impressed by his behaviour and so he goes up to him and the bloke says –

Deb Is this some kind of test?

Kevin Na, it's a joke, babe.

Deb I don't get it.

Kevin That's 'cos I ain't finished it yet. So the bloke says to the inspector, 'You've got to get me out of here. I'm perfectly all right, I've been locked up by a mistake.' The inspector talks to him a bit more and he tells him how sorry he is that he's been locked up and promises that as soon as he gets back to the office he'll make arrangements to get the bloke out of there. The bloke is very pleased and goes with the inspector to the door. The inspector is just about to get into his car when the bloke throws a brick through the car window. The inspector turns around and says, 'What did you do that for?' The bloke says, 'You won't forget to tell them, will you?'

Deb (*laughs*) You're deranged, you are.

Kevin Yeah, but you're not. If you was, you wouldn't have got the joke. Mad people don't understand jokes. Do they? No, 'cos their minds are not there, are they? And you're all here, ain't you? See?

SCENE TEN

On the escalator. Music: 'See Amid the Winter's Snow'.

Susannah They make up the symptoms as they go along if you ask me.

Deb Let me put Action Man in my bag, Harry, while we're on the escalator?

Harry No, me hold him.

Deb (*to Susannah*) I weren't right though, was I? (*to Harry*) Come on 'cos we have to jump off soon. See there the café at the top. You don't want to fall off, do you? There, I'll put him safe in my bag.

Susannah If you follow that logic, all photographers would be locked up.

Deb Eh? Yer what?

Susannah Your taking photographs. Everyone has to start somewhere.

Deb Oh, don't start that up again. Here we are, Harry. Oops, off we get. That's it.

They get off the escalator and walk towards the entrance to the café.

No, leave that alone, Harry. (*to Susannah*) I don't half envy you being able to go shopping on your own. Is Thomas with Ben or have you got a child minder?

Susannah I've still got the photo you took of Thomas in that hospital carry cot. I had it framed.

Deb You're like a dog with a bone, you are.

Waitress Table for two and a high chair?

Harry No, proper chair. Mum, proper chair.

Susannah Table for three, please.

Waitress If you'd like to follow me.

They do so.

Susannah (*to Deb*) Well, where does it state that wanting to take photographs is evidence of personality disorder?

Deb If it didn't before it probably does now, thanks to me. I mean I ain't even got an art GSCE. No, take it from me, it was definitely part of the purple side coasters.

Waitress This one all right, ladies?

Susannah Fine thanks. (*to Deb*) The what?

Deb Sorry, I wasn't going to mention it.

SCENE ELEVEN

Past. Deb and Kevin's flat. Deb is very agitated, pacing up and down. The GP (male) and the Health Visitor (female) are talking to Kevin in the adjoining room.

GP It would be much better, Kevin, if you could persuade her to come of her own accord.

Kevin I'll try, Doctor, but she's not making no sense.

H. Visitor Would you like me to –

Kevin No. Let me. I'm the only one she seems to recognize. Why's it happened to her?

GP There are a lot of big hormonal upheavals after a woman has a baby and it can have a very strange emotional impact.

Kevin But she's been buying stuff like it's going out of fashion and she thinks her mum's alive and her mum died over two years ago. How can your hormones do that?

H. Visitor We don't really know. But what we do know is that she needs help to get her back to –

Kevin What did you say it was called again?

GP Puerperal psychosis. I think we should make a move.

Kevin What about Harry? I can't just –

H. Visitor We'll bring him with us.

Kevin goes into the other room.

Deb (*still pacing the floor, muttering to herself*) Don't cross over the line. If you stay behind the sofa, they won't see you. Don't touch it, don't touch it. Leave that there. They can't see you, anyway. They are the . . .

Kevin Deb? Deb? Hey, put your coat on, babe.

Deb (*urgent conspiratorial whisper*) You must get them out of the flat. They are police squatters with cameras –

Kevin They're going.

Deb They've come to the wrong house. I told them I didn't need anything. They want to know what we've got. They are going to come back and burgle us.

Kevin Deb. It's the doctor and the health visitor.

Deb They're pretending to be. What's the matter with you? Can't you see? Can't you see? They just want what we've got.

Kevin (*weary*) Just put your coat on, Debs.

Deb (*desperate*) I can prove it to you. Listen, I heard them. They said I think she's got purple side coasters. But we haven't! All we've got is these coasters your mum brought back from Spain. (*triumphant*) And they're red and yellow.

Kevin (*upset*) Debbie, you're talking rubbish.

Deb (*aggressive*) It's you. You're so thick you can't see. You believe them. You believe anything anyone tells you. You traitor. Go on, then, betray me. You can do what you want. I don't want anything to do with you.

GP Come on Debbie. Let's get in the car.

Deb (*very frightened and very aggressive*) Don't come near me.

Don't touch me. (*She throws a glass which smashes against the wall.*) Leave me alone.

Kevin Debs. Debs. (*to the others*) It's OK. I've got her.

Debbie is screaming, shouting and struggling.

Deb Bastard . . . shit . . . piss . . . bastard . . .

GP I think I'd better ring for an ambulance.

Kevin Give us a sec. Deb. Deb. It's Kev. I've got yer. I've got yer. It's only me. How 'bout we go out shopping? Eh? We're going to go out shopping. You want to do that, don't you? Come on, then. Let's get a move on before the shops shut.

Deb Can I have a new lens? So I can take photos of their insides?

Kevin You can have what you want, babe, but only if you're good.

SCENE TWELVE

Present. Busy café area. Lot of background chatter, crockery clanking. Susannah and Deb are laughing. 'Silent Night' either without words or German version.

Harry Why are you laughing? Mummy? Mummy?

Waitress (*clears her throat to get their attention*) Are you ready to order, ladies?

Deb I think we need another couple of minutes –

Harry Cake . . . cake . . .

Susannah (*still laughing*) We were just wondering if you have any coasters . . .

Deb (*still finding it funny*) Shush, Susannah. I thought you didn't want anyone to know.

Waitress Coasters?

Susannah Yes, to put drinks on at the side of –

Deb Susannah, you'll get us thrown out.

Waitress We don't need coasters, madam. Our tea is served in cups with saucers.

Susannah What a shame, we'd like coasters at the side –

Waitress I could see –

Deb Take no notice of her.

Susannah They would have to be purple . . .
Waitress (*confused*) You want purple side coasters?
Deb No thanks. We've already had it.

They both laugh.

SCENE THIRTEEN

Past. Outside the entrance to the mother and baby unit.

GP Here we are, Debbie. We've just got to ring the bell and get them to open the door.

Doorbell.

Kevin It's not like I imagined.
H. Visitor The grounds are really beautiful.
Deb (*whispers*) Why are they coming shopping with us, Kevin?
Kevin Shush, Deb. Just try and keep calm for me, eh?
GP Come on. (*He rings the bell again.*)
Deb Do they have to open specially for us? Like they do for the Queen?

The door opens.

GP Hello, Sister. This is Debbie Stevens. I'm her GP. I phoned earlier.
Nurse Hi. Come in. Hello, Debbie. Let's go into the office.

They go in. The door slams shut behind them with a final-sounding clunk.

Deb This is a hospital.
Kevin It's okay. I'm here.
GP Why don't you wait here with Debbie, Kevin, just for a couple of minutes while we go into the office and have a word with the duty psychiatrist?
Kevin Oh. All right.

The Nurse, Health Visitor and GP go towards the office.

Deb I told you they were mental. Why did we have to bring them here?

The others go into the office and shut the door behind them.

Kevin They brought us here.

Nurse (*background*) This is Debbie Stevens's GP and Health Visitor*.

Deb *What are they saying?

Dr D. (*background*) Do please take a seat. Where is the patient?+

Kevin +I can't quite make it out. Be very quiet.

GP In the reception area. Her husband's with her.

Dr D. So what's been happening?

GP On the two occasions I've seen her this week, *her behaviour had been increasingly odd* . . . *the first time, was last Wednesday when she was convinced that I was a policeman.

Deb *I told yer. I told yer. They are out to lunch.

H. Visitor With me she's been completely *manic** . . . shouting, laughing, deluded, then increasingly paranoid . . . She's been on manic shopping sprees.

Deb *Two sandwiches short of a picnic but as much fruitcake as anyone can eat. (*She laughs manically.*)

Dr D. And she's described these *Delusions?*+

H. Visitor Yes, she believes her mother, who died two years ago, is still alive and staying with them. There have been *periods of lucidity.*

Kevin +Keep it down, Deb. I can't hear.

GP *Rapidly decreasing though.* *This afternoon she didn't recognize either of us. She refused to cross the room. She thought if she did, she'd disappear.

Deb *Go on, Kev. You spy on them. Give them a taste of their own medicine. (*She laughs loudly.*)

Dr D. So what are we looking at?

GP Thirty-six hours for assessment?

Dr D. *You definitely think the only way we can keep her in is on a Section?*

GP Yes.

Dr D. OK, let's take a look at her.

Kevin (*alarmed*) We've got to get out of here, Debs. Just take me hand and run.

Deb I told you.

Kevin Run, run.

They run through the corridor. Kev tries to open a door but finds that it's locked.

Shit, it's locked. Come on, this way –

Deb Kev. Kev, close your eyes and we can walk through it.

Kev Keep them open, Deb. You'll bash into something.

They pound down another corridor.

GP (*calls*) Kevin? (*to the Nurse*) Where are they?

Nurse They've run into the other wing. Do you want me to sound the alarm, Doctor Daintith?

Dr D. Not just yet. They have to come back this way. (*to GP*) I thought you said he was willing to bring her here.

GP He was. (*Pause.*) There, they're over there –

Kevin Oh shit, we've gone in a circle.

Deb The devil has run rings around us. (*Laughs.*)

The GP, psychiatrist (Dr D.) and Nurse run after them.

GP (*calls after them*) Kevin? Kevin? What are you doing?

Kevin (*kicking the door*) They're all bleeding locked. This way, Debs. Don't go back to them. We're going home.

Deb (*calmly*) It's all right. I can get us out. (*She smashes her hands against the glass reinforced with wire and succeeds in cutting her hand.*)

Kevin You've cut it. You've cut it. Debs –

Deb It's all right. It doesn't hurt.

H. Visitor Debbie, we've got to clean that up for you. Please come with me.

Deb Wash away the sins of the world.

Kevin (*on the verge of tears*) You can't keep her here. Please let me take her home.

Deb (*as she allows herself to be led away*) It's all right, Kev.

Kevin (*desperate*) Debbie –

Deb What they don't know is that I can walk through walls –

GP Kevin, what do you think you're doing? You agreed to us bringing her to the unit.

Kevin I thought you were just going to give her an injection or something to calm her down.

Dr D. That's probably what we are going to do, Mr Stevens.

Kevin And then I can take her home?

GP She'll need to stay here a little while just until she gets well.

Kevin I'm not having her sectioned.

H. Visitor It's best if we –

Kevin No, please, please. (*desperate*) I can look after her. Just let me take her home –

H. Visitor But you've seen how she is. You know yourself that what she needs is some proper medical care.

Kevin You can't just lock her up and throw away the key.

GP No one's going to let that happen. But we do need you to sign the form to –

Kevin What do you think I am? I ain't going to sign my wife into a nuthouse. No way.

GP We don't need you to, but it would be easier.

Kevin It's all my fault. We needed the overtime. I didn't even realize anything was wrong for ages. I thought it was me – see. That I didn't understand what having a baby meant. I didn't – Shit, I let it get to this state –

GP You did your best, Kevin.

Kevin And what poxy good was that? Useless.

GP Let's go into the office, Kevin. This is Doctor Daintith, by the way.

Kevin Doctor, you really don't have to keep her in here, honest.

SCENE FOURTEEN

Café. Susannah, Deb and Harry. Music: 'When a Child Is Born' by Johnny Mathis (not the talking section).

Susannah (*laughing*) D'you remember how humourless Doctor Daintith was?

Deb Do I? What about when he threatened to increase my medication because he reckoned I was too happy.

Harry I've done a picture. Mummy? Mummy?

Deb That's nice, Harry. What about putting another person there?

Harry OK.

Susannah In one session he asked me if I could remember the events which led up to my being sectioned. Well, I actually felt sorry for the poor sod, having to listen day in and day out to stories of women going bananas so I tried to make it as entertaining as possible and ended up killing myself laughing. Big mistake.

SCENE FIFTEEN

Susannah remembers as she tells Deb. Dr Daintith's office in the mother and baby unit.

Dr D. Just try and tell me what you remember, Susannah –

Susannah In a nutshell, I became convinced that Thomas, or rather his innocence, would be able to save the world in a way that Jesus hadn't been able to. I don't know why. I didn't even have a religious upbringing. Anyway, in this higher state of awareness, I put Thomas in the car and drove through town convinced that Thomas would give me a sign. Sure enough, this man in a Rover pulled out in front of me in Magdalene Square and Thomas started to cry. So, assured that this was the celestial signal, and that we'd all be catapulted into the perfect world if I slammed my foot on the accelerator, I did. And, of course, went smack into the back of the car. I remember that I couldn't work out why things hadn't gone according to plan but rationalized that this must have been merely a test and not the real thing.

Dr D. Sorry? You're saying you were rational?

Susannah No, I was completely barmy but the barmyness had its own rationale, pertaining to good and evil. Sorry, am I boring you?

Dr D. No, no, then what happened?

Susannah The driver got out of the Rover. Certainly, he seemed to personify evil. What he wasn't shouting at me was nobody's business, no expletive left unturned. So, of course, I took this as another indication that greater forces were at work and God told me, or I thought, in my rational barmy state, that God was telling me, to get the hell out of there. So I put my foot down and as I went past his car, I took his door off. (*Laughs*.) Of course, the police came round that night, and the rest, as they say, is history.

Dr D. You and Thomas could've been killed.

Susannah But we weren't. And, I'm no psychiatrist, but I expect that driver has to think twice for the rest of his days before he pulls out in front of someone. What do you think?

Dr D. I think that maybe finding things amusing is one of your defence mechanisms.

Susannah That is interesting because I've always been ridiculed for my lack of humour.

SCENE SIXTEEN

In the café. Deb, Harry and Susannah.
The two women laugh at the story.

Susannah Honestly, Deb. He'd have taken it less seriously if I'd taken out a gun and shot myself.

Deb He could drive yer nuts but he weren't a bad old stick really.

Susannah What about when that what-was-her-name, married to a vicar, Emma. Do you remember when she punched him in the face?

Deb That was terrible.

But then they both laugh uncontrollably.

Harry Look, Mum – finished.

Deb That's really nice, Harry.

Harry (*whispers*) For her.

Waitress Pot of tea for two, chocolate milkshake and a selection of cakes.

Deb Thank you.

Susannah At last. You might have saucers with the cups, but judging from the state of the table you don't provide plates.

Waitress Pardon?

Susannah Could you wipe the table, please?

Waitress I'll just go and get a cloth. Do you mind what colour it is?

Susannah Have you got a purple one, then?

Deb (*to Waitress*) Take no notice of her. (*to Susannah*) Don't start that up again. Look, Harry's got a picture for you.

Susannah Oh, thank you very much, Harry. What is it?

Harry Mummy.

Deb You're s'posed to say, 'Can you tell me about it?' Least that's what the health visitor told me.

Susannah Oh. Can you tell me about it?

Harry It's Mummy. I just told you.

Susannah Well, thank you. Would you like your milkshake?

Harry grabs the milkshake and starts to drink it through the straw.

Harry Thank you.

Deb Good boy. Take it easy –

Harry Cake, Cake . . .

Susannah (*to Harry*) Which one would you like? (*to Deb*) I always thought you thought I was a snob.

Deb I did. (*to Harry*) Yes, you can have this piece. (*to Susannah*) You were rather po-faced, at first. But I never knew what you saw in me.

Harry No! That one. And that one. Not one. More.

Deb Harry, will you just behave.

Susannah Why don't we cut a little piece of each of them and then you can see which one you like best.

Harry No, big piece.

Deb Don't be greedy.

Susannah Your being outrageous.

Deb He can't have everything. He'll be sick.

Susannah No, I meant that's what I liked about you. Your outspokenness. But I always felt like I was like the unpopular swot of the class.

Deb D'you know, I reckon, I'd probably still be stuck in there if it weren't fer you.

SCENE SEVENTEEN

Past. Deb's room in the mother and baby unit.

Dr. D. How are you feeling today, Debbie?

No response.

How's she been, Nurse?
Nurse She's refusing to come out of her room or speak to any of the staff.

Susannah barges into the room.

Susannah You've got her on too many drugs.
Nurse Please go back to your room, Susannah. Doctor Daintith is here to see Debbie.
Susannah Then he needs his eyes testing. He's the one that's made her like this. Can't you see what's happening to her? Why isn't she being offered therapy? Because you think she's too inarticulate? The only thing you can conceptualize her doing with her mouth is swallowing drugs.
Dr D. Debbie?
Susannah Of course she can't respond to you now. That dose of chlorpromazine would make an ox fall over. The patient's advocate is coming to see me and –
Dr D. Go back to the ward, Susannah. You are violating a patient's rights by interrupting a confidential consultation.
Susannah On your own head be it. (*She goes, slamming the door behind her.*)
Dr D. Let's have a look at your notes, Debbie, and see how much we've put you on.

SCENE EIGHTEEN

Present. Café. Music: 'Unto Us a Son Is Born'.

Harry Play with Action Man? Play with Action Man!
Deb He's for Christmas.
Harry No, now.
Deb No.

Harry Please?

Deb All right. Here, now play nicely with him. What do you say?

Harry (*sing-song*) Thank you. Thank you. Thank you.

Deb That's enough, thank you. Good boy. (*to Susannah*) Do you and Ben ever think of having another one?

Susannah No. There's no way I'd ever risk putting myself through that hell again.

Deb I don't want him to be the only one –

Harry (*to Action Man*) Quick. Find him. (*Starts to make Action Man perform dastardly deeds with the cruet set and crockery.*) Bang. Blow up.

Deb Although, I must still be a bit insane to even imagine coping with two of them. (*to Harry*) No. Let's put those back upright before they get broken. Oh dear. Would you look at that? Action Man is worn out now. I think he needs a big sleep, don't you?

Harry No. He's got no bed.

Susannah Use these napkins. Here's the mattress and here's the duvet.

Deb Yes, yes, put Action Man bye-byes.

Harry He wants cake.

Deb He wants a little sleep. See, look, you can tuck him up.

Harry No! Take clothes off. First.

Deb Yes, that's right. Go on then.

Harry proceeds to take Action Man's clothes off.

Susannah But you're thinking seriously of taking the risk?

Harry (*to Action Man*) Whoops-a-daisy. Take your arm out.

Deb When I came out of hospital we never talked about it. Then when we did, it was like we both felt it was like impossible, as though we'd accepted that we couldn't biologically or something. But there's no reason. I mean, the side coasters might not happen again –

Susannah But it might –

Deb At least I know what it's like now. I've a feeling that I'd handle it better, knowing I'd been there before. Or maybe it's just a case of forgetting with time.

Susannah The only way I'd have another is to adopt, though that's out of the question for anyone with any sort of history of mental health problems. Anyway, it's all academic.

Deb What d'you mean?

Harry Look. Mum. Look.

Deb Well done, Harry. Now he's undressed you can put him to bed.

Harry No, look.

Deb What?

Harry He's got no willie.

Deb Well, don't let everybody see.

Harry How will he go for a wee wee?

Susannah We must make sure he doesn't drink anything.

Deb (*to Susannah*) If your Thomas was here, we'd have Tom, no Dick, and Harry. (*She laughs.*)

Harry Don't laugh at him.

Deb I weren't laughing at him. I was laughing at me own jokes as per usual. You tell him a story. Gently. (*to Susannah*) I 'spect Tom's with his nanny, en he?

Susannah Actually –

Deb I didn't mean it nastily –

Susannah No. I know. I was going to say, Ben and I are separated –

Deb Oh, sorry –

Susannah It's . . . well . . . understandable. I mean, I understand. If he'd been like I was, I don't think I'd have wanted to stay with him.

Deb But you couldn't help it.

Susannah No, but then, I suppose, you never really know how deep feelings are until they're tested.

Deb How d'you mean?

Susannah It's quite easy to love someone or fool yourself into thinking you love them when you're having a good time. If you never have a crisis then you never really have to put it to the test.

Deb Do you still miss him?

Susannah It's worse.

Harry Mum? Mummy?

Deb Shush, Harry. (*to Susannah*) Worse? Than what?

Susannah Ben got custody.

Deb But they can't do that. You were ill. They understand –

Susannah No, it wasn't because . . . It wasn't quite that simple – (*She discovers that she's got some jam from the table on the sleeve of her jacket.*) Oh God.

Deb What? What?

Susannah Damn this table. Where the hell is she with that cloth? Now I've got jam and God knows what on my sleeve. I'll just go to the loo and wipe it off.

Harry Mummy, me? Wee wee . . . me . . . me . . .

Deb Wait a sec'.

Harry Now!

Susannah I'll take him. Come on, Harry. Don't worry about Action Man. We'll leave him with Mummy.

Harry He can't go. He's got no willie. (*Laughs.*) Quick! Quick!

Susannah Won't be long.

She and Harry go.

SCENE NINETEEN

Past. Hospital grounds. Birds singing.

Deb I'm actually going to miss it here.

Susannah Don't tell them, they'll change their minds about letting you out next week.

Deb Won't you?

Susannah I'll miss you. I'd forgotten what a good laugh was.

Deb I don't quite know how to take that.

Susannah As a compliment. I'd have gone mad if it wasn't for you.

Deb You wouldn't have had far to go. (*Laughs.*) Go and get Thomas and we'll take them for a walk out here.

Susannah Let's just sit here and listen to the less intrusive creations of nature in peace.

Deb Eh? Oh, you mean the birds singing and the bees buzzing and the grass growing an' that. (*Pause.*) D'you know I don't reckon I've ever been anywhere where you couldn't hear traffic noise.

Me and Kev went to Lanzarote before we was married but that
was more noisy than the M25.

Susannah We've got double glazing. (*Laughs.*)

Deb What's so funny about that?

Susannah (*laughing*) I don't know . . . it just seems so pathetic
. . . it's funny . . .

Deb Don't let them see you laughing, they'll give you an
injection.

Susannah I know who I'd like to give an injection to –

Deb Yes. Doctor I'll-be-the-judge-of-when-you're-better
Daintith?

They both laugh.

Susannah No, Thomas.

SCENE TWENTY

*Café. Music: 'Come Unto Him'. Deb, alone at the table, still
waiting for Susannah and Harry to come back. Waitress comes
up to her.*

Waitress Have you finished, madam?

Deb No. I'm . . . err . . . just waiting for my friend to come back
from the ladies'. Then we'll go –

Waitress Do you think you'll be needing anything else?

Deb Umm . . . No . . . Thanks.

Waitress I'll get your bill then, shall I?

SCENE TWENTY-ONE

*Deb's memory. Deb and Kevin's kitchen. Kevin is holding Harry,
who is grizzling.*

Kevin What are you doing, babe?

Deb ignores him.

Debs, leave that. The cutlery don't need cleaning, not in the
middle of the night. It's so clean you can eat your dinner off of

228

it. (*Laughs.*) Debbie? Debbie? Leave it. Don't look at me like that. What is it? What is the matter with you? You can pretend I don't exist if you want but you just can't ignore him. Listen to me. Scrubbing the bleeding cupboards ain't as important as him. You got all your priorities arse about fricking face, you have. He comes first!

SCENE TWENTY-TWO

Present. Café.

Waitress There you go –
Deb Would you just look after the bags –
Waitress I can't do that. Actually, we need the table. We're very busy.
Deb Don't worry then, I'll take them –
Waitress The bill –
Deb Blimey, just for that? Here – (*She gives the Waitress a note and goes.*)
Waitress (*calls after Debs but not too loudly*) Your change?

SCENE TWENTY-THREE

Deb's Memory. Mother and baby unit.

Nurse You did the right thing in telling us, Debbie. Susannah's very ill.
Deb But I thought you'd help her, not take him off her.
Nurse We're just giving her some space. When she's better she can have him back.
Deb S'pose she still wants to kill him?
Nurse Don't you remember that you were frightened that you were going to drop Harry?
Deb But I just didn't want to have to cope with him. I never wanted to hurt him.

SCENE TWENTY-FOUR

Present. Ladies' toilets. Deb opens the door and rushes in. There is a long queue. Music: 'In Dulci Jubilo' by Mike Oldfield.

Deb (*calling*) Harry? Harry? Susannah? (*banging on doors*) Harry? Harry?

Woman 1 Excuse me. There is a queue, you know.

Sound of toilet flushing. Door opens.

Deb Susannah? Sorry, have you seen a woman in a navy suit with a little boy?

Woman 1 No, I haven't.

Woman 2 What's happened?

Deb I've lost them. Has anyone seen them? He's three. About this high with a red sweatshirt with Power Rangers on it.

Woman 1 If he's with your friend he'll be all right.

Deb I hardly know her. Really.

Woman 2 If I was you I'd get them to put out an announcement –

Deb Where, where d'you do this?

Woman 1 There's a security desk just by the side of the restaurant.

Deb Right, right. (*She goes.*)

SCENE TWENTY-FIVE

The security desk. The Security Officer is dealing with a male customer who's lost his wallet. Music: 'Oh, Little Town of Bethlehem'. Deb runs up and tries to push in.

Security Officer The front desk are going to ring the police, sir.

Deb Excuse me –

Man What can they do?

Deb Excuse me –

Security Officer I'm just dealing with this gentleman, madam. (*to Man*) I've already explained that we can't search everyone in the shop. You never know, it might be handed in.

Man Oh, yes, and Tinkerbell's still alive.

Deb (*breathless*) Help me. You've got to help me.

Man I was here first –

Deb Sorry. Please –

Security Officer I'll be with –

Deb But I've lost my little boy. I've lost my little boy –

Security Officer I'm sorry, sir, but lost children are a priority. (*to Deb*) All right, love, now can you give me a description?

Man For God's sake. It had over two hundred quid in it –

Deb (*still trying to catch her breath*) His name's Harry. Wearing a red Power Rangers sweatshirt. He's three and he's with a woman called Susannah Westlake who's wearing a navy suit.

Security Officer You mean they're together?

Deb Yes. Make an announcement. They could be anywhere.

Security Officer I'm sorry, madam, but if he's with a friend of yours –

Deb He's my little boy –

Security Officer Yes, but if you just temporarily mislaid –

Deb (*panicky*) You're not bloody listening –

Security Officer Just catch your breath and let me finish –

Man Then maybe you can get on with finding my wallet.

Security Officer Just a second, sir. (*to Deb*) We don't put out announcements for adults who lose each other. It's our policy. We'd never be off the PA system. Especially this time of year.

Deb You don't understand, you must –

Security Officer I'm sorry. There's nothing I can do. It's company policy.

Deb But I hardly know her. Not really. He might be. (*Breathing gets worse.*) Oh God . . .

Security Officer Then why is she with your little boy?

Deb (*gulping for breath between sentences*) We were having a cup of tea. She went to the loo. She took him with her.

Security Officer Without you knowing?

Deb No, no, he wanted to go. But I –

Security Officer I suggest you take a deep breath and go look there then.

Deb I have –

Security Officer You've probably just missed them. That's what usually happens. I'd go back and wait in the place where you left them.

Deb I've not seen her for years. We just bumped into each other.

Security Officer As you can see I'm very busy –

Deb We met in hospital.

Man How nice for you. (*to Security Officer*) Where are the police, then?

Deb A mental hospital.

Security Officer I don't see –

Deb (*breathless and hysterical*) For Christsakes, she was put away because she couldn't cope with her own child and she's had him taken away from her and now she's taken mine.

Security Officer Why on earth did you let her go off with your little boy?

Deb I thought she was better –

Man (*knowingly to Security Officer, about Deb*) I'd make sure she has a little boy in the first place. If they were both in . . . hospital.

Security Officer (*to Deb*) Now, let's get this straight. You were –

Deb Just put out an announcement. Just do it! (*Shouts.*) For Christsakes, what do I have to do, throw a brick through the window?

Security Officer There's no need for threats. Now, let's all just calm down –

Deb (*shouts*) Do something! (*Screams.*) I've lost my child!

Security Officer (*now very weary about her*) OK, OK, madam. Give me a description and I'll get it relayed.

SCENE TWENTY-SIX

Susannah and Harry in the electrical department. Music: 'Away in a Manger'.

Harry Mummy, Mummy, Mummy –

Susannah I think we should go now.

Harry For Mummy –

Susannah All right, we'll buy her this. Then we must go and no fuss, promise?

Harry Yes.

Assistant 2 Would you like it gift-wrapped, madam?

Susannah No, we've not got time.

Assistant 2 How would you like to pay?

Susannah Damn, I've not got enough cash on me. It'll have to be a credit card. Here.

Assistant 2 Thank you.

Card put through the machine. The announcement comes over in the background over the music and runs underneath the next line.

Announcement (*mumbled*) Would Susannah Westlake who is in the store with a little boy, who answers to the name of Harry and is wearing a red sweatshirt, please come to the security desk which is situated (*fade*) next to the restaurant.

Assistant 2 Sign here, please –

SCENE TWENTY-SEVEN

Susannah's memory. Dr Daintith's office in the hospital.

Dr D. I'll need your signature, Mr Westlake.

Ben (*signs his name*) If you want to extend the Section you will inform me?

Dr D. Of course.

Susannah Don't give me away, Ben. Don't throw me out with the rubbish. It's a trick. Ben. They're divorce papers. Up to capers. The people in here are rapers with papers and drugs and mugs.

Den Darling, it's all right. I'm not going to leave you.

SCENE TWENTY-EIGHT

Present. Electrical department as before.

Assistant 2 If you wouldn't mind holding on a moment.

Susannah Hasn't it gone through?

Assistant 2 No.

Susannah How come? I've just signed for it.

Assistant 2 I am sorry –

SCENE TWENTY-NINE

Susannah's memory. Ben and Susannah's house.

Ben I'm sorry.

Susannah So, in the words of the song, how long has it been going on?

Ben Not that long.

Susannah You've just been waiting for me to get the all clear from the hospital so that you can go with a clear conscience?

Ben Susannah.

Susannah It must have been some time, then.

Ben It doesn't matter.

Susannah No, you're right, nothing does.

Ben Don't start that again.

Susannah Do you love her?

Ben Yes.

Susannah You don't know the meaning of the word.

Ben Do you?

SCENE THIRTY

Electrical department. Background noise of music and TVs as before.

Susannah Would you please hurry it up?

Security Officer 2 comes up behind her.

Security Officer 2 Excuse me, madam, are you Susannah Westlake?

Susannah What is this?

Assistant 2 Yes, she is.

Security Officer 2 Didn't you hear the announcement?

Susannah What announcement? Is something wrong with my credit card?

Security Officer 2 (*to Harry*) And what's your name, son?

Harry Mind your own business.

Susannah (*laughs*) It's a phrase he's picked up at nursery.

Security Officer 2 (*carefully*) Ah. Would you mind coming with me?

Susannah We can't, his mother will be worried sick.

Security Officer 2 She is, madam.

Susannah What do you mean? I only took him to the lavatory.

Security Officer 2 That was nearly half an hour ago.

Susannah Now, listen, I only stopped on the way back to buy –

Security Officer 2 Save the explanation for your friend, Mrs Westlake.

SCENE THIRTY-ONE

Susannah's memory. Susannah and Ben's house.

Ben When will you learn that you can't solve everything with money?

Susannah Oh, don't be so trite.

Ben Me? If your feelings weren't so empty and superficial, you probably wouldn't have had a breakdown in the first place.

Susannah You can't use that in court against me. It's a recognized illness.

Ben I don't want to use anything against you. I really don't. I only want what's best for Thomas –

Susannah Then why didn't you stay with me?

Ben I am sorry I hurt you. I really am. But it's Thomas we're talking about here.

Susannah I know. I know.

Ben And threatening me with the best barrister money can buy isn't the point, is it?

Susannah (*sarcastic*) Oh, I'm so sorry. I thought I was doing my best to retain custody of my son, but it seems I've not even got that right.

Ben (*gently*) All I'm saying is that we should try and put our feelings aside for a bit and talk about this by putting him first for a change.

Susannah Go on then.

Ben If you're going to be like that –

Susannah I'm not being like anything. Go on.

Ben I know it's been difficult since he was born –

Susannah Oh, you mean me being sectioned, by *you*, to a psychiatric unit.

Ben Oh well, if you're saying that was all my fault –

Susannah No. No. I'm not. I know I was ill. But it didn't help when you left almost as soon as I was well.

Ben But I have done my fair share of childcare, more –

Susannah And?

Ben And you insisted on going back to full time.

Susannah And you didn't. The only reason you can even consider custody is that your girlfriend works from home.

Ben Actually, she's just landed a very good job so as from next month I'm going to work at home – part time. And that's my choice. I want to make the most of Thomas growing up and not have the nanny know more about him than his dad.

Susannah Oh.

Ben Look, you'd be able to see him whenever you wanted. You'd be involved in all major decisions. Look, you know I'm talking sense.

Susannah You talk like some bloody advert.

Ben (*sighs*) What's the point?

Susannah You tell me. You're the one with all the answers.

Ben We're just going to have to wait and deal with it in court.

Susannah Take him. Take him, then. Go on, you can have custody.

Ben Don't, don't just make a decision out of spite.

Susannah How can it be out of spite? I'm giving you what you want.

SCENE THIRTY-TWO

Security desk. Music: 'Mary's Boy Child' by Harry Belafonte.

Security Officer 2 Found them in the electrical department.

Security Officer Thank God for that.

Harry (*runs to Deb*) Mummy . . . Mummy.

Deb (*picks up Harry*) Harry . . . Harry . . . Where have you been? Are you all right?

Susannah Of course he is. Debbie, what on earth's the matter? I only took him to the loo.

Deb You didn't. I went after you. You weren't there.

Susannah There was an enormous queue in the one next to the café. Then I remembered that the ladies' near the electrical department is nearly always empty so we went there.

Deb Oh.

Pause.

Harry Broken. Air broken.

Deb What?

Susannah The hand dryer wasn't working.

Deb Oh, right. (*Pause.*) Here's your shopping.

Susannah What's happened? I don't know about you, but I was actually enjoying myself. It's been a really nice afternoon. Then I take him to the toilet and the next thing I know I'm being carted back here by a man in uniform.

Deb How was I to know what had happened?

Susannah But he was with me.

Deb I know, but I didn't know – (*Stops herself.*) What were you thinking of? You were gone for bloody hours.

Awkward silence.

Harry Present. Present.

Deb You've had enough presents to last you until next Christmas.

Harry Amera. Amera.

Deb What are you on about?

Susannah He insisted that we bought you a present, that's why we were a bit longer – Here –

Deb I don't –

Harry Say thank you.

Deb Susannah. Oh, shit. I thought –

Susannah It's all right. I know what you thought.

Deb I don't know what I was thinking. My mind was racing. I imagined all sorts of things. I was out of my mind. Somehow I just got it into my head that you –

Susannah Don't worry. No harm done.

Deb Na?

Susannah No. It was nice to see you.

Deb Please, you don't have to go –

Susannah You know what it's like. I've got loads to do. (*She turns to go.*)

Deb (*calls*) Susannah.

Susannah turns back.

I'm sorry.

Susannah (*turns*) It doesn't matter. Really. (*She goes.*)

SCENE THIRTY-THREE

Past. The mother and baby unit.

Kev Come on, Debs. What are we hanging about for? For months you've said you couldn't wait to see the back of the place.

Deb I just got to say goodbye.

Kev You've said a million of 'em. If you go back in there now they'll probably lock the door behind you.

Deb Just hang on to Harry a sec' and stop being so paranoid, otherwise you'll be joining me. (*She runs back into the unit.*)

Nurse Have you forgotten something, Debbie?

Deb Yeah. (*Calls.*) Susannah? Susannah?

Nurse (*laughs*) You're just as loud when you're well as when you were ill.

Susannah I thought you'd gone.

Deb Na, not until I've said goodbye. What did old Daintith reckon?

Susannah If I keep this up and don't allow myself to lapse into silly behaviour, I'll be home very soon.

Deb You'll be out quicker now I'm not here to encourage you to mess about.

Susannah I don't know how I'm going to stand it without you.

Deb Come here. Give us a hug. You're like the sister I never had.

Susannah I've lived through more with you than a lifetime with my sisters.

Deb We'll be like step-sisters, eh?

Susannah Do you mean that?

Deb 'Course I do. You know me, when have I ever bothered saying anything I don't mean. Waste of breath. I bet it's you who forgets me.

Susannah Never.
Deb Then we'll always know each other, won't we?
Susannah Promise?
Deb On my life.
Susannah Promise.
Deb Promise.

End.

Generations

JACKIE KAY

Generations is one chapter of a long poetry sequence entitled *The Adoption Papers*, written between 1980 and 1990.

The Adoption Papers was originally broadcast on BBC Radio 3 in 1990 as part of the *Drama Now* series. It was produced by Frances Anne Soloman.

Jackie Kay was born in Edinburgh in 1961 and grew up in Glasgow. She has published two collections of poetry, the first of which, *The Adoption Papers* (Bloodaxe, 1991), won the Saltire and Forward prizes. The Second, *Other Lovers* (Bloodaxe, 1993), won a Somerset Maugham Award. Her plays include *Every Bit of It* and *Twilight Shift*. Her first novel, *Trumpet*, was published by Picador in 1998.

Generations

The sun went out just like that
almost as if it had never been,
hard to imagine now the way it fell
on treetops, thatched roofs, people's faces.
Suddenly the trees lost their nerves
and the grass passed the wind on
blade to blade, fast as gossip

Years later, the voices still come close
especially in dreams, not distant echoes
loud – a pneumatic drill – deeper and deeper still.
I lived the scandal, wore it casual
as a summer's dress, Jesus sandals.
All but the softest whisper:
she's lost an awful lot of weight.

Now my secret is the hush of heavy curtains drawn.
I dread strange handwriting
sometimes jump when the phone rings,
she is all of nineteen and legally able.
At night I lie practising my lines
but 'sorry' never seems large enough
nor 'I can't see you, yes, I'll send a photograph.'

I was pulled out with forceps
left a gash down my left cheek
four months inside a glass cot
but
she came faithful from Glasgow to Edinburgh
and peered through the glass
she would not pick another baby.

I don't know what diseases
come down my line;
when dentist and doctors ask

the old blood questions about family runnings
I tell them: I have no nose or mouth or eyes
to match, no spitting image or dead cert,
my face watches itself in the glass.

I have my parents who are not of the same tree
and you keep trying to make it matter,
the blood, the tie, the passing down
generations.
We all have our contradictions,
the ones with the mother's nose and father's eyes
have them;
the blood does not bind confusion,
yet I confess to my contradiction
I want to know my blood.

I know my blood.
It is dark ruby red and comes
regular and I use Lillets.
I know my blood when I cut my finger.
I know what my blood looks like.

It is the well, the womb, the fucking seed.
Here, I am far enough away to wonder –
what were their faces like
who were my grandmothers
what were the days like
passed in Scotland
the land I come from
the soil in my blood.

Put it this way:
I know she thinks of me often
when the light shows its face
or the dark skulks behind hills,
she conjures me up or I just appear
when I take the notion, my slippers
are silent and I walk through doors.

She's lying in bed; I wake her up
a pinch on her cheek is enough,

then I make her think of me for hours.
The best thing I can steal is sleep.
I get right under the duvet and murmur
you'll never really know your mother.
I know who she thinks I am – she's made a blunder.

She is faceless
She has no nose
She is five foot eight inches tall
She likes hockey best
She is twenty-six today
She was a waitress
My hair is grey
She wears no particular dress
The skin around my neck is wrinkling
Does she imagine me this way?
Lately I make pictures of her
But I can see the smallness
She is tall and slim
of her hands, Yes
Her hair is loose curls
an opal stone on her middle finger
I reach out to catch her
Does she talk broad Glasgow?
But no matter how fast
Maybe they moved years ago
I run after
She is faceless, she never
weeps. She has neither eyes nor
fine boned cheeks

Once would be enough,
just to listen to her voice
watch the way she moves her hands
when she talks.

Mary Medusa

SHAWNA DEMPSEY *and* LORRI MILLAN

Shawna Dempsey and Lorri Millan have been collaborating in a variety of media since 1989. Their performance art, video, film and book works make use of humour in order to articulate feminist concerns. They are best known for the performance and film *We're Talking Vulva* (1990), which has shown all over the world to an estimated audience of one million people, and the award-winning video and book project *A Day in the Life of a Bull-Dyke* (1995). Dempsey was born in Toronto in 1963, and Millan was born in North Bay in 1965. Both now make Winnipeg, Canada, their home.

Mary Medusa is a thirty-five-minute media and performance piece. All of the characters referred to are the Medusa, performed by Shawna Dempsey. Her snakey head remains the same throughout, while she presents herself in different guises and incarnations. The only exception is Athena, performed by Sharon Bajer in the slide/audio section 'Classical Lines'. The entire piece is composed of nine parts: one video, two slide/audio pieces, five short performances and one short story. Each part is designed to exist autonomously, for exhibition independent of the whole, as well as grouped together forming the entirety of the piece.

The first components of *Mary Medusa* were presented at the Winnipeg Art Gallery on 25 January 1992. A subsequent version was performed at Prairie Theatre Exchange, Winnipeg, 18–23 February 1993. The finished piece was first presented at the Western Front, Vancouver, 3 April 1993, and has since been produced in Canada at: Galerie Sans Nom, Moncton; Centre for Art Tapes, Halifax; University of Calgary; The Banff Centre for the Arts; Oboro Gallery, Montreal; Niagara Arts Centre, St Catherine's; and Gallery 101, Ottawa. *Mary Medusa* has also been performed at the Angry Women Live Festival, Berlin and

Vienna, and Distant Skinship Women's Performance Project, Tokyo and Yokohama. The script has been published in its entirety in *Canadian Theatre Review* 76 (Fall 1993).

Funding for the development of this project has been received from the Canada Council, the Manitoba Arts Council, the Winnipeg Arts Advisory Committee and Video Pool's First Video Fund. Special thanks also to the Banff Centre for the Arts.

Please note: the text which follows is the ancillary short story, *not* the performance or video texts.

ONE

My parents made Goodland their home because of the inexpensive real estate, good gardening soil, and absence of anything remotely Turkish. In fact, Goodland is perhaps most notable for its absence of many things. Situated on the treeless plain, it lacks geographical features, municipal monuments or indeed anything to mark it as remarkable or unique. It boasts no peculiar rock formations, wildlife or weather; no war monument, or statues of giant turtles or potatoes; no eccentric lawn ornament displays. Daunted by the challenge of filling the vast prairie, the prudent townsfolk have striven to maintain in Goodland a sense of void – and not only in the physical appearance of the town. The existence of the unusual or the unexplained is emotionally and philosophically negated by most every man, woman and child. Hence crime is low and miracles are few, making Goodland a safe place to raise a family.

The late Fifties was a notorious time for enforced conformity, and nowhere was this more evident than in the town of my birth. Equally white souls took part in equally wholesome bonspiels, auctions and church suppers. As swarthy immigrants of non-Presbyterian faith, my family was not invited. So alien did we seem to the people of Goodland that no attempt at peer-pressure was even made. The life of the community went on around us, at a safe distance.

But this isolation is a faint memory compared to the smell of my mother's cheese pies, or the sound of my father's voice as he told the stories of vengeful gods and goddesses. Our kitchen was the centre of my world. As an only child I was allowed to bask in the full power of my parents' love. I was their hope for the future, their cream of the new world. I was somebody. Sitting on my mother's lap I learned that Jesus died for me, Mary. Sitting on my father's lap I learned pride. I was a Papadoplous. I was a Greek. I was a descendant of Zeus.

The idyll that was my childhood was unblemished, and would

have remained so, had the Cuban Missile Crisis and mounting Cold War hysteria not allowed Goodland's collective denial to reach its zenith. Difference, in the town, on 12 November 1962, simply did not exist. The vortex created in the minds of Goodland's citizens was so successful that my parents were sucked into it, never to be seen again. Also reported missing on that date were Li Lo and his family, proprietors of Café Air Conditioned, and a travelling salesman with an unfortunate facial birth defect. They all simply vanished, as if they had never been. I was the only remaining evidence of the tragedy.

Orphaned in this way at the age of eight, I learned the importance of fitting in. I feared the black hole that claimed my parents, and actively fought against it. I always changed my underwear. I always ate everything on my plate. I believed what adults told me.

I was fortunate to be adopted, after the disappearance, by Miss Gartiner, an elderly spinster and breeder of dwarf hogs. And I became just like everyone else – to the best of my ability. I had no particular passions or foibles. My grades were average. I had neither friends nor enemies. I couldn't resist the thought that I too, had vanished, but the event had been so unremarkable that no one had noticed, not even me.

I undertook a variety of experiments designed to prove or disprove my existence. I later learned to name these: anorexia, bulimia, slashing. Several near-death experiences reassured me that I was alive. This wasn't particularly good news, but I decided to make the best of it.

On the eve of my grade twelve graduation Miss Gartiner's hiatus hernia got the better of her. By the next morning she had passed on, and I was once more an orphan. Her last will and testament bequeathed the hogs, the house and a hundred shares in Manitoba Hydro to her only living relation, her nephew Lesley. I received the household effects and a strongly worded recommendation that I marry Les before I was too old or he found someone better suited to the job. I carefully examined all my options before withdrawing my $75.00 in life savings from the Credit Union, and got on the first Grey Goose bound for anywhere else.

In Manitoba, most roads lead to nowhere, with a few

exceptions which lead to Winnipeg. It was in Winnipeg I ended up. I was eighteen, blessed with neither wealth nor beauty, friendless, skill-less, and with no idea what I'd do next.

TWO

On rare occasions adversity inspires new wellsprings of courage. Despite the sad state of affairs, I felt positively exhilarated. I was, after all, free.

From the bus depot I marched, stopping at each business to ask for a job. At last, at the local perogy house, I was successful in obtaining gainful employment.

In no time I had a cozy apartment, real friends and an inner sense of fulfilment. What I did was important. I was making the world a better place. I even began taking night courses at Red River College in accounting. I could see credits and debits as perogies not eaten, and not paid for; monthly balance sheets as links of sausage, unique unto themselves, but together forming a harmonious continuum. I was an A+ student. I was no longer dieting. For perhaps the first time in my life, I was happy.

It is true that I've never been a lucky person. I have often wondered if the gods present me with ill fortune to test me. Or perhaps I am paying for the sins of my kin, or a misdemeanour I have committed unwillingly. These musings aside, my happiness was short-lived.

What happened was not exceptional. Worse horrors have been endured by many, many women. And yet it is painful, so I will be brief and use plain language.

My friend and employer Irenie was married to a big, jolly man named Burt. One night I was working late, trying to figure out a way to maximize perogy flow and minimize inventory, when Burt came round to pick up his wife. As she cashed out, Burt took me to the back of the shop and raped me. When he had finished, he collected my dear Irenie, who had been waiting patiently, and drove her home.

The next morning I returned to the store, battered and confused, to console my friend and be consoled by her. Instead, I was handed my separation papers and my final pay.

That's all. That's the end of that story.
I finished my courses. I ate little and slept less. I stopped talking.

THREE

It was at this point in my life that I decided to become a man. Not physically, of course, but behaviourly. I realized my upbringing had taught me to be passive, and not assertive; to play the piano, and not hockey; to feel too much, and take too little. Miss Gartiner had betrayed me. Irenie had betrayed me. Even my mother, in her disappearance, had betrayed me. I hated women. I loathed the feminine. I was committed to being male from here on in.

I realized that before I could become a man, I must become a boy. My childhood had been a complete waste of time. I must begin again. I got a new wardrobe. I caught reptiles and tortured them mercilessly. I spat. I swore. I never cried. I went fishing on weekends, and drank beer 'til I puked. No one could tell me what to do. It was my world. I was one of God's chosen people. I was a male child.

I got a job at the meat-packing plant, driving a fork lift. I was making three times what I had at the perogy house. I bought my first gold chain.

Notwithstanding my dubious gender, the men at the plant accepted me. We had so much in common. We'd talk about the virtues of a slant-6 over a V-8 engine; who'd won the game?; what a bitch the floor manager was. I think what really endeared me to them was my newfound sense of humour. I'd make farting noises with my armpit. I learned to sing the chorus of 'Taking Care of Business' while belching. I bought T-shirts with funny sayings on them. Finally, I belonged. I was one of the boys.

But despite my outward air of self-confidence, there lived, deep within me, a tiny voice that said, 'I'm afraid.' I feared that people could see through me, and would know that my macho bravado was an affectation I'd assumed for self-protection. Perhaps my female-to-male transformation was incomplete. Or perhaps it is part of being a man, that hidden, inner voice of self-doubt. I had no way of knowing.

Of course one of the most popular topics of talk among my buddies was women. Following their lead, I began to hang out in the all-female packaging department. Strangely, it irritated these girls when I dominated the conversation, and talked constantly about myself. I'd tell them to get me another cup of coffee, and they'd remain impassive. Jumbo, our foreman, would wink at the gals and say, 'Nice tits,' sending them into peals of laughter. When I tried it, I was reported to the plant manager for sexual harassment. It was at this point that things changed. I was banned from the packaging area. A wall of silence met me when I entered a room. My old jokes didn't work any more. Even my friends would have nothing to do with me. I felt almost as if they were somehow afraid.

Shortly thereafter my employment was terminated, not by management, but by vigilante justice. As I came around the outhouse corner of the warehouse that Friday afternoon, they were waiting for me. Armed with frozen legs of lamb, which they held like clubs, stood Jumbo, Vincent, Hassam and Pinkie. 'Come here, bull-dyke,' they taunted. 'Come here, cunt.'

Obviously my masculinity had been misinterpreted. I did not love women. I just wanted to be a man.

As I faced my impending bludgeoning, I was forced to make a difficult choice. Would I stay and fight, as any proper male would? What was to be gained? The end result would leave me neither virile nor feminine, but simply bloodied.

In that moment I rejected the concept of gender altogether. I would adopt neither male nor female role. I would simply survive.

FOUR

Quick to put theory into practice, I ran for my life. I ran until I was safe, and continued to run for good measure. I never returned to the packing plant for either pay or possessions. I still have a hard time eating that company's meats.

Being neither male nor female is difficult in this world. How do you get dressed in the morning? What do you eat for breakfast? How do you walk down the street? Without gender, do you in fact exist? Maybe this was the void I'd feared for most of my life. Maybe this was my personal black hole. Just as my parents had been swallowed by the small-mindedness of a community that had failed to recognize their identity, I was being swallowed by my own lack of self-definition.

I would get up in the morning and look in the mirror, only to face a blank image. Nowhere could I find myself reflected. For what are we taught to see, beyond biological norms? Just freaks and monsters.

Only in our dreams can gender and form change, and change, and change, with sensual ease. In my dreams I can be boy, camera, lightning, sword, woman, and myth, simultaneously and in succession. So it was into my dreams I retreated, though I remained awake.

Like a sleepwalker I moved through the next three months letting images flow over me like a river. The stories and legends that my parents had told me as a child resurfaced during that time, and slowly they began to have meaning. Slowly, slowly they washed away illusion and began to show me who I truly am.

'Was it painful,' one might ask, 'this process of self-revelation?' To the contrary. Although I hesitate to admit it, an unexpected sensation made the process compellingly pleasurable. Deep, successive orgasms welled up inside of me, night and day, making it impossible to worry. I felt unashamedly sensual. True, my desire did surprise me: its strength was unmistakable, immutable, HUGE. But I did not hide from it, or the images it brought. I felt proud of the power between my thighs. I knew it had the strength to move mountains.

One morning I awoke with the confused emotions of a newborn: abandonment, anger, anticipation, wonder. The metamorphosis was complete.

As I turned to greet my true self in the window's reflection, each snakey lock reached out to me. 'You're invincible,' they said, 'You're horrible. You're safe.' A smile grew up from deep within me, and spread like the mask of a jack-o'-lantern across my face. My eyes bulged and my tongue grew. I laughed as I thought that now, anything was possible. I could go forth into the world simply as me, unquestioned and unassaulted, my resplendent ugliness as my shield.

As I gazed on the face of Medusa, I felt peace.

FIVE

Suddenly my clothing seemed vastly inadequate. The starched smocks of my perogy days, and the plaid shirts of my meat-packing months: both seemed beneath the magnificent creature I had become. I took myself to the most expensive women's clothier I knew of, into whose windows I'd previously only dared to glance. As I entered, fresh-scrubbed clerks snapped to attention, and rushed to supply me with my every wish and whim. I bought only the latest, the 100 per cent, the designer labels, and was fearless as I paid with money I did not have.

Next, I realized I needed a job. It didn't even occur to me to spend hours waiting in lines at the unemployment office. Armoured in Alfred Sung, I took a cab downtown, to the city's tallest building. I marched into the lobby and asked to see the president of the company. Phones rang, guards bowed, and the receptionist personally escorted me to the ninety-ninth floor. Doors opened magically before me as I strode into an office larger than my entire apartment, and confronted a small withered man behind a large granite desk. I would be his personal assistant, I informed him, and entranced, he shook my hand in agreement.

Each day I would use the brisk, half-hour walk to the office as an opportunity to go over my personal goals. Once there, I guided the elderly Mr Cassady through his day like a terrible angel. There were no obstacles we did not brush aside. Advertisers, lawmakers, plant managers and stockholders all magically bowed to Mr Cassady's will, just as Mr Cassady bowed to mine.

I would forgo lunch in favour of meditation and Tantric chanting, and at 6.00, as the other employees left for the day, I stayed at my desk, poring over sales profiles and flow charts. I learned every nut and bolt of the industry, late at night in that glass tower. I learned so much that within a year I knew more than anyone in the company.

This was fortunate, because within a year dear old Mr Cassady was dead of a heart attack, locked in rigor mortis behind his granite desk.

My promotion from personal assistant to president was smooth and painless. After the funeral I returned to the office rather than attend the reception. When the other mourners arrived for work the next day, I was already ensconced in Mr Cassady's office and the stationery had been changed. Not that anyone would have questioned my right to leadership. I was the logical choice for the job. I had simply spared them the formality of asking me.

SIX

Aside from the larger desk and improved view, very little has changed in my life.

My lack of physical beauty in no way dampens the contentment I feel. I am able to maintain what few assets I have, and I am happy to report that I am blemish-free, cellulite-free and polyester-free. I strive for a look that *Cosmopolitan* describes as assertively feminine. I am not above perfume and décolletage in the boardroom, for I understand from experience that people cannot accept powerful women if they do not at least appear 'fuckable'.

My behaviour is not radically different from when I was trying to be a man. But because I look very much like a woman (with the exception of my snakey hair) it is accepted that I know my place. Since my appearance actively seeks male approval it is assumed that I am not an unnatural monster, but a gaping playmate-bunny-vagina like any other. They accept me because I let them think that they can conquer me in their fantasies. Whereas in reality my business acumen turns them to stone.

Although I let many consider the possibility, I let no man into my bedroom. It is the sacred shrine of my transformation. Besides, the vile bumping and grinding on the perogy-house floor remains fresh in my memory, and always will. I have no desire to have the performance repeated, however sensitive, or skilled or heaven-forbid long the Romeo promises it will be.

Now some would say that working eighteen hours a day, having no interpersonal relationships, and earning a six-digit salary does not constitute a path to fulfilment. I, on the other hand, would beg to differ. I trust no one and am betrayed by no one, and have control over all aspects of my life.

Except . . .

Except Perseus. I know there are many who would like to see my head severed from my neck. It's a dog-eat-dog, hero-slays-monster, kill-the-bitch world. Realistically, my days are numbered.

Although I am willing to fight for life, I do not fear death. The possibilities of forevermore fascinate me. Will my parents be there? Will they even recognize me? Will they be proud? I am not the same as when I was a child. There have been so many necessary changes.

But I have no regrets.

Finally, I am able to see myself – Mary – clearly, and accept myself for what I am: demanding, singleminded, and even repulsive. I am truly a self-made woman. Or am I?

Did I choose this fate, or it me? Do we choose our dreams? Am I born from a collective will? A repressed desire? Or am I just a girl from Goodland, where choices are few and miracles don't happen?

Medusa? Medusa Black!

DOROTHEA SMARTT

Extract from *Medusa*, which was first presented at Sauda – An Event for Black Women, London Women's Centre, London, 5 October 1991, performed by Dorothea Smartt with photo slide images from Sherlee Mitchell and Ingrid Pollard, and technical assistance from Sherlee Mitchell.

Subsequent presentations include: Sheffield Women Performers' Club, November 1991; Apples 'n' Snakes Poetry, London, April 1992; Oval House Women's Post-Pride Serenade, London, 28 June 1992; Gay Sweatshop One Night Stand, London, October 1993; Institute of Contemporary Art *Respect* season, London, September 1994; and the Centre for Contemporary Art, Glasgow, April 1996.

Dorothea Smartt, poet and live artist, was born in London in 1963. *Medusa* is her first solo work. In 1994 she collaborated with photographer Sherlee Mitchell to create their ICA Live Arts Commission *From You To Me To You*, premiered at the Institute of Contemporary Art, London, November 1994. She also performed her work in *Fo(u)r Women*, a collaboration with Adeola Agbebiyi and Patience Agbabi, Institute of Contemporary Art, London, May 1996. Her poetry appears in several anthologies. She was a 1995–6 ICA Attached Live Artist. She is currently developing *Medusa Play*, with dramaturg Bryony Lavery, for the Talawa Theatre Company Women Writers' Project.

medusa? medusa black!

Medusa? Medusa Black!
Medusa was a Blackwoman!
afrikan dread
cut she eye at a'sistamirror
turn she same self t'stone
she looks really kill?
ask she nuh Medusa would know
she terrible eyes leave me stone coal
Medusa is a Blackwoman lost
looking for love
kept behind icy eyes
fixed inside the barricade
for anybody who come too close
runnin' from she own
'case the worse thing happen
an' she see she self like them see she
the blood haunted
If you black, get back
If you brown stick around . . .
Is that okay? being black your way
whitewashed an' dyed back black
am I easier to hold in an acceptable role
. . . and if you white comelong y'alright
make it go away the nappiheaded nastiness
too tuff too unruly too ugli too black
get back
scrub it bleach it operate on it powder it
straighten it fry it dye it perm it
turn it back on itself
make it go away make it go away
scrub it step smiling into baths of acid
and bleach it red raw
peel skin of life sustaining melanin

operate on it
blackskin lying useless discard it powder it
head? fuck it wild haired women
straighten it fry it desperately burn scalps
banish the snake-woman
the wild-woman
the all-seeing-eye woman
dye it
remembrances of Africa fast-fadin'
in the blond highlights
turn us back on ourselves
slowly making daily applications
with our own hand
my hair as it comes
is just not good enough
the blood haunted
if you black get back
if you brown stick around
and if you white comelong y'alright
say
make it go away make it go away
daa nappiheaded nastiness!
is too tuff too unruly too ugli too black
too tuff too unruly too ugli too black
get back
Medusa!
Black get back.

Girl

JAMAICA KINCAID

Jamaica Kincaid's first book, *At the Bottom of the River*, a collection of stories that received the Morton Dauwen Zabel Award of the American Academy and Institute of Arts and Letters and was nominated for the PEN/Faulkner Award, was published in 1983. Her other books include *Annie John* (1985), *A Small Place* (1988) and *Lucy* (1990). Her most recent novel, *The Autobiography of My Mother* (1996), was a nominee for the National Book Critics Circle award in fiction, a finalist for the PEN/Faulkner Award, and the winner of the Cleveland Foundation's Anisfield-Wolf Award as well as the *Boston Book Review*'s Fisk Fiction prize. *My Brother* (1997), a work of non-fiction, was a finalist for the National Book Award. She is presently at work on her own book about gardening.

Jamaica Kincaid lives with her husband and two children in Bennington, Vermont.

Wash the white clothes on Monday and put them on the stone heap; wash the colour clothes on Tuesday and put them on the clothes line to dry; don't walk barehead in the hot sun; cook pumpkin fritters in very hot sweet oil; soak your little cloths right after you take them off; when buying cotton to make yourself a nice blouse, be sure that it doesn't have gum on it, because that way it won't hold up well after a wash; soak salt fish overnight before you cook it; is it true that you sing benna in Sunday School?; always eat your food in such a way that it won't turn someone else's stomach; on Sundays try to walk like a lady and not like the slut you are so bent on becoming; don't sing benna in Sunday school; you mustn't speak to wharf-rat boys, not even to give directions; don't eat fruits on the street – flies will follow you; *but I don't sing benna on Sundays at all and never in Sunday school*; this is how to sew on a button; this is how to make a buttonhole for the button you have just sewed on; this is how to hem a dress when you see the hem coming down and so to prevent yourself from looking like the slut I know you are so bent on becoming; this is how you iron your father's khaki shirt so that it doesn't have a crease; this is how you iron your father's khaki pants so that they don't have a crease; this is how you grow okra – far from the house, because okra tree harbours red ants; when you are growing dasheen, make sure it gets plenty of water or else it makes your throat itch when you are eating it; this is how you sweep a corner; this is how you sweep a whole house; this is how you sweep a yard; this is how you smile to someone you don't like too much; this is how you smile to someone you don't like at all; this is how you smile to someone you like completely; this is how you set a table for tea; this is how you set a table for dinner; this is how you set a table for dinner with an important guest; this is how you set a table for lunch; this is how you set a table for breakfast; this is how to behave in the presence of men who don't know you very well, and this way they won't recognize immediately the slut I have warned you against becoming; be sure to wash every day, even if it is with your own spit; don't squat down to play marbles – you are not a boy, you know; don't pick people's flowers – you might catch something; don't throw stones at blackbirds, because it might not be a blackbird at all; this is how to make a bread pudding; this is how to make doukona; this is how to make pepper pot; this is how to make a good medicine for a cold; this is how to make a good medicine to throw away a child before it even becomes a child; this is how to catch a fish; this is how to throw back a fish you don't like, and that way something bad won't fall on you; this is how to bully a man; this is how a man bullies you; this is how to love a man, and if this doesn't work there are other ways, and if they don't work don't feel too bad about giving up; this is how to spit up in the air if you feel like it, and this is how to move quick so that it doesn't fall on you; this is how to make ends meet; always squeeze bread to make sure it's fresh; *but what if the baker won't let me feel the bread?*; you mean to say that after all you are really going to be the kind of woman who the baker won't let near the bread?

Poems for Men Who Dream of Lolita

KIM MORRISSEY

Kim Morrissey is Canadian. She has published two books of
poetry, *Batoche* (Coteau, 1989) and *Poems for Men Who Dream
of Lolita* (Coteau, 1992), and two plays, *Dora: A Case of
Hysteria* (Nick Hern Books, 1994) and *Clever as Paint: The
Rossettis in Love* (Playwrights Canada Press, 1998).

Tuesday, June 6, 1947

I

Mr Humbert Humbert
Mr Humbert Squared
likth to do everything twithe
twithe
which drives my mudder mad
mad

he has two cups of coffee
and two slices of toast
he brushes and shaves
and flushes
twice just to be sure

once,
when I had an eyelash
he closed mummy's door
and licked my bare eye
like a snail

and then licked the other
and then two times more

and then Mr Hum
Bert Humbert Squared
blinked twice and said
not to tell Mother

tell her what?

II

Last night in the hammock
he called me 'Lolita'
playing hand over hand over hand

No. My name is Dolores, age twelve
grade six, size three
my friends call me Dolly

Lie still little apple pie sweet
your name from now on is Lolita
leg over leg over leg
and you need your cheeks pinched
like a pie crust   pressed down
two fingers two fingers two

Just a prick and she's done
says my mother and purses her lips
peering into her mirror
as she puts on her eyes
Dumpy Dolly

My name is Dolores

My friends call me Dolly, but
my name's really Dolores

My name is Dolores, age twelve

III

stepfather

somewhere between the dark stain
on the tiles
and the towels
heaped on the back of the toilet
you rest your case:
I may leave if I want
today you are giving me choices

I watch my head turn in the mirror
thin hair finger-brushed back
tied low on my neck like a bone
taste your hair at the back of my throat
tightly wound wires
riding the tip of my tongue

today is the day we make choices:
you or the foster home
you or the jail

IV

when I remember
I remember sorrow
sad eyes waiting

you will leave me you will
leave me like a rosary
you rubbed

the small blister of truth
the sore you picked red
never wanting it to heal

Lift and Separate

VICTORIA WORSLEY

Lift and Separate is based on pages 174–5 of the Burlington Lycra Warehouse's mail-order catalogue for spring/summer 1966, on display in the twentieth-century design galley at the Victoria & Albert Museum, London.

Victoria Worsley was born in London in 1966 and works as an actor as well as a writer. She began devising plays with performance company Tattycoram in the mid-Eighties and founded the new writing theatre company Jade in 1992. Other plays include *And All Because the Lady Loves* and *Night Train*.

Lift and Separate was produced by the Soho Theatre Company at the Cockpit Theatre, London, in March 1993 with the following cast:

The Woman Mary Pegler
Apricot Robyn Lewis
Black Jenny Lynch
Midnight-Blue Melanie Hudson
Pink Josie Ayers
Primrose Maria Gough

Directed by Alex Perrin
Choreographed by Kate Brown

Overlapping dialogue is indicated by a solidus at the point where the interruption occurs.

It's dark. Enter a woman in a Sixties suit and heavy-rimmed glasses. (Note: she shouldn't be a cartoon figure, she should be played for real.) She is just visible in some offstage light. She staggers in with a stack of files under one arm and as many full grocery bags as she can carry in both hands. She stops to turn on a light switch. A small pool of light comes up front right or left and she staggers into it. Exhausted, she dumps the bags on to the floor.

Woman Groceries. (*She looks at the files with distaste.*)
Tomorrow's typing. (*She looks at her wristwatch.*) Six-thirty.
(*double-take*) 6.30! AAAAARGH! FOOD! (*She panics, starts to struggle with the bags again and is just about to leave the pool of light when something catches her eye. She puts down the bags again and picks up a note off the floor. She reads it aloud.*) 'Dear darling,
(*She smiles with pleasure.*) Don't bother to cook tonight. We haven't been out for a while. We ought to go out. I've decided to take you out. Somewhere a bit exciting. Somewhere I particularly like. Love, Your loving husband.'
   The love.
'PS. Pick you up at seven sharp.' AAAAAARGH! (*She panics. Hurriedly she pulls off her office clothes. She is wearing sensible, substantial underwear. She stuffs her office clothes into a grocery bag and pulls out a dress. She holds it up to herself. Too smart. She pulls out another. Too sexy. Finally she pulls out something flowery and pretty. Just right. She begins to struggle into it. However, she has only got it over her head when she stops with a sudden realization.*) Oh no. I haven't got a . . . I need to have a . . . I can't wear this without a . . . I can't go out without a . . . (*She searches madly in the grocery bags. No luck.*) Oh dear. (*She rushes offstage and comes back immediately in some triumph clasping some large catalogues and dragging a chair. She sets the chair in the light and sits*

275

down with the catalogues on her knee. She reads their covers.)
Spring '66. HARRODS. (*Too expensive. She discards it.*) THE
BIBA BLUE CATALOGUE. (*Too wild. She discards it.*)
JANET REGER LINGERIE. (*Interested, she takes a quick
look. Far too sexy. She throws it out. The next one meets with
her approval and she reads the title with relish.*)
BURLINGTON LYCRA WAREHOUSE ltd SPRING/
SUMMER 1966. Lycra, the revolution in underwear. (*She
delves into it with delight, turning the pages faster and faster
until she hits the right one.*

*Then, very slowly and smoothly, she begins to lift something
out of the catalogue. It is a short nylon slip with wired cups
which she lifts out bit by bit, holding it by the tips of the
shoulder straps. [The centre of the catalogue needs carving out
to accommodate it.] She puts it on slowly and with great care,
as if the garment is the most precious and delicate object in the
world. As she does all this she speaks the following, enjoying
every word.*) Beautifully fashioned (30-denier) nylon slip. A
superbly fitting garment with body profusely styled in stretch
lace with LYCRA. The strategically placed inserts of s-t-r-
e-t-c-h tricot give superb form-fitting qualities and the
shoulder-hugging straps allow for complete freedom of
movement. Neatly scalloped lace adorns the hemline. Apricot,
black, midnight-blue, primrose, pink or white. Bust 34, 36
inches, twenty-two and six, twenty weeks at one and tuppence.
Bust 38, 40 inches twenty-four and six, twenty weeks at one
and threepence. Bust 42, 44 inches twenty-six and six, twenty
weeks at one and fourpence. State bust size and colour
required. Terms to suit you.

*She is very pleased with herself. She looks down at herself. The
effect isn't quite what she had had in mind. She tries a more
elegant pose. She's not quite satisfied with the result. She goes
back to the catalogue to see how she should pose for
maximum effect.*

*She takes the pose of one of the models in the picture. It isn't
easy to get it right. When she has got it to her satisfaction, a
Model in a slip with a fantastic Sixties hairdo and false
eyelashes, etc., walks on and takes up the pose immediately*

behind her. The Woman steps away and looks back at the
model approvingly. She goes back to the catalogue and tries
copying another model in the picture. Again it is tricky and
again, when she is ready, another Model dressed like the first
(except in a different-coloured slip) walks behind her (or
beside her) and takes the pose from her. This repeats another
three times, speeding up as it goes until the stage contains five
women in Sixties hairdos and different-coloured nylon slips
making up the picture in the catalogue.

The Woman is surrounded.

The rhythm of the Models' entries should build so that the
following comes at the top of a crescendo.

Male Voice SMILE!

Huge photo flash.

Models (*each introducing herself in turn to the audience with*
enthusiasm, waves, smiles, etc.) Hi! I'm Apricot!
I'm Black!
I'm Midnight-blue!
I'm Pink!
I'm Primrose! But you can call me Blonde.

Or other names according to the colour of their slips.

Primrose (*as if advertising herself to the audience, not the slip*)
You're safe with –
Models S-T-R-E-T-C-H LYCRA, For the 'modern girl',
Black or your mother,
Pink your wife,
Apricot Easy,
Midnight-Blue unrestricting,
Models For your daily life.
Primrose Suits your every need,
Midnight-Blue Gives the freedom one expects,
Black Superbly fashioned body
Models with a little hint of –
Apricot – lace.
Models S-T-R-E-T-C-H LYCRA!
Pink It's pretty and it's pink,

Apricot apricot!
Primrose primrose!
Black black!
Midnight-Blue brunette!
Models Most adaptable accessory from club to kitchen-sink.
Male Voice SMILE!

Photo flash.
   *The Woman has been trying to keep up with their poses but
failing. Now she exits in a hurry to continue getting ready and
should reappear on occasions during what follows, crossing
the stage at appropriate moments in various states of
preparation, e.g. with a cup of tea, in a pair of boots, doing her
lipstick, etc.*
   *The models relax their poses, shake out a stiff leg, stretch,
look around. Midnight-blue is still smiling hard. They look at
her.*
   *Note: none of the women should be played as stupid. All the
conversations they have with each other can be given plenty of
room to breathe.*

Midnight-Blue I think it's frozen.
Apricot I'm not surprised.
Primrose I'd like a cup of tea.
Pink Oh, yes.
Midnight-Blue I'd like a hot bath.
Black I'd like a cigarette.
Apricot I'd like a trip to the Bahamas.
Black (*to the back of the auditorium*) Could we have a tea-break
   please?

Pause. There is no response.

Midnight-Blue How are your straps?
Primrose Bit slippy.
Midnight-Blue It's this nylon isn't it?
Primrose Is it?
Pink Yes.

Pause.

Black Fuck, it's cold.

Pink Could you check my eyelashes?
Primrose Don't you think we could go inside at least?
Black Is this a tea-break?
Pink I think one's coming off.
Black Been up for hours.
Pink I rather like the morning light.
Apricot So do they. Apparently.
Midnight-Blue What make are these?
Pink Mary Quant.
Midnight-Blue Really?
Apricot BRING BACK THE LASH!
Midnight-Blue (*to Apricot*) I'm sorry? (*to Pink*) It's fine.
Apricot The advert, isn't it?
Midnight-Blue Oh, yes.
Pink Goose pimples.
Black Yuk.
Midnight-Blue Does this wire poke into your tit?
Primrose Yeah. A bit.
Midnight-Blue (*to the audience*) I don't usually wear this, actually.

When speaking to the audience, each character should find a distinct rhythm and quality of their own so that each speech is clearly distinguishable from another (e.g. Pink could relish and stretch her words while Primrose could be quite matter-of-fact). Each actor should find her character's own particular relationship to the audience (e.g. Midnight-Blue could be quite confidential whereas Black could be off-hand). It is also crucial that the actors listen to and play with the overall rhythm of the piece, working absolutely as one. At the same time they need to think of their pieces to the audience as part of one continuous speech of their own and play it for real, not just for the musicality. It is a fine balance. I would suggest that the actor playing Black think in terms of the character's uneasiness rather than her anger.)

Primrose I'd like a cup of tea.
Pink Yes, please.
Black I'd like a cigarette.
Apricot I'd like a soft-top.

Midnight-Blue (*to the audience*) I expect you guessed.

Apricot In the Bahamas.

Midnight-Blue (*to the audience*) Not that there's anything wrong with it.

Primrose (*to the audience*) Personally, I don't do it.

Midnight-Blue (*to the audience*) It's fine.

Black It's cold.

Apricot It's what we're paid for.

Pink Better money than *Vogue*.

Black It's still cold.

Midnight-Blue (*to the audience*) I just wanted a chat. I wanted to ask . . . Do you think I look . . . boring?

Black Fuck it, I'm going to have a cigarette. (*She fishes one out of her wig and a lighter from her knicker elastic. She proceeds to light the cigarette and smoke it.*)

Midnight-Blue (*to the audience*) Or something. Old-fashioned? Do you?

Apricot (*to the audience*) You know, I still have my first Gossard's Wonderbra.

Midnight-Blue (*to the audience*) I hope not.

Primrose (*to the audience*) I just don't buy underwear.

Black (*offering the pack*) Anyone?

   The following dialogue is all to the audience.

Pink (*really enjoying the word*) SILK.

Primrose Not me.

Midnight-Blue I mean I'm not.

Pink SILK.

Midnight-Blue Am I?

Primrose Never.

Pink SATIN.

Primrose Not at all.

Apricot In purple.

Pink SILK.

Apricot Obligatory.

Primrose Nothing wrong with that is there?

Midnight-Blue Do you think I should branch out?

Primrose It's a personal thing.

Midnight-Blue Or not?

Primrose It's private.

Midnight-Blue I can't tell. Can you?

Pink Not nylon, Bri-nylon, Lycra, Spandex.

Midnight-Blue I'm just being silly –

Pink Elastomerics.

Midnight-Blue – I/know.

Pink /No.

Apricot And a Janet Reger number.

Midnight-Blue I mean it's –

Apricot In red.

Midnight-Blue Inconsequent. I just don't know what you'll
    think. You see, well, I like –

Apricot Ungmo's metal bra,

Midnight-Blue It's just –

Apricot A little cold.

Midnight-Blue I like cotton knickers. Still. OK?

Black Personally I don't care.

Midnight-Blue No frills.

Black About underwear.

Pink Don't follow 'the LOOK'.

Midnight-Blue No slinky, scanty, lycra briefs./I don't like the
    feel –

Pink /follow the feel –

Midnight-Blue And cotton bras.

Apricot Frederick's BATTLE DRESS.

Midnight-Blue Substantial. OK?

Apricot The best.

Following not to audience.

Black Could we have a tea-break now?

Pause while they all wait for a response. It doesn't come.

Pink I could do with a sit-down.

Apricot Can I scrounge a fag?

Primrose You'd think they'd let us go inside.

Midnight-Blue What's he up to anyway?

Black Fiddling with his flash.

Pause. Following to audience.

Primrose Excuse me, do you mind not looking at me while I pick my knickers? Choose my knickers. I mean choose. That's what I'm doing. Do you mind averting your eyes? Does it matter which I pick? I'd prefer if you didn't watch. That's all.

Pink SILK (*a beautiful sound*). Nylon (*a nasty sound*). SILK. NYLON. SILK. SKIN (*all beautiful sounds now*). SILK. SLIP.

Apricot I have a transparent ensemble trimmed with fur.

Primrose Please don't.

Pink Who says it's indulgence?

Primrose It's none of your business!

Pink It's your second skin.

Primrose Don't look!

Pink It makes sense.

Following not to audience except where shown.

Apricot Winter coats.

Midnight-Blue What?

Apricot We should be modelling winter coats.

Midnight-Blue Not for summer.

Primrose (*to the audience*) One woman's bra is another woman's poison.

Black It isn't summer.

Apricot You're telling me.

Pink (*to the audience*) What's closest to you matters most.

Midnight-Blue Well, they have to shoot in advance, don't they?

Black Here?

Pink (*to the audience*) And nothing's much closer than pants.

Primrose (*to the audience*) MIND YOUR OWN KNICKERS!

Apricot Freeze my tits off.

Pink Ooh, my back.

Midnight-Blue My feet.

Black My shoulders.

Primrose My legs.

Pink I could do with a sit-down.

Black I could do with a break.

Pause. Following to audience except where shown.

Black Why should I worry about underwear?

Midnight-Blue You see, I like something solid that won't let me down.

Pink Enjoy, enjoy.

Black No one sees it.

Pink What's underneath counts.

Black And the rest is bad enough.

Apricot A 'no-bra bra' and a 'none-in-one' in my favourite colour –

Midnight-Blue Something I can trust. Something –

Apricot – nude.

Midnight-Blue – warm. Is that all right?

Black I can't be bothered with bras.

Apricot See-through jumpers with nothing underneath.

Black My undercover revolution.

Primrose NO DISCRIMINATION ON THE GROUNDS OF UNDERWEAR.

Black 'Rebel without her drawers.'

Pink Treat yourself.

Black I wear my knickers till they hang on by a thread.

Pink Just yourself.

Black And then a bit more.

Pink Treat yourself well.

Black And that's all.

Pause.

Primrose Well, what the hell. What does it matter if you don't like my pants? You don't have to wear them. You don't have to look at them.	**Pink** SMOOTH. SOFT. COLD.

Black (*not to audience*) Do you like this garden?

Primrose I'd prefer it if you didn't.

Apricot (*not to audience*) Be better with some flowers.

Pink It's the parfait of underwear.

Black (*not to audience*) And a bit of sun.

Pink (*not to audience*) I quite like the fresh air.

Primrose Didn't look.

Midnight-Blue I mean something slight and light never feels like enough, if you know what I mean. There's the insecurity; the nagging doubt that it might not be enough to keep it together, to hold it up.

Primrose How strange to see you here in underwear.

Midnight-Blue Is that dull?

Primrose Underwear department, I mean. I guess the food-hall's next door. Found the fish-stall? Got your steak? Yes, these are my knickers. Let me introduce you: Harry knickers, knickers Harry.

Apricot A transparent bra with flowers on the nipples.

Primrose I don't think I like them now.

Midnight-Blue God, I hate things that are dull.

Following not to audience.

Black I'm going for a walk.

Primrose Me too.

Apricot I wouldn't. Not now.

Pink He's nearly ready.

Midnight-Blue Oh, good.

Primrose OK.

Black Oh, fuck.

Following to audience except where shown.

Apricot I even have stick-on sequin breast-cups from Valentine's.

Midnight-Blue I just don't like it all fancy, silky, sporty, lacy, racy, wired up, lift and separate, cross your heart, hope to die.

Apricot A lot of fun but . . .

Midnight-Blue None of that.

Black (*not to audience*) I'm cold.

Apricot He doesn't like them.

Black (*not to audience*) I'm fed-up.

Midnight-Blue Should I consider acid?

Apricot Why not? I do.

Midnight-Blue Will it give me a proper taste in lingerie?

Black (*not to audience*) I don't like this.

Apricot I love it.

Midnight-Blue The wilder side?

Apricot I thought he was meant to like that sort of thing?

Midnight-Blue Should I like it?

Black (*not to audience*) Right!

Apricot Aren't they?

Midnight-Blue Should I?

Black (*not to audience*) If we don't break soon, I'm walking out.

Pause. The pace increases.

Midnight-Blue I'm sorry, I just don't like it dressed up, messed around, squashed in, sorted out.

Black Cotton, Lycra, nylon, dacron.

Apricot Leather, lace, suspenders, corsets.

Midnight-Blue Someone else's shape.

Black I don't care!

Midnight-Blue Oh dear, I'm letting myself go,

Apricot He zips up quick.

Midnight-Blue Exposing my failings.

Black So long as it's minimal, practical/and goes in the washing machine.

Apricot /and disappears.

Primrose I asked you not to watch.

Pink No knickers?

Apricot Such a /pity.

Pink /pity.

Primrose Don't look.

Pink Silk slip, silk knickers, silk skin.

Primrose Got Sunday's pudding? EAT MY PANTS.

Midnight-Blue I like it secure /I like it simple.

Apricot /I like a little experimentation.

Midnight-Blue And I like it cotton.

Black Fuck the rest.

Following not to audience.

Male Voice SMILE.

Models LYCRA. The underwear revolution made for YOU.

Photo flash.

Male Voice That's tea.

They all run as fast as possible offstage, leaving the Woman revealed behind them. She comes forward smiling, puts on her dress and sits on her chair ready and waiting. All the while she intones quietly as if reminding herself.

Woman
You're safe with S-T-R-E-T-C-H LYCRA
For the modern girl,
Your mother or your wife.
Easy, unrestricting
For your daily life.
Suits your every need,
Gives the freedom one expects,
Superbly fashioned body
With a little hint of . . . lace.

S-T-R-E-T-C-H LYCRA
It's pretty and it's pink
Most adaptable accessory
From club to kitchen-sink.

The lights narrow down and then fade slowly on her as she sits waiting to be picked up.

Faith and Dancing

Mapping Femininity and Other Natural Disasters

LOIS WEAVER

Lois Weaver was born on 26 October 1949 in Roanoke, Virginia, and raised in rural southwest Virginia in Southern Baptist country. Her first theatrical experiences were church plays for the Mount Pleasant Southern Baptist Church. She attended Radford University (then Radford College) and graduated in 1972 with a Bachelor of Science degree in theatre and education. She was a founding member of Spiderwoman Theatre in 1975, co-producer of the WOW Festival in New York in 1980 and 1981, co-founder of WOW, performance space for women in New York in 1982, and founding director of Split Britches in 1981. Split Britches work includes: *Splitbritches* (1981), *Beauty and the Beast* (1982), *Upwardly Mobile Home* (1984), *Dress Suits to Hire* (written by Holly Hughes, 1987), *Little Women: the Tragedy* (1988), *Anniversary Waltz* (1990), *Belle Reprieve* (written with Bloolips, 1991), and *Lesbians Who Kill* (1992). Won Village Voice Obie Award for ensemble acting in *Belle Reprieve* in 1993. Appointed joint artistic director for Gay Sweatshop Theatre Company in London, 1992. Currently Resident Artist at Queen Mary and Westfield College, London.

Faith and Dancing was co-commissioned by Gay Sweatshop and It's Queer Up North and first performed at the Green Room, Manchester, as part of the It's Queer Up North festival, 15 May, 1996.

Darkness. The sound of a strong wind that diminishes as if a storm is departing as the lights fade up. Faith is sitting on a swing. She is an adult in a child's imagination. She's wearing a red and white dress made of paper, a pale blue apron, pale blue socks and ruby slippers. The swing is a child's red swing set but the seat has been replaced by an adult-sized bench tied to the frame with oversized rope. The swing set is placed slightly right of upstage centre and is secured to the stage with sandbags covered in blue silk. Pink geraniums are scattered on the floor under the swing. Behind the swing is a pile of laundry arranged in a semicircle that resembles both a crescent moon and a mountain range. The laundry is various shades of blue and is arranged with the darker shades at the bottom and the lighter shades towards the top. Upstage left several children's balls in various sizes and colours are suspended from the ceiling to resemble planets or stars in the firmament. Downstage left is an ordinary lawn chair surrounded by Yellow Pages, encyclopedias and dictionaries. After a brief silence Faith speaks directly to the audience.

I want to go home. I want to go home but I can't find my way. I left a trail of corn bread but the wind has come and scattered the crumbs. It was more than a wind. It was a tornado, a pink tornado. It wasn't pink to start with, when it hovered over Virginia. Virginia is a state, you know. But it is also the name of my mother. I think this tornado had something to do with her because I haven't seen her since. It started over the west ridge. I should have known this was different. Storms usually come from the east. Do their dance of terror and temptation on the east ridge appearing from the backdoor just beyond the lilac and the clothes line. No, this one came from the west, from the end of the day, a winter's day. Winter is an unusual season for tornadoes but there had been blizzards and the warm spell and terrible ice storms and there would be the flood so a tornado was odd but not impossible. It was at the end of the day. Just after the sun had dropped behind the nearest mountain beyond the west ridge a halo, no, more like a tiara, appeared on the head of the mountain. So we were expecting it. We were waiting. The air stilled. The hawk inhaled and I pretended everything I could but then I would, you see, because my name is Faith. Faith, who had always lived in the state of Virginia. Until the tornado.

It looked like an ordinary tornado. You know what that looks like, don't you? Fuzzy, grey and blue even though it isn't. Like the Blue Ridge Mountains look blue even though they are not. Tornadoes start out as colourless droplets of moisture and turn blue from all the debris that gets sucked up into their souls, like white clothes in a dark wash. And they dance on one leg, on one pointed toe. They only have one leg, tornadoes, and yet they can be such good dancers. Spinning on one toe – what is that called in dance? (*Answers her own question.*) Pirouetting. So, pirouetting down the road, they can, like discriminating neighbours, destroy all the houses on one side while leaving those on the other side completely unscathed. I never studied dance, although I did pay a lot of attention to the weather. I looked it up in the Yellow Pages once, dance that is, and marked the place with a pencil. I referred to the place, pointed it out, suggested it as a possibility but never actually asked. It was the FLOYD WARD SCHOOL OF DANCE. (*Faith stands. Cornmeal pours from a hole in her apron. She uses the cornmeal to trace the outline of the state of Virginia around the entire set while she performs the following lines and illustrates the dances.*) 'What? You haven't gone dancing lately? Why not? It's another great indoor sport for two. Your Floyd Ward dance coach moves you to music, cha cha, rumba, salsa, tango, waltz and, of course, the lindy. Join the Floyd Ward Ego Booster club and spoil yourself a little. You can afford it.' (*Removes her apron and tosses it on the pile of laundry and returns to centre stage.*) Floyd Ward taught social dancing to the few people in Virginia who had ever heard of such things. They also taught little ballerinas, not well but enough to give them a passion for pink. Now I had never seen a ballerina but I had some experience with modern dance. (*Performs a short dance phrase in the style of Martha Graham.*) Like most things, I found modern dance by accident. I stumbled on to semi-classical music while working at Sears department store. It's only because the hi-fi section was right near the big appliances and they had this semi-classical category on sale at the end of the aisle just down from the refrigerators. So I brought home a high-fidelity recording of the *Grand Canyon Suite* and my body exploded all over the wall of my room. I bounced and leapt from bed to window, from the door to Virginia's room to the door of the bathroom while Virginia and the milkman were watching Lawrence Welk in the living room. I exhausted my body in the *Grand Canyon* and went in search of more semi-classical inspiration. For me that turned out to be bootlegged versions of *West Side Story* and *South Pacific*. What I mean is, they weren't the original cast recordings. They were selections of the greatest hits with *South Pacific* on one side and fake Hawaiian songs on the other. I had never dreamed of Hawaii then, only dancing. So I looked it up in the Yellow Pages just like I looked up the word lesbian after I heard two boys spelling it out behind me in a voice that made me think it must be something unlawful. I was only ten and couldn't find the definition in the dictionary. But I got my answer. Without asking I got my answer. 'How can you be a good Christian and think about dancing?' she said. What Virginia meant is that she didn't understand how to manage this. How would I get there for a start? She didn't drive and the milkman had two jobs. Also the only dancing she knew about had been prohibited, not because of God but because of economics. It had been the Depression and all such social gatherings had been cancelled. But to put the record straight, it wasn't God or the Baptist preacher she cared about really. She just didn't know what else to say. She would have had to admit then and too soon that Faith had a body and that body could take flight and leave the state of Virginia. Which brings me back to the tornado and how I lost my way home.

It started out as an ordinary twister as it made its way towards our ridge which was the one that sat between east and west. That reminds me of a joke. (*Walks down left towards the audience.*) What's the difference between a Baptist and a Buddhist? Baptists do nothing and kneel down and Buddhists kneel down and do nothing. (*Returns upstage right.*) So the volcano, I mean, tornado was heading east. They always do, you know. They always head east and they blow in counterclockwise spirals because they are deflected by the rotation of the earth. That is if you happen to be in the northern hemisphere, otherwise your spirals will be clockwise. So heading east and slightly south, it came down our dirt road just like I had many times. And like me it stopped for a split second, just long enough to be late for dinner or considered missing or possibly even long enough to get a naked switch across the back of the leg. It stopped like me for second at Ame's house. (*Walks towards audience.*) Ame's other name was Lucy but I called her Ame because she had one. The main one I think was to tempt me away from Virginia. She tempted me with cornbread. Hard, coarse, crunchy cornbread. Not that fake cakey sweet kind. Oh, she had nothing against sugar. Put sugar in just about everything including a handkerchief tied in a knot so I could suck on it. A sugar tit she called it. But she never, never, never, never put sugar in her cornbread and ironically it's that recipe for cornbread that gave me the map I needed to navigate my way home. Until the tornado. (*Sits on swing.*) What is that word that sounds like the French word for ice cream or gizzard, chicken's gizzard? (*answering the question*) Glissade. The tornado did a glissade. It sidestepped just when it got to Ame's house who was sometimes called Lucy, although now we might call her Aunty Em. Because this mighty tornado stopped at her house, danced delicately around the African violets in her basement and turned a violent pink when it pulverized her yard full of geraniums. That's the last thing I remember, the tornado turning pink and the sky full of the smell of geraniums.

Blackout.
    Lights up. Faith is standing centre stage.

When I came to, Virginia was gone and now I'm looking for a way back home. (*Crosses down stage left to the lawn chair.*) That's why, in spite of my dyslexia, I have taken up cartography. One of the most interesting things about maps is that they lie. I come from a family of liars. That's because we are optimists. In the face of most things we either imagine a way out or tell an untruth. In fact I have already told you a lie and there will be six more before the performance is over. A total of six because no one works on Sunday, not even elephants. If you ever hire an elephant to make a movie you should know that they only work on a six-day contract. They refuse to work on the Sabbath. I don't know if they pray but I do know they suffer and they teach their children to grieve. They take hold of their little trunks and teach them to carefully trace the bones of the dead, memorizing the shape of their remains, mapping the memories of distant relatives. But memories, like maps, lie about shape and distance. Just like maps lie about size and direction. Maps lie because they are flat. (*Sits in the chair.*) Maps lie on the table in their untruth. They tell stories of places unvisited and state a closeness that doesn't always exist. Richmond can't possibly be that close to St Petersburg. And don't you think it's odd how there can be so many places with the same name. Salem is a good example. There's one in almost every state. In Virginia it's the county seat. I went there with Virginia when the milkman died. I went with her because she doesn't drive. She did once in the '48 Chevrolet. She drove around and around the field, not the one between us and Ame but the rough one, the garden one on the other side. She drove while he watched Sunday baseball. He had no particular interest in her being able to get someplace on her own. The service he provided was quite enough. His schedule could be her schedule and she could be just as dependent as he was on unexpected bowel movements. He wouldn't leave the house until he was sure that either that possibility was taken care of or that he could get to his destination before he had to go. I wonder if he ever messed his pants or if the fear kept him far from it. Like me, the fear of messing myself has kept me close, not to home, but to the silent corners of my tent. (*Stands.*) I can't seem to keep Faith indoors. She always wants to camp out, pitch a tent. I like tents. Tents are like maps. You can fold them up and take them with you. Not like globes. Even though globes tell the truth about shape and distance, they are expensive and difficult to carry and store. (*Performs another movement sequence that is obviously inspired by Martha Graham. She stops midway and refers to her performance.*) I don't like being watched. Faith is the evidence of things not seen. I'd much rather watch myself. I'd rather watch myself in the bathroom mirror because the bathroom is where I keep my evidence.

Blackout.
Lights up. Faith is swinging.

One of the things I knew when I was growing up was that the sky
was bigger than my head. I would look up and deep into a blue
that you hardly ever get on a map, although sometimes you
might see it on a globe but then it's the ocean and not the sky.
Maybe that's what they mean by deep blue. A blue that plunges
you into that place where there's no form, only texture, like being
inside a velvet painting of Elvis singing 'Blue Hawaii'. One or
two stars are all that I can remember. That and the first time I
really heard the words to the third stanza of 'Amazing Grace'.
(*singing*)

When we've been there ten thousand years, bright shining as
the sun
We've no less days to sing God's praise than when we first
begun.

That was my first awareness of poetry, or infinity for that matter.
But then maybe that is the power of poetry. It pulls up the skirt of
infinity. I saw this from the swing. I realized so many things while
swinging on that swing. Almost too tall to make you believe it
would stand on its own. (*Stands on swing with head appearing
over the top of the frame.*) But not so tall that I couldn't image
swinging high enough to gain enough centrifugal force to wrap
myself around the cross piece at the top. It was in those fantasies
of flight or actually orbit that I had thoughts. I thought, for
instance, both suddenly and surely that I must have been an
accident. I am not sure why I thought that. Perhaps it was a
disaster fantasy. While swinging I might have imagined letting
go. Unwrapping my fingers from the chain and catapulting
through the air and landing on the back steps. Virginia was
standing at the door. She had on her hat and coat and gloves. It
was her fortieth birthday. She had just killed the pigs and made
the sausage. It had been ten years last July since she finished
canning an acre of peas on her way to the hospital with her
second and what she thought would be her last child. So now she
was on her way out. She was going to learn to drive. And just as
she pivoted on that cement step, turned back to make sure the
coffee was off, I landed in her arms. And unlike me, she didn't

fall. She simply went back in the house and started over. (*Leans across the swing on her stomach, pushing the swing up and out towards the audience.*) Now I'm almost certain that this knowledge came before my knowledge of sex. Which came to me almost as suddenly but from the cold security of the kamode. Don't you feel funny about that word? Kamode? It would be a better proper name than name for an object. Lacy Kamode. I think that was the name of one of Virginia's boyfriends. That is before she met the milkman. Anyway it was all a matter of logic. I sat there safely with no notion of flight in this, one of our most grounded positions, the closest we get to squatting into the earth to give birth. Squatting in this civilized way, I discovered two things. (*Pulls feet up and squats on the swing.*) One, how it feel to have breasts pushed up against your skin. I found this out by leaning into my thighs. My thighs were me and my breasts were someone else's. This is what it feel like to hug me. I said. And if the ten thousand years on the swing was my first experience of poetry, sitting on the kamode in this position was my first experience of logic. It was simply two plus two. (*Sits in swing.*) I thought of my body. I thought of how I was shaped and then I thought of the short short-stop who was younger than me and let me sit on his hand as it caressed the cool stiff frame of his bicycle. I'm not sure if it was his hand or the steel pipe inside it that felt so good between my legs. But the logic of it exploded in my brain. It was a mechanical situation. One thing simply fitted inside the other. Oh my God, I said to myself. Of course. That's it! Oh my God! I said to myself in the privacy of that room, the only room in the house that wasn't a throughway to another room. That's how it works and I was both exhilarated by this new information and horrified that it might have something to do with me.
(*singing in a sweet voice*)

Amazing Grace how sweet the sound that saved a wretch like me.

I once was lost but now am found, was blind but now I see. So here I am on the swing, singing 'Amazing Grace', not because Aretha Franklin sang it and not because Virginia taught it to me. Because, you see, I discovered religion or rather the Church the same way I discovered sex and infinity, and modern dance; by accident. It became a social necessity. I would swing alone.

Virginia would be in the kitchen and Ame would be on her way
down the path and I knew there must be others. So I followed
Mrs Neighbours over the hill to the Mount Pleasant Baptist
Church where I could practise my personality. That is where I
learned about power and what it meant to maintain power and
still behave like a girl, a good girl. I was going to try this out. I
would be good. Even better than my family could have imagined
or demanded. I would invent their demands.

Music in. It is a song from the Fifties in the style of 'The Twist'.
Faith illustrates various popular dances of the Fifties and
Sixties as she performs the following lines.

I had a few clues, though. Virginia called me in one afternoon. I
was wrestling with the boys. I was wrestling and I was winning. I
was enjoying the force of winning but I was also enjoying the
physical contact. Virginia in her house could feel that pleasure.
What went through her mind and body? Did she see something
she knew she may not be able to keep for herself very much
longer? She called me in and said I was getting a little old to be
roughhousing with the boys like that. Like with the dancing, she
didn't really mean it. They weren't her words. They were stories
she heard, lies she told, ideas she had from the neighbours she
didn't even particularly like. Ame was different. Ame could tell a
dirty joke.

Blackout.
Lights up. Faith is leaning on the poles of the swing set.

Virginia was fixed. Virginia stayed put. She was the patch of
earth where the chickens scratched and the tomatoes grew and
the dogs died but the cats lived too long. She would put on a pot
of coffee when she saw Ame, who she called Lucy, heading down
the diagonal path from her house. Every day, once and
sometimes twice, Lucy travelled to and for Virginia. Hurricane
Lucy, I sometimes called her because she walked fast and brought
a windstorm of stories. Stories about things like adultery and
divorce which like earthquakes only happened in places like
California and about malignant tumours which could lie
dormant and then erupt almost anywhere and catch people in the
gesture of daily life. I would sit outside the window and listen

and think about Pompeii and wonder when and if that could happen in Virginia. Then I didn't know the difference between dormant and extinct. (*Straddles the swing.*) Ame was tall and because she bent in the middle when she laughed and she laughed a lot I knew she must know something I didn't. She was constantly in motion like the needle of a compass hungry for north, not true north, which is fixed and represents a climate too cold for her southern bones, but magnetic north that points in a northern direction, that allows for variation. Anyone who uses a compass soon masters the task of allowing for variation. (*Faith gathers the scattered geraniums and lays them on a diagonal line between the swing and the chair.*) Sometimes I'd follow her when she'd start home with her long stride and swinging arms like a hurricane heading up the coast. She'd trace a diagonal line through the field at a declination of forty-five degrees. Declination is another word for variation and describes the angle between magnetic north and true north. At a declination of forty-five degrees, Hurricane Lucy marked the way out. Sometimes I'd run away on my own and I would find her with her hands pushed deep in the bed of geraniums that followed the cement wall most of the way up the dirt road. She knew a lot about geraniums. 'Geraniums hold the smell of the past,' she said, 'slightly sour and musty like basements and old ladies.' I stood on the high end of the cement wall on my way up the road and felt the rush of fear and possibility. I knew Ame would be there to catch me with hands that smelled of geraniums. But I didn't like the smell. It reminded me of a place I wasn't ready to go. (*Climbing over the back of the chair and sitting.*) Ame also raised African violets and did other people's laundry. She took me in her basement and showed me the Himalayas in the mountains of sheets piled high by her children's laziness and a tender rainforest reflected in the last watering of her violets. African violets take their water from below, drink their coffee from the saucer. 'What can I tell you?' she'd say, pouring her coffee from cup to saucer, with that look on her face that meant she'd found a bit of news in the pocket of the jeans tossed carelessly into her pile. Ame's house was different. It teetered on the edge of disaster. It was a mess and wouldn't go to church to clean itself up. 'Sorry' was what Virginia would say. That girl or this man is 'sorry', which means they wouldn't pick up after themselves. If you look it up in the dictionary, sorry means apologetic, repentant, asking forgiveness. When Virginia said someone was sorry they weren't usually the kind of person who would apologize for their behaviour. You wouldn't find them on their knees except maybe for sex and I'm not sure they would care to have your forgiveness, let alone ask for it. So these sorry people were the opposite of sorry. Although in the dictionary sorry also means worthless, just like Virginia meant it. Then the opposite of sorry could be worthy. So to me, if these sinful people are not sorry for their sins, if they are not sorry, then they are worthy. That's how dyslexia functions.

(*standing and tracing the letters in the cornmeal*) D-y-s-l-e-x-i-a. Why does a word that describes a difficulty with the order of things have to be such a difficult word to spell? That is how I learned to be a good girl. Dyslexia. I turned it inside out. I kept the frame of good and girl but reversed the picture. Pretty is as pretty does. I built a character. (*Crosses up right along the diagonal line using the geranium as a tightrope.*) I wore an Easter bonnet, dotted Swiss dress and carried a lavender patent-leather purse. Although at a certain point that purse disappeared. I kept it in a drawer, one that was becoming easier and easier to reach. And when Virginia and I were on our way to town one day, I went for the purse and it was gone. I searched for many years after that and never found it. Like with the wrestling. Virginia had to make a decision. Was it too small for my dreams? Was it filled with too much imagination or was it the one bag she knew I'd pack before I'd go. It was a symbol and, like symbols on a map, rivers aren't blue and roads aren't red and purses aren't lavender, at least not on the map of Virginia.

Blackout.
   Lights up. Faith is standing stage left of the swing.

Virginia used to say that a woman is judged by how she hangs out her laundry. She didn't actually say that but she implied it. She never directly said very much at all. But she did instruct. Be economical with the clothes pins. Let the panties share the pins. Sheets are doubled and hung with at least three pins. They too must share. (*illustrating the action of hanging out laundry in the style of Martha Graham modern dance*) Towels are not folded in any way but hung straight and together with all the other towels. Shirts are hung from their tails at the side seams. It is more difficult to share pins with shirts but may be necessary to save space and equipment. Pants are hung front on at the waist. Although some like Miss Connor hung them from the cuff. Some even dried them on a stretcher, creating a peculiar effect of many working husbands floating like kites at the end of the yard. The most important thing to remember is category. Hang things in groups. Sheets with sheets, towels with towels and underwear together always on the back line. Keep in mind that people can see these details of your life. What I mean is, people can see how you manage your private affairs in the way you hang out your laundry. The other women will notice if the sheets are smooth and stretched and if there are gaps in the underwear. (*Crosses far stage right and squats in the curve of the mountain of blue laundry.*) I used to sit in the wicker clothes basket under the clothes line just behind the lilac bush while Virginia would hang out the wash. She wore pants on those days. I guess it was because the clothes line was on a hill and she thought a dress might blow over her head. And she never did, except on Sunday, wear any underwear. Maybe that's what I was thinking, sitting there in that basket. I wanted to see. I wanted her to have on a dress and I wanted it to blow over her head and I wanted to see her, naked and hairless. I knew it was hairless because nothing would show through the white briefs she wore to Sunday school and I knew it was naked because when she did the laundry and I would sit in the cool dark basement next to the coal bin and watch and occasionally be asked to help pull something through the wringer, I would stare at her wet belly. I especially remember that belly on the day before her only son went to Japan. She stood in the damp basement with a wet belly and she cried for her only boy leaving home. Don't worry, Mama, I'll be your boy. I'll even be your husband. I would be your lover if the idea had ever occurred to us simultaneously. The closest we ever got was in the kitchen after returning home from Bible school or after going to town. We'd come home and sit down for a minute. Virginia would light a cigarette and I'd be near her or on her lap, but only if there were others there. It was too frightening to be alone and that close. I would remember the smell and force of the rubber in her girdle. It smelled like something sweet and tight. I would hear the sound her stockings made when she rubbed her tired legs together. I would watch the smoke curl up and under her arm because she held her cigarette in the palm of her hand so she'd have to kiss her fingers each time she took a drag. She held it there because she didn't want anyone to know. She couldn't show it, just like I couldn't say it. I couldn't say the word cigarette for the longest time. Just like I couldn't say the word cab until I changed it to taxi and took one. (*Crosses to the swing.*) Just like I would take a pack of Virginia's unsmoked Lucky Strikes and hide between the wall and the buffet in the dining room. I liked the smell of the unsmoked tobacco, the feel of the crisp cellophane, and the hard shape of the square package in my hand. I fondled them but I never lit them. (*Straddles swing.*) I never lit them because I was afraid of fire. I would stand for hours in the garden side of the yard trying to get up enough nerve to light the match to burn the trash. Virginia would wonder what took so long but I could never tell her. I could never tell her I was afraid of fire. Although she knew I was scared of the dark. At night I would call her to my bed. Until I was well past thirteen, I wanted her in my bed. I would wait 'til I could stand it no longer and then I would call Mama. Funny how her name changed throughout my life, more a naming of myself than her: Mama, Mom, Mother. Virginia was lying on the diagonal in the next room sighing when I began my mantra. (*lying on the swing*) Mama, I can't go to sleep. Mama, I'm scared of the dark. Mama, I'm afraid of fire. Mama, I want you in my bed. I want the fountain of your body pressing into the mattress so that gravity will pull me towards you, into the valley at your side.

Blackout.

Music in. It is a country and western song in the style of the Willis Brothers' version of 'Tattooed Lady', which describes a woman who has a map of the United States tattooed on her body. Faith does a fake hula to the song and rips her paper dress to reveal the body parts mentioned in the song. At the end of the song she tears her skirt into small bits of paper and scatters them on the floor behind her like a trail of crumbs.

Digging for Ladies

JYLL BRADLEY

For Jack Bradley, my father

Digging for Ladies is the story of four women's journey from innocence to experience told through the lore and language of gardening – a 'pursuit' that is a means of self-expression for many women. The play first appeared at The Drill Hall, London, in 1996 as *On the Playing Fields of Her Rejection*. Reworked, it then toured site-specifically to some of the most beautiful gardens in England through the summers of 1998–99.

Digging for Ladies is a theatrical pleasure garden inhabited by four budding women gardeners. It tells the story of their employ on the estate of a revered local lady, employ which entails the careful tending of particular areas of her garden. They each work earnestly at their designated jobs to win the lady's approval. When their efforts fail to bear fruit they become disenchanted and, setting forth under the magical light of a solar eclipse, they begin to consider creating their own gardens. Gardens in which they might plant fresh seeds.

The play as it appears here was the centrepiece of a wider evening's 'garden masque' which also included a specially written 'parodic' guided tour of the garden, performed by the actors. The audience were invited to come dressed in their gardening gear and a prize was awarded nightly for the 'Best Dressed Gardener'. *Digging for Ladies* was co-directed by Emma Bernard and Grainne Byrne and described by *The Times* as 'a hybrid formed by grafting Joyce Grenfell with Sarah Bernhardt, Vita Sackville-West with Enid Blyton: a specimen whose charm is in proportion to its rarity'.

Jyll Bradley writes for stage and radio. Her stage work includes *The Fruit Has Turned to Jam in the Fields*, for Scarlet Theatre. Recent radio work includes *Filet de Sole Veronique*, and the first radio dramatisation of Kate Chopin's *The Awakening*.

Act One

SCENE ONE – FOUR BUDDING GARDENERS SEEK EMPLOYMENT

The gardeners enter the garden on a rousing rendition of 'English Country Garden'. Each proudly carries a garden tool. All wear identical Liberty floral frocks.

Henriqua Henriqua!

Bello Bello!

Idele Idele!

Ursule Ursule!

Henriqua Our beloved queen and huntress!

Bello Our beloved queen and huntress!

Idele Our beloved queen and huntress!

Ursule Our beloved queen and huntress!

Henriqua We stand together at her service! Gardeners all!

Bello We stand together!

Idele We stand together!

Ursule We stand together!

Henriqua We stand together! We have waited so long to stand here together in these gardens that now we are aquiver with nerves. For these are gardens of one, our beloved queen and huntress, who lives in the house yonder.

Ursule Shall we play hockey?

Henriqua No, we shall not play hockey. We have waited so long to stand here together in these gardens that now our time has come we are aquiver with nerves. Since these are the gardens of one, our beloved queen and huntress whose herbaceous borders we have for so long longed to ponder and tend.

Bello Shall we go on a cross-country run? Across field and down dale, racing each other in a mad dash for the garden gate?

Henriqua No we shall not. We have waited so long to stand here together in these gardens that now we are afroth with anticipation. These are the gardens of one, our beloved queen and huntress. (*Pause.*) A lady ambitious for her gardens. A lady whose gardens are renowned far and wide! Look at her splendid roses, admire her shrubs and conifers, her attendant

303

parklands and woodlands. Her luscious lawns! Not to
mention her intimate alpine garden. In short, her sizeable
estate. Yes –

Bello What about her hedges and topiary?

Henriqua Yes, yes, her hedges and topiary –

Idele Yes, you forgot to mention her paradise of dwarf
rhododendron.

Henriqua Her paradise of what?

Idele Her paradise of dwarf rhododendron.

Henriqua Look at her splendid roses, admire her shrubs and
conifers, her attendant parklands and woodlands. Her
luscious lawns! Not to mention her intimate alpine garden, her
hedges and topiary and her paradise of dwarf rhododendron
. . . yes . . .

Ursule You've forgotten something. Her vegetable patch!

Henriqua People don't want to know about her vegetable patch!
Anyway, it is situated in a private part of the garden. That is to
say beyond a gate clearly marked 'private'.

Ursule People particularly like to know of those parts.

Henriqua Look at her splendid roses, admire her shrubs and
conifers, her attendant parklands and woodlands. Not to
mention her intimate alpine garden, her hedges and topiary
and her paradise of dwarf rhododendron and . . . her
vegetable patch! Yes, as far as the eye can see and the tongue
can reach these are the gardens of one, our beloved queen and
huntress!

Pause.

Ursule Shall we ping on the kettle for our tea-break?

Idele Oh, yes! I bought a pint of milk on my way in.

Ursule We should get a kitty going for that sort of thing . . .

Idele Yes, then it's fair dos all round!

Bello Did you remember to buy the custard creams?

Idele I'd marked you down as more of a digestive person!

Henriqua We have waited so long together in these gardens that
now our time has come we are aquiver with nerves. Since
these are the fertile and fecund gardens of one, our beloved
queen and huntress. As you can see her gardens lie at the foot
of her house. A house as high as one's greatest aspiration!

Idele Do you take sugar?

They all grow serious again.

Henriqua We had heard mention that there were situations vacant in her extensive gardens, openings for employment.

Ursule Jobs for the girls!

Henriqua looks disdainfully.

Henriqua Thus, by way of application, we were discovered one morning on the lawn, dew up to our knees, staring at the house. We stared so hard, so intently, that her ladyship flung her windows wide and asked us of our business. Then she rode out on her steed, her face a blur of fury and curiosity and, hats in hands, we bluffed our way into her gardening employ after she had engaged us in this rigorous and searching interview. (*Henriqua takes up the role of their beloved queen to relive the interview they went through. Pause as she composes herself in the guise.*) If you discovered a species of plant, any species, uprooted and lying on a grassy knoll, what would you do?

Bello I would gather it up and replant it myself, then sprinkle water on it at regular intervals.

Henriqua I see. And if you discovered a species of plant, any species, uprooted and lying on a grassy knoll, what would you do?

Idele I would trim it where it lay at regular intervals.

Henriqua I see. And if you discovered a species of plant, any species, uprooted and lying on a grassy knoll, what would you do?

Ursule I would eat it where it lay at regular intervals.

Henriqua I would do exactly the same as you. Then I would go for a stroll through the alpine garden. And if it rained what would you do?

Bello Catch the rain in a bucket.

Idele Catch the rain in a floppy felt hat.

Henriqua Catch the rain in a floppy felt what?

Idele Catch the rain in a floppy felt hat.

Ursule Catch the rain in a drain.

Henriqua Are you afraid of earwigs? I must hurry you.

Bello Are they the ones with the . . .? (*Puts fingers up to head to mimic earwig.*)

Idele (*screams*) Yes!

Bello No, no I don't mind them.

Idele Yes.

Ursule No.

Henriqua Aphids?

Bello Yuuck!

Idele Yes.

Ursule Yes.

Henriqua Do you suffer from hayfever?

Bello Yes.

Idele Rarely.

Ursule No.

Henriqua Name this plant . . . think carefully –

Bello A *cornus controversa.*

Idele A *begonia hybrida erecta superba.*

Ursule A gaudy vulgar bedding plant.

Idele Did you hear that, the very cheek . . .

Henriqua And what is the rule of thumb when judging the amateur vegetable category at the village show? (*Pause.*) It will be one of your duties . . .

They converse, Idele is pushed to answer.

Idele Mere size, without quality, is no merit.

Ursule With the exception of onions which should be as big as your head.

Idele (*to Bello*) Oh, this is just like that programme on the radio. What's it called? Now, it's just after the shipping forecast on a Sunday lunchtime and just before the classic serial adaptation. At least it was there the last time I tuned in. By the way, how are you finding the new schedule?

Henriqua If one were anxious to grow peas for the supper table as late into the season as possible, what is the latest date they could be sown?

Bello The third week in June. Sow a miniature early variety for it matures more quickly than the taller ones. Thereby guaranteeing a bountiful crop.

Henriqua What is this tool used for?

Idele Would you repeat the question?

Henriqua What is this tool used for?

Bello Pruning.

Idele Hoeing.

Ursule Eating.

Henriqua And how would you train a runner bean?

Bello On your marks, get set, grow!

Idele With gentle persuasion.

Ursule Nibble at its roots until it races laughing up the climbing frame.

Henriqua What would you wear for your duties?

Ursule Garden hose!

Idele I would wear a floppy felt hat.

Henriqua A floppy felt what?

Idele A floppy felt hat.

Bello A jerkin, a kerchief tied around my neck, a peaked tweed cap, round spectacles, corduroys, laced bruised brogues, a greatcoat for winter . . . digging stirrups when necessary.

Henriqua What is a compost heap?

Idele (*to Bello*) By the way, I do like your hothouse pelargoniums.

Bello Oh, thank you, they're just something I do in my spare time. Have you been complimented on your helleborus?

Idele Not recently, no. What's your secret with them. Do tell.

Bello Trussing them up properly after flowering.

Idele Oh!

Bello Then twice-weekly feeds with well-rotted liquid horse manure, diluted to the colour of weak tea. And a thorough sulphurous fumigation . . . kills the greenfly.

Pause.

Idele Oh! . . . Look, I don't suppose, no . . . it's a bit of a cheek. . . .

Bello Don't suppose what?

Idele That . . . I could have a cutting?

Bello walks off to get a cutting for Idele. Idele follows.

Ursule (*following Bello and Idele*) Can I have one too?

Henriqua What is a compost heap?

Idele, Bello and Ursule run back to their places.

You!

Bello Oh . . . a warm place to sleep at night.

Idele A place to pass by quickly with one's head held high.

Ursule A delegation of plant matter returning home from exile.

Henriqua What is a ha-ha? Ha, ha, ha, ha (*dissolving into laughter at her own funniness*).

Ursule A place for laughing at your own jokes.

Idele and Bello join the mirth at Henriqua's expense.

Henriqua And your greatest –

The other three are still laughing.

– I've started so I'll finish. Your greatest gardening ambition . . . tell me about that.

Idele To serve your gardens all my days!

Bello Yes! To tend, to hoe, to scythe, to mow, to prune.

Ursule To get my hands on one of the head gardener's prize specimens.

Henriqua looks very disapproving.

To serve your gardens.

Pause.

Henriqua And finally, what would you do in the event of an eclipse?

All (*as though chanting a mantra*) Under whose terrible eye, as all gardeners know, all plants do wither and curl and die.

Ursule Watch the moon as it creeps gradually across the face of the sun, then stare at its totality.

Idele, Bello and Henriqua look at her as though she is quite mad.

Idele Scream out loud then run for cover until it's all over.

Bello Stand in such a position as to throw my own shadow across the plants under my care. To protect them from the shadow of the eclipse.

Henriqua You have answered just as I would have answered. I pronounce you employed.

The gardeners jump for joy and congratulate each other.

Your working hours will be dawn till dusk, come rain or shine, all year round. Payment will be in arrears. Once a year, on my birthday, all will get the afternoon off! Breaks will be one per day at noon for ten minutes. Tomorrow at dawn you will commence work in the following areas of my garden, yours will be the rhododendron –

Idele Oh joy!

Henriqua – and yours my hedgerows and topiary –

Bello Excellent!

Henriqua – yours my lawns and (*as if to herself*) yours my vegetable patch! (*Henriqua steps back into herself to receive her appointed area.*) Yes'm, thank you'm. Very good'm. (*Then back to her regal persona*) Tend my gardens well. Seize every opportunity to further their cause . . . your tools are your responsibility – they must be kept well oiled at all times. I will inspect them weekly on a Wednesday. Any breakages thereof will be docked from wages. (*Henriqua returns to herself.*) We stand together at her service! Gardeners all! Our beloved queen and huntress!

Bello Our beloved queen and huntress!

Idele Our beloved queen and huntress!

Ursule Our beloved queen and huntress!

Bello, Idele and Henriqua don't hear what Ursule says next.

I hear the moon rising in the west. It will creep stealthily out of the night to describe an arc in the sky. Plants, animals and gardeners beware for I foresee an eclipse!

The gardeners celebrate their new jobs with a joyful gardening ballet, dancing with their tools to uplifting music. When the music ends they each take up their new-found jobs.

CENE TWO – CELEBRATION ON FINDING EMPLOYMENT

Idele Emploi! Emploi! Emploi! Emploi! Employ! Employ! Employ! Employ! Em-ploi! Emploi! Employ! Emploi! Emploi! Emploi! Emploi! Emploi! E-mploi! Emploi! Employ! Emploi! Employ! Employed!

Bello I have found employment!

Idele Where have you found it?

Bello I have found employment. I found it in a hedgerow, in that little bit of the garden that could whimsically be described as a wilderness. I held down a branch and stepped inside that hedge. Then on standing tall I found employment. It was noon, yet twilight reigned within. All around, the rest of the world was dry. Yet deep in secret side, the hedge fuzzed darkly wet. I stood tall within the hedge. I laughed out loud to find myself so hidden, yet so tall. The hedge quivered with my laughter. I laughed some more. Then the sun glanced in and trickled. I nibbled at the leaves. Evergreen! I nibbled at the leaves then I chomped. The cellulose dribbled down my chin and off my chin and fell to the ground in a froth. I chomped for some time and finally I stopped to admire my work – I had created a hedge in the distinct shape of a peacock! Topiary the envy of gardeners everywhere!

Idele I have found a situation!

Bello A situation!

Idele A very bright situation! Down amongst the grass, I spied a globe of dew. In it my face was reflected. Perfectly framed! Perfection! So I lapped it up and from it quenched my thirst. Then I surfaced to find my lips in the vicinity of what I now know to be a fragrant rhododendron flower.

Ursule (*trying to pronounce*) Rho-do-den-dron.

Idele That's what I said. I confronted that flower full face on. I shook it. I confronted it. I shook it. I smelled it. (*She inhales deeply.*) Then I snogged it.

Ursule How do you spell snog?

Idele I snogged it. Then I gathered a bevy of those flowers fully in my full hands, until my hands were full. And I snogged each flower in turn. Lingeringly. For a full five minutes each to be sure that no flower had cause to rejoice over preferential treatment over the other flowers. So there would be no grotesque posturing or showing off or exhibitionism. No condescension or affectation. I confronted first one flower, then another. My face was covered in pollen and I glowed yellow until the day broke and then I dusted myself down. In my care the rhododendron flourish. Into a rioting paradise of perfume and colour, rivalled bar none! Envied by all!

Bello You're kept busy, then!

Idele Yes.

Henriqua We stand together at her service!

Idele We stand together!

Ursule We stand together!

Bello We stand together!

Ursule I have found an opening!

Bello You have found an opening?

Ursule I have found an opening! On the wide sweep of lawns in front of the house. The grass was a bit unkempt. But I soon saw to it! My lips and teeth puckered over those shoots. And I found my lips and teeth rushing across the surface of the grass in one long furious munch. My mouth frothed green with cellulose. Then I munched my way back, in a similarly straight line then back and forth and back and forth and back and forth until I had perfectly grazed the lawn.

Henriqua Our beloved . . .

Ursule Now on Wednesdays she plays croquet upon it. I found an opening. The lawns bask under their new close crop. The lawns grow. They grow and I graze.

Henriqua Our beloved queen and huntress! We stand together at her service! Gardeners all!

Bello We stand together!

Idele We stand together!

Ursule We stand together!

Henriqua I have found a vacancy. I have found a vacancy. Behind the house. To the rear of the house. On the reverse side of the house.

Idele Where is that exactly?

All laugh except Henriqua.

Henriqua Beyond the gate marked private. Yes, I have found a vacancy. The vegetable patch! Legumes. All was still. First I grew a courgette. Afterwards a cucumber. Then a marrow. Recumbent friends, they lay twitching on the surface of the soil. Bewitching . . . Quite often I harvest my finest and modestly display them in local competition at the county show.

Idele The village show, in the amateur category.

Henriqua My marrows regularly win first prize. Whereupon I swell with pride.

Hints of rivalry and jealousy begin to sprout among the gardeners.

Bello What about your cucumbers, then?

Henriqua Highly commended.

Bello Our beloved queen and huntress!

Idele Only highly commended? Better luck next time et cetera. I received a royal blue rosette for my rhododendrons! Special mention was made of their exquisite fragrance. Her ladyship was most delighted at my success.

Henriqua As she was with the size of my courgettes, which were highlighted for praise by the judges.

Bello Size isn't everything and all that.

Idele Except with rhododendrons, of course. Mine are soon to be photographed, you know, for one of the better Sunday supplements.

Henriqua Oh, congratulations! Of course, *Country Life* featured my courgettes last week in a full-colour double-page centrefold splash. And, did I tell you . . . I have been asked to submit a paper on 'Practical Brassicas for All'.

Bello To what publication?

Henriqua *Down to Earth*. The journal of the Co-operative Vegetable Worker.

Bello I don't subscribe.

Henriqua Not a paid-up member? You surprise me.

Idele I'm afraid I'm not terribly interested in hobby plants myself. At any rate my prize-winning blooms leave me very little spare time these days.

Ursule Well, my lawns are shortly to be immortalized on celluloid.

They are all taken aback.

Henriqua You what?

Ursule Yes, they are shortly to be filmed for *Gardener's World.*
From three different angles and I have been asked to endorse a
new fertilizer. For which my agent is currently negotiating a
seven-figure sum.

All others taken aback.

Henriqua We stand together at her serv –

*The ballet music comes in again and Henriqua for a while tries
desperately to get them to dance together again. It fails with
Idele's interjection. Ursule leaves, horrified.*

Idele (*to Henriqua*) Did I mention that I am to open my
rhododendron dell to the public for select dates next year – on
the personal request of the county secretary of the National
Garden Scheme. We lunched late last week. She laid on a
buffet. And overlooking her prize-winning patio she begged
me to do so . . . of course, by the time we had reached dessert I
simply had to say yes . . . for the sake of charity . . .

Bello I had a similar experience with the chair of the Royal
Society of Topiarists, of which I am to be made honorary
fellow at an extraordinary general meeting . . .

Idele Of which I am already a fully paid-up life member . . . By
the way, will you be exhibiting at Chelsea, this year? I hear
they have a dwarf topiary section this year.

Bello leaves, shocked.

Henriqua (*to Idele*) The only exhibits these days at Chelsea are
showy, rampant climbers, don't you find? No, I am kept busy
with my talk 'Grass Roots Management of Parsnips'. Actually,
I delivered it to a rapt audience of the Townswomen's Guild
last week. It was hailed by all as a great success. A notice was
written up in the paper, you may have seen it?

Idele How quaint! A talk! That must have been the night I was
invited by the WI to give an illustrated presentation with
illuminated slides.

Thunder fades into sombre music which sets in as they ask the following questions, as though they are asking questions of life itself.

Idele I worked so hard on my brassicas, why did they fail this year?

Bello Why do my salvias so often disappoint?

Henriqua How did the frost get to my fruit trees?

Bello Was I over-ambitious for my sunflowers?

Henriqua How can I stop convolvulus choking my passion flower?

Idele Why do my rampant climbers never get past go?

Bello How can I stop my roses swarming with greenfly?

Henriqua Why won't my wisteria flower?

Idele How can I stop my tulip bulbs from rotting?

Their voices become a rising cacophony of gardening discontent. As the cacophony continues, Ursule recites William Blake's poem 'The Sick Rose'. It focuses their sadness.

Ursule
O Rose thou art sick!
The invisible worm
That flies in the night,
In the howling storm,
Has found out thy bed
Of crimson joy:
And his dark secret love
Does thy life destroy.

Time is passing. The mood is sombre. The music continues. Ursule finds a gardening manual, written by a famous woman gardener. She starts to study it.

Henriqua How can I protect my bedding plants from frost?

Ursule (*looking at the book*) It seems you can't always.

Henriqua Why does my greengage never bear fruit?

Ursule There's not always an explanation.

Henriqua Was it too early to sow my antirrhinums? Tell me, how can I stop my paeonies being blighted by disease? Why is my bedding display not as fine as last year? Why do my neighbours' hollyhocks always grow taller than mine? Why

only a highly commended for my cucumber? Why weren't my
marrows filmed for *Gardener's World*? Why wasn't I invited
to address the WI? Why do my evergreens always turn out
deciduous? Why do my seeds so seldom take root? Why is my
blossom always nipped in the bud?

Ursule (*reading from the book as though it is a book of life*) You
must not, any of you, be surprised if you have moments in
your gardening life of such profound depression and
disappointment that you will almost wish you had been
content to leave everything alone and have no garden at all.
Some time ago I heard the moon rising stealthily in the west. I
foresee an eclipse.

*Overlapping with the fading out of the music, thunder is
heard. It gives way to rain. The music fades out. The moment
is held. A wind of change has swept through the garden.*

Act Two

SCENE ONE – DISILLUSIONMENT WITH WORK

The gardeners regroup.

Henriqua Henriqua!
Bello Bello!
Idele Idele!
Ursule Ursule! (*sarcastically*) Our beloved queen and huntress!
She brushed by me this morning without one good word for
my work. I held out my hand. The leaves were aching. I
withdrew my hand.
Henriqua I will call a meeting. I hear murmurings of dissension.
We will have a minute-taker. We must elect a representative.
Bello I will take the minutes. You are elected.
Idele I'll plate up the biscuits.
Ursule I'll make the tea!
Bello Are there any sandwiches?
Idele Potted crab do you?
Henriqua May I venture corned beef?
Ursule Anyone seen the corned beef?

Bello There's some left under the hedge over there.

Ursule Seize the time! Organize!

Idele Anyone prefer orange squash?

Henriqua This isn't a Tupperware party!

Idele No, it's a real hoot!

Ursule (*shouts*) The gardeners united will never be defeated!

Henriqua Members only will attend the meeting. Enlist the members!

Bello Your names? Bello!

Idele Idele!

Ursule Ursule!

Henriqua Henriqua! Members! Members! Are we quorate?

Bello Bello!

Idele Idele!

Ursule Ursule!

Henriqua Henriqua! We are quorate! Right, down tools all!

The gardeners all lay down their tools.

Everybody out! Everybody out!

Idele, Bello and Ursule troop out.

(*exasperated*) Everybody in!

They troop back.

No one's to cross the picket fence! Now let us have the first of many representations and grievances. Of which I know there to be several.

Bello takes out a notebook and pencil. She records the grievances.

Ursule She brushed by me this morning. She had not one good word for my work. I held out my hand. The leaves were aching. I withdrew my hand.

Idele She constantly criticizes where praise would be politer.

Ursule She brushes by me. Daily. The leaves lie on her lawn. Then I rake them up all blushed and wrinkled and worn and build a bonfire as sad as myself. And then I graze. I graze and graze her lawns. I graze. I graze and graze her lawns. I graze. I graze and graze the lawns in front of her house. The lawns sweep right up to the great glass doors. The wind rushes them open. I graze and graze. The curtains flutter and the dust mutters under the carpet. I graze and graze the lawns. I graze until my mandibles drip with cellulose and my teeth are worn. I graze and graze. I graze the lawns, I graze. I graze the lawns. The lawns I graze and graze. I graze the lawns until I am docile and domesticated and until I am a shadow of my former glorious, ridiculous, irrepressible self. Then I graze the shadow that I cast hoping, praying, wishing, desiring a different taste, a deeper taste, a shadow taste and then the sun sweeps out and up and in and I am left with leavings and piles of leaves shrunken embers of their former glorious, ridiculous, irrepressible selves. I graze the lawns. On Wednesdays she plays croquet on the lawns I've grazed. The bright balls roll unchecked across the perfect green baize. She always wins. I graze and graze. I graze the lawns. I graze and graze and graze and graze and graze . . .

Idele I wear a floppy felt hat.

Henriqua A floppy felt what?

Idele I wear a floppy felt hat. This is my representation. I had been working the rhododendrons all day and all night. In readiness for a forthcoming opening under the National Garden Scheme. As dawn broke I saw her approach me from the house. She looked straight through me. She swerved along the path where I stood. A puddle lay in her route. I went to lay my coat across the puddle. But she did not wait. She ploughed through the puddle fluttering the mud to create a neat fan across my jerkin, my jauntily tied kerchief, my round spectacles, my laced, bruised brogues and my corduroys thonged from the knee to the ankle. I went to lay down my coat. But she waved me aside to create the aforementioned fan of mud. She stepped into the puddle, her dainty feet, ankles and legs up to her thighs were wrung with slush and her hands as light as bells, their fingertips muddied by her course through the puddle. As she proceeded through the puddle she became more and more muddied until I could barely see the top of her head, just a neat circle of brown crown and then she emerged, calm and berobed in mud. She did not look at me. Instead she carried books and she carried nuts.

Henriqua My representation is similarly brief. It is that I am never allowed to wear corduroys when working her brassicas. She says it interferes with her music practice.

Idele, Bello and Ursula all cry 'Shame!'.

The meeting is dissolved! Our minute-taker has made a note of these many and varied representations and grievances. You will each be copied copies. Then you will be balloted.

Idele, Bello and Ursule are not impressed. Bureaucracy is not the answer to their distress.

For now the meeting is dissolved as a sugar lump plopped into a hot cup of tea. That is to say it is adjourned, run its course, retreated into hibernation, left us for the foreseeable future, evaporated.

Idele, Bello and Ursule remain still. They are not satisfied.

Your copied copies will be delivered in due course. You will be balloted shortly. Up tools all!

They remain still.

Ursule I graze and graze the lawns. I graze the lawns.

She continues in an angry lament to the hard work she does; the scant reward. Idele and Bello join in. This is directed at Henriqua.

I graze, I graze and graze the lawns, oh, I graze, yes, I graze . . . on Wednesdays she plays croquet, yes I graze . . . They film my lawns for *Gardener's World.* Oh, I graze . . . (*and on*)

Idele I tend the rhododendrons, I tend them, I tend them into a rioting paradise of perfume and colour, rivalled bar none, envied by all! I water them, I trim . . . they flourish . . . (*and on*)

Bello I prune those hedges, I trim the topiary, rivalled bar none, I win prizes for my hedges, I prune, I trim, I nibble, I chomp . . . (*and on*)

The mood of revolution, of eclipse, grows.

Ursule I graze till dawn . . .
Idele I hoe past noon . . .
Bello I scythe to dusk . . .

Henriqua (*joining them*) I mow, I mow, I mow . . .

Ursule I mulch . . .

Henriqua You what?

Idele I prune . . .

Bello Till kingdom come . . .

Idele Then I prune a little more . . .

Ursule And then I graze on top of those grazings . . .

Idele And I hoe on top of those hoeings . . .

Bello And I scythe and I scythe and I scythe and I scythe . . .

Henriqua I mow, I mow and still my marrow seeds don't always grow . . .

Idele And still my rhododendrons are often ruined by rain.

Bello And my hedges grow awry.

Ursule And my lawns are scorched by sun.

In their anger they all begin to get a glimpse of what life could be like; at last they speak their innermost desires.

Idele (*shouting and startling herself and others*) I want my own garden! I want a garden where I can drift around my own sunny beds, felt hat on head and trug in hand pausing to lift a lettuce for a light supper.

Bello And I want a garden where desirable wild natives can run rampant through my herbaceous borders!

Ursule A greenhouse, where I can grow a –

Henriqua at last rises to the call of her troops. The sun is reaching its zenith.

Henriqua There will be an eclipse!

All Hurrah!

Henriqua Some time ago I heard the moon rising in the west. It will sail over our heads and describe a great arc in the sky. En route there will be a solar eclipse as it passes in front of the sun. Up tools all!

They up tools.

Ursule The moon's shadow will sweep over the face of the earth.

Idele Do you really think so?

Ursule Enveloping all. At first, the disk of the moon will just lightly touch that of the sun at its western rim. Then slowly,

slowly all sunlight will vanish. And the earth silenced by shadow.

They all begin to look up into the sky, fearfully, expectantly.

Bello It will be noon, yet twilight will reign!

Henriqua We must prepare for the eclipse! To the lawns, to the wide sweep of rhododendron, to the ever proficient hedgerow, to the vegetable patch!

Ursule In the darkening sky, all the brightest stars will shine. As the moon obliterates the sun there will be a great flash! And the eclipse will be crowned all around by a solar corona shining as finely etched frost against a deep blue darkened sky . . . People will stare, animals will cower . . . plants will wither and their shoots grow warped.

Bello What of my hedges and topiary?

Idele My rhododendron?

Henriqua We must prepare for the eclipse!

Ursule Under the shade of the eclipse anything is possible. Nothing predictable! All will suffer a sea change, into something rich and strange. Dreams, hopes, fears, desires!

Henriqua To the lawns! To the wide sweep of rhododendron! To the ever proficient hedgerow! To the vegetable patch! Scatter! Lay down your winter coats then stand with your back to the sun and cast a great long shadow, ample shadow. A shadow to bathe your respective charges – the lawns, the rhododendron bushes, leguminous growths. Lean long and watch and wait for the moon to clip the corner of the sun. Clip and eclipse. By your own shadow stand blinking into the flame, fringed umbra. Scatter! Scatter!

The gardeners speak their dreams.

Ursule Dreams, hopes –

Idele I want a garden where I can one day drift around my own sunny beds.

Bello Desirable wild natives!

Ursule To grow a melon from seed, in a greenhouse!

Henriqua To win first prize for my cucumbers!

Ursule A garden I can call my own . . . A garden I can call my own!

All The eclipse! The eclipse! The eclipse! (*and on*)

Darkness sweeps the garden. A worm squeaks out from within a rose; a prize cucumber moans; hedges gossip nervously. Suddenly a fountain that ran dry years ago sputters with life and the garden erupts with wild music. A new dawn breaks over the garden.

Act Three

SCENE ONE – AFTER THE ECLIPSE, DEBRIEFING

The gardeners regroup, dishevelled, and blooming, to tell their stories.

Henriqua Henriqua!

Bello Bello!

Idele Idele!

Ursule Ursule!

Henriqua We will no longer hear the moon rising stealthily in the east! We need no longer prepare for the eclipse!

Bello I stood at such an angle as to cast my shadow. I shook it in my palm and it trembled there, then I threw it long and low. It tumbled out across the hedgerows.

Idele I apologized in advance to the rhododendron that for their own protection I must needs stand with my back to them. This did not appeal to their vanity. I covered them gently with my shadow.

Henriqua I hurried to my vegetable patch. But I was late, so in advance I threw my greatcoat high into the air. It twisted and turned, then delicately embraced the leguminous plot.

Ursule I graze and graze the lawns. I graze. I graze the lawns. I graze. I laid down my greatcoat upon the lawn, but I threw my jerkin, my jauntily tied kerchief, my peaked tweed cap, my round spectacles, my laced bruised brogues and my corduroys thonged from the knee to the ankle, I threw them high into the air.

Bello The eclipse occurred.

Idele We saw each other eye to eye. My brows were singed by ringlets of fire. I sighed. Then the disk dislodged and rolled to the side.

Henriqua Now a marrow has made its home from the left-hand sleeve of my fallen coat; a courgette its home from the right-hand sleeve and a cucumber has snugly nosed its way into the lining . . . Perhaps this year my highly commended will win first prize!

Ursule The grass is singed. Its shoots are frazzled. Now the garden has only a healthy part in the shape of ourselves. Voluptuous as it may be. Sensual to the T as it may be. Amusing, mysterious, deep and delicious as it may be, all else is singed.

Idele One day I may drift around my own sunny beds, felt hat on head and trug in hand pausing to lift a lettuce for a light supper . . . but for now . . .

Ursule The wind carried my clothes far and far. Our beloved queen rode out upon her horse to view the eclipse. Moments later my clothes fell, my jerkin, my jauntily tied kerchief, my peaked cap, my round spectacles, my laced bruised brogues and my corduroys thonged from the knee to the ankle. They flew straight into her face. Then her horse, startled by the eclipse, reared up and threw her from her mount. Suddenly, the sun shone again. I mounted her horse. I galloped across the lawns which I once grazed. The windows of the house were open. I rode inside. I took up residence. The next day I bought a houseplant. It is easily managed and its year-long blooms bring me great joy. All who pass through are welcome to water it. And many do.

Long pause.

Henriqua We stand together! Gardeners all!
Idele We stand together!
Bello We stand together!
Ursule We stand together! I may yet grow a melon from seed.

Lights fade. Exeunt.

Ophelia

A Comedy

BRYONY LAVERY

Ophelia writes play revealing the 'real' reasons for her suicide
(among them, incest with her brother Laertes, whose child she is
carrying). The play within the play inverts and becomes the main
event. The Player King (a female actor) opens the play. Ophelia is
actor and author. This is an extract from the latter part of the
play to the end, showing scenes 15, 16, 18–21 and 23.

Bryony Lavery is a playwright, director, performer and teacher of
playwriting. Her plays include *Bag*, *Flight*, *Two Marias*, *Wicked*,
Origin of the Species, *Witchcraze*, *Calamity*, *Kitchen Matters*,
Her Aching Heart, *More Light*, *Goliath* (adapted from the book
by Beatrix Campbell) and *Frozen*. Her plays for children include
Madagascar, *Sore Points*, *The Dragon Wakes*, *Down Among the
Mini-beasts*. Her cabaret includes *Floorshow* (with Caryl
Churchill), *Time Gentlemen Please*, *The Wandsworth Warmers*
and *Female Trouble*. Her work for radio includes *Laying
Ghosts*, *The Twelve Days of Christmas*, *Velma and Therese* and
adaptations *My Cousin Rachel*, *Wuthering Heights* and *Hacker*.

Ophelia was first presented by the Stantonbury Campus and Collage Theatre Companies at Stantonbury Theatre, Milton Keynes, in November 1997.

SCENE FIFTEEN – TIDYING

Gertrude attended by Portia and Goneril.

Gertrude
O, that I had not given birth!
That I had kept him within me . . .
attached to me by leading reins of blood!
From this unhappy accident we know
mothers should never let their children go!

Portia
Madam, he has killed and you must think
how to bestow him safely for himself
and others . . .

Goneril
Lady,
I have a ship stands in the harbour;
hold him at arm's distance there,
till these storms die and cease to whisper
when I will bear with him to England . . .

Gertrude
Away from me?

Claudius enters, the Scribes are with him.

Claudius
Your mad son is held, our poor dead Polonius
found . . . what's to be written
what's to be done?

Gertrude
These ladies have arranged it.
Write that my son, distracted by his father's death
is sent to England till he find his noble
mind again.

Portia
I will give you the addresses of some kindly hearts,

with clever brains who'll listen Hamlet back to
himself . . .
Goneril
I'll have my captain put a lock upon the door
of a stout cabin in the womb of my ship.

Portia and Goneril exeunt.

Claudius
(*to Scribes*) Go write this firm . . .
in many copies bound, that our dear visitors
may carry away our royal version to the
far-flung world.

*As Claudius dictates, Scribes write, Visored Guards convey
Hamlet through Elsinore . . .*

Scribes exeunt.

Gertrude . . . while your son walks we are not safe!
Gertrude
I cannot let this poison in my ear!
You rid me of my husband,
you'll not also have my son!
Claudius
No, you'll have mine! (*He seizes Gertrude. Starts to undress
her.*)
The berry's blighted on my brother's vine,
so let us grow a hopeful rose on mine . . .
Gertrude
tho my heart protests, my blood louder sings,
I am a royal woman, I make Kings!

They are practically procreating as the lights dim . . .

SCENE SIXTEEN — WEAPONRY

*To be created . . . The arms chamber of Elsinore. Various
weapons . . . swords, daggers, guns, etc., on display. Ophelia
appears in the centre of the chamber. From the four corners of
darkness Katherina, Celia, Nurse, Raag and Tottir edge warily*

*up on her. Ophelia takes a cutlass from the store, slashes it
widely. The others move back.*

Raag
  Shit!

Ophelia
  This will do!
  I'll cleave the arm that thrust . . . separate it from its trunk,
  just as it separated my father
  from his life!

Katherina
  Sweet friend, put down the sword,
  this anger dangers you . . .

Ophelia
  Oh, here's daggers too! (*Takes one.*)

Tottir
  Shit!

Ophelia
  This will do to enter his empty breast!
  For no heart beats there, that is sure!

Celia
  Good pupil, here's a lesson poorly learned!
  Act not without thought,
  We've heads as well as hearts!

Ophelia
  Why, here's a musket!

Raag/Tottir
  Shit! Oh shit!

Ophelia
  I'll fire this at his head,
  show Man's Invention unto Man!

The others become very still.

Oh I am fortunate!
I know these weapons well!
My brother Laertes taught them
all to me!
He knew without a mother by
I'd not be safe!
Stand back, there's vengeance must be done!

They start forward . . .

I'll kill the first one stops my way!

She points the musket at them. They stand back. All but . . .

Nurse
No *mother* . . . now what's this?
no *noble* one that's sure,
but she who gave her life to bring you here!
And what of that low *ewe-sheep* that your
father bought, said 'here's a poor lamb needs suck'
was not she baby Ophelia's dam? (*Nurse is standing close to
Ophelia, the barrel of the gun at her heart.*)

Did she not love you like a mother true?
Ophelia
She was *paid* so to do, by this knife . . .
Nurse
And *did* and *does*, no extra charge, for life.
Give me that nasty toy, baby . . .

This softens Ophelia. She puts up the musket.

Raag
My lady . . . I'll take the musket . . .
Tottir
And I the knife . . .
Katherina
I'll order these tools of death locked up
until this misery is past . . .
Celia
(*shows keys*) Madam, it is done.
Ophelia
(*to Nurse*) There's nothing left!
Nurse
There's sleep.

Exeunt weaponry. Light fades.

328

SCENE EIGHTEEN – HOUSEKEEPING

To create . . . a laundry. Nurse supervising Raag and Tottir
washing bedlinen. A steaming copper. Piles of soiled laundry.
  Raag and Tottir hold up various sheets for Nurse's inspection.

Nurse
  (*first sheet; pristine white*) Lady Capulet's.
  She lies a-dying, little life there.
  Gentle wash.
  (*next sheet; white; great rip in it*) Lady Katherina's. In sleep she
  still is fighting.
  Sewing pile.
  (*next sheet; white; torn in three*) Lady Goneril. Quite torn in
  three?
  Sewing pile.
  (*next sheet; white; ink-stained*) Lady Portia. *Bed-linen* not
  parchment,
  lady scribe!
  Bleach.
  (*next sheet; white; stained with blood*) Lady Macbeth. (*Sighs.*)
  Bleach.
  (*next sheet; white*) My girl Ophelia.
Raag
  From the night my lord Hamlet stayed
  with her till dawn.
Tottir
  Such cries and yells through the door . . . .
Nurse
  (*removes the sheet from Raag and Tottir*) Handwashing.

  They stand.

  Bleach!

  They go back to work. Nurse covertly examines the sheet.

  My girl Ophelia grows with child
  yet no virgin blood the night of Hamlet *wild*
  so who's the father, that is who *pays*?

the one has *most* makes childhood happy days!
On this blank sheet there's nothing writ. (*She exchanges
Ophelia's sheet for Lady Macbeth's bloodstained one.*) I'll
take *this* to the Queen, there's coin in it!

SCENE NINETEEN – DEPARTURES

*To be created . . . the great hall of the castle . . . a great door
open to the improving weather. Sounds of travel . . . horses
stamping . . . wheels on roads, etc. Gertrude and Claudius are
bidding their guests goodbye . . . and a group of Scribes is
writing.*
Goneril comes forward.

Goneril
Your son is on my ship . . . close-watched.
When the tide turns and welcomes late tonight,
I'll take him hence across the sea to England.

We see Hamlet, pacing a small square.

Gertrude
We thank you for your royal kindness
and wish you joy upon your native shore.
Goneril
My father calls me back; there's change in th'air;
he's old and grey and aching to take ease . . .
I am the eldest, mine the forked crown, the royal chair
I'll lift them from his tired arms if he please.
Claudius
King and Queen of Denmark content will be
when you with husband reign across our common sea.

Goneril retires. Her place taken by Lady Macbeth.

Gertrude
Madam, for you our hearts are heavy as stone . . .
you came carrying joy, you leave alone.
Lady Macbeth
I take nothing with me but an empty space,

fear not, some germinating seed will soon,
occupy its echoing place . . .
tho 'nothing nothing nothing' it's only sound
twill grow within me and once more make me round . . .

Gertrude
Ah, madam . . .

Lady Macbeth
No more! I cannot! I cannot!

*Lady Macbeth retires. Her place is taken by Lady Capulet,
helped by Lady Katherina.*

Katherina
So great a debt for your kindness as we bear
The impudence I employ here I scarce dare . . .
You gave so much, so ere your kindness end
give us as parting gift Ophelia, our sorrowing friend.

Claudius
Our doctors attend her, practise all their healing arts
We anoint her in the salve of our loving hearts.

*Light on Ophelia. Celia administering medicine. Ophelia
resists. Her reluctance is overcome by Guards.*

Lady Capulet
My lord, in Italy we live beneath a ripening sun
which from dawn to dusk beams its warming light
the girl is filled with darkness, mistakes ghosts for friends,
let us give her ease from her perpetual night . . .

Gertrude
Lady, I've lost a son, his sad deeds take him
from me o'er the sea,
you lost a daughter, take not mine,
tho not of my flesh, she's that to me.

Katherina and Lady Capulet retire. Lady Portia takes their place.

Portia
King, Queen, you have entertained me well,
your learned tomes have been my pillow reading,
they tell me we of this sex were never here
save for our task of gentle breeding!

She bows, goes to the open door. Turns to the Scribes. They write.

And I agree. I review our defence and find it thin
We pleaded womanliness and let this old house take us in
We held high rank, yet used it to lessen other's pain
We let the storm fright us, we merely watched the rain . . .

Scribes finish writing. They wait, their pens poised.

Let this be writ, it is morn, the day is new,
all females lift their eyes, walk into the sun
we must leave our old quiet habits, stand in clear view
and ride to do the deeds that must be done!

The visiting dignitaries depart into radiant light. Scribes look to Claudius. He shakes his head. They write nothing. Gertrude and Claudius prepare to retire. Nurse sidles up.

Gertrude
Yes.
How is your mistress?
Does she sleep?
Nurse
Well, considering she sleeps not alone.
Gertrude
Why, who's with her?
Nurse
A baby, madam, but it cries not,
being still within.
Gertrude
She bears a child?
Nurse
Ay, madam, though who's its sire's not writ.
Here's her bedsheet, the one Prince Hamlet pressed,
perhaps he's it?
Gertrude
This tells us nothing.
No evidence is here . . .
except this night Ophelia was virgin pure . . .
Nurse

And good Prince Hamlet showed himself a man . . .
there's pleasure *untold* when *mum* becomes a *gran*!
Whatever's the truth, one thing is chapter and verse,
the babe will surely need a *nurse*!

Gertrude
Leave this intelligence with me.
Nurse none of this elsewhere. (*Gives krone.*)
If this stays secret till I give it out,
your future employment will never be in doubt.

Nurse retires.

In Denmark's garden now two rose trees grow,
I planted this red one with Hamlet, my first spouse,
on its thorny branch grew Hamlet, my one son,
'tis the family tree of a Royal House . . .
I planted this white one with Claudius my fragrant love,
its perfume draws me to it across the air,
no white-petalled flower yet nestles in the green,
but God, I want to see it there!
Now from the red tree's grown a branch
and let down into the bed another tree,
and soon, all I see is red,
where my white rose should be!

Charmian comes to Gertrude.

Charmian
My lady, my time here is brief,
my mistress waits for the turning tide,
this morn I heard her in my heart speak 'Gertrude'
so I came to you . . .
you said there's mischief to be trapped,
regarding why my sister Iras died . . .

Gertrude
Sad Charmian, there is, I've got a tale of woe,
a tapestry bag of envy, wicked threads shot through.
I loved your sister Iras, who, tho she served me
I thought of her as dear as daughter,
this my sweet loved Ophelia liked not well,
and turned her jealous gaze at your sister's quarter . . .

333

I said 'there's love for all within this breast'
Iras was content, but Ophelia could not rest
and when I bid them to the fields to gather herbs,
for hues, for lotions, all the lea to comb . . .
I sent them both to open up their hearts,
but only one, with heart of stone came home.

Gertrude/Charmian

Ophelia! . . .

Gertrude

. . . who held far higher rank than your sad kin
and so Polonius used his estate to keep this secret in.

Charmian

Ophelia!

Gertrude

My wished-for daughter.

Alarums. Guards rushing about. Claudius enters.

Claudius

Gertrude . . . is the Lady Ophelia with you?

Gertrude

Why no. She's in her chamber with her sewing frame,
singing sad songs, and counting out her woes.

Claudius

So thought my Switzers when they took her sup.
The chamber's empty . . . nought but air.

Gertrude

She flies to madness, a frenzied, limed Jay . . .

Charmian

I'll bring her down, I am now bird of prey!

Exuent to find Ophelia.
  We leave the castle for . . .

SCENE TWENTY – PARTING GIFTS

*To create . . . a ship's hold. Awaiting the tide. Bound for
England. Horatia is bidding Hamlet farewell . . . she gives him a
book.*

Horatia
  My Prince, we know the nights at sea are long,
  Here's a stout book, many many pages long,
  and full of argument and sides and several
  points of view . . .
Hamlet
  (*takes it*) Here's an anchor. Here's a holding lead
  . . . that I'd never cast myself from learning!
Horatia
  When you return, you'll come to Wittenberg
  and we'll make a citadel of these
  and observe the world far far below
  from our book-built ivory tower!
Hamlet
  I will some English book bricks bring with me
  and crenellate the ramparts with white Dover
  chalk!

  They smile at one another. A pause. They shake hands.

  Why cannot all intercourse between our sex
  be warm as this?
Horatia
  Sir, I know not.
  Save 'Sex' is catalyst somehow!
  We'll debate on it at Wittenberg. (*Horatia departs.*)
Hamlet
  There'll be no more debate, Horatia,
  all books lie
  nothing happens as we intend
  then we die.

  *He puts the book aside. To be created . . . a sound of water,
  the ship tilts as if something has just pulled at its side. Strange
  sea cries. Hamlet goes still.*

  What's that?
  Some creature come from the watery deep
  to swim through my reef-surrounded mind?

  Ophelia, dripping wet, climbs into the hold.

Ophelia

A mermaid, sir,
come with a coral gift.
The Switzer Guards hold sway on land.
I, born of water, took the watery way.

Hamlet

When we were children and we played in the sea,
it seemed you could live in the water . . .
when you dived, you stayed for ever till I
thought you drowned . . . then up you'd burst,
and I would, laughing, call you fish!

She has a waterproofed package in her hand. She gives it to him. He slowly opens it.

Hamlet

I deserve no gift from you.

Ophelia

It's true, but we are out of water here.
Women give gifts, men deserve them not.
It is the custom here on land.

The package contains a sampler.

I have been confined within my room.
A trifling ailment . . . a daughter's grief.
I've whiled the lonely hours with needlework.
Here's a sampler . . . a child's first gift.
It's for your son, when dawns that joyous day.

Hamlet

Ophelia, I travel light. All's Emptiness!

Ophelia

Then you are fortunate.
The tapestry is Adam and Eve beside a tree.
The fruit is knowledge. A bitter berry.
Why, here's a needle still threaded within! (*She removes it from the sampler.*)

Wise women say there's a future in your hand,
if you can read, there's lines upon your palm.

Let's see if such diligent students as us
can see the lesson, sir, Life has in store . . .

*Hamlet holds out his hand. Ophelia jabs the needle into it once,
then many times. Hamlet continues to hold out his hand.*

This is the only weapon I have left.
A woman's arsenal is small,
lest she borrow from man's.

*He puts out his other hand. She jabs that viciously until she is
spent.*

You killed my father because you loved not yours!
You took my love and gave not yours!
You gave your grief to me but took not mine!
You told me all your nightmares
You talked of love
then said your words were play.
You gave me hope . . .
then snatched it straight away!

Finally, she is exhausted. There is silence. Stillness.

Hamlet
Ophelia, look on my palm.
No wounds.
Look on the marks writ there.
The lines are short.
There is no future.
I am dead already.

Ophelia
I am content.
It is what you deserve.
What comes to me as yet is hid.
Go, cold dead man, to England.

Hamlet
Warm, living Ophelia, stay.

*It seems they will part. At the last moment, they bend and
forgive one another. They are quaking tight within each
other's arms as . . .*

SCENE TWENTY-ONE — UNDERWATER

To create . . . the seashore before the castle. Gertrude and
Charmian wait . . .

Charmian
  You're sure she comes this way?
Gertrude
  As sure as Elsinore stands before the breaking sea.
  All ships departed now with their arranged cargoes
  My son to England is safely sped . . .
  Ophelia was apprehended in his cabin,
  bidding her fond farewell to my scornful Prince . . .
  but she, being slippery water fish,
  slithered from out the Guards' clutching grasp . . .
  and into the sea dived where it is deep . . .
  look, here she comes . . .

Ophelia comes wading out of the sea.

  I'll call her to me, wait by . . .
  I'll offer her my hand and warmth . . .
Ophelia
  Who's there?
Gertrude
  It is Gertrude, mother to Hamlet and to you,
  if you would come into my embrace . . .
Ophelia
  Madam, your family has not served me well.
Gertrude
  I know it . . . but I am here to offer reparation . . .
  come within my cloak, here all is dry and warm . . .
Ophelia
  I'm tired. I am alone.
Gertrude
  I'm here. I'll take you.

Ophelia comes into Gertrude's embrace. Charmian traps her
with the cloak.

Ophelia
Oh, what is happening?
Charmian
A sisterly embrace!
Gertrude
A mother's love!

Together, Gertrude and Charmian wrestle to drown Ophelia.
Ophelia resists mightily.

Ophelia
I never did you harm!
Charmian
Then do our betters lie!
Gertrude
Your seed lays weeds within my garden,
their burgeoning tendrils choke my
nurtured tree . . .!
Ophelia
Oh, I am killed by Lies!

Gertrude and Ophelia overcome her . . . Charmian drowns
her . . . Gertrude watches for a little.

SCENE TWENTY-THREE — THE MANUSCRIPT ENDS

Player King walks tentatively on to the scene. She is holding her
prompt copy. Looks for Fortinbras.

Player King
Sir, Good lord Fortinbras,
there the manuscript ends . . .
what happens next . . . the terrible scene
whose bloody ends you entered on . . .
this fearful family expunged . . .

Player King and Scribes execute a bow. Fortinbras claps.

Fortinbras
The poetry's uncertain, the action strange,

the women too angry and the men too few,
but it passed a time, and if she'd lived
she'd have made . . . a *woman* playwright,
by my word!
More pity it is she took the child with her
to the grave . . .

*He stares again at Ophelia. Player King and Props put arms
around her.*

Player King
Ay sir . . . we humble players thank God our
daughter here is lowborn . . .
Props
And with us still to take the family on . . .
Fortinbras
If it were that sweet Hamlet's son,
I could raise up that royal house once more
in Elsinore!

Fortinbras departs as Player King calls after him . . .

Player King
And if it were that sweet Laertes' one,
double house of Polonius could take the
floor! (*She watches him depart.*)
He's gone.
Pack up!

We're on our way!

*Scribes take off their costumes . . . the dismantling of Elsinore
begins . . . as props, everything is cleared . . . Greasepaint
removed . . . all the space is cleared . . . the light grows and
grows to a wonderful, hopeful brightness, presaged by that of
Portia's departing speech earlier . . . Player King administers,
as Ophelia changes . . . simply dressed and towelling dry her
hair . . . she is smiling at something the disrobing Gertrude
and Charmian are telling her . . . a burst of laughter.*
Player King
Well, lady Ophelia,
how did you like your play?

340

Ophelia
'The poetry's uncertain,
the action strange,
the women too angry and
the men too few;
but it passed a time . . .
and if she'd lived . . .'
Player King
Which mercifully she *did* . . .
Ophelia
Because she held her breath
and swam and fought against the tide . . .
Player King
She'd have a life, a future, and a child . . .
Ophelia
All of which she has . . .
and friends to travel with . . .
Props
Who, though low-born and poor,
are rich and bounteous with love . . .
Ophelia
Then 'Tragedy of Ophelia' it is not
and she must rewrite
and bend her pen to scrawl its ink
upon the next page blank and white . . .

The stage is bare of all the Elsinore effects.

And there she'll find the rainbow images
to fill with dreams this empty space,
and all lies, betrayals, unkindness, woe
will henceforth happen only here upon the stage,
and in no other many-blessed worldly place!

The light is now wonderful. Music has started, and grows.
Ophelia sings.

the dawn
a new fresh day
the dew is fresh upon the grass

we rode with fire
your hayrick burned down
last night

the dawn
a stiffening breeze
sand swirls across the shore

we sailed with fire
your ship burned out
last night

the dawn
with crumpled sheets
lovers wake in each other's arms

we dreamed with fire
the sky was red
last night.

*The players and Ophelia carry cases, boxes, carts into the
future. Music swells . . .*

Lear's Daughters

Based on an idea by Elaine Feinstein
and written in workshop by members of the
Women's Theatre Group

Elaine Feinstein is a poet, novelist, biographer and playwright. Her work includes *Selected Poems* and *Daylight* (both Carcanet Press). She has written twelve novels, of which the most recent is *Lady Chatterley's Confession*. In 1980 she was made a Fellow of the Royal Society of Literature and in 1990 she received a Cholmondeley Award for Poetry.

Adjoa Andoh is an actor, writer and co-founder of Wild Irish Theatre Company.

Janys Chambers is an actor and writer with over twenty plays produced and four published.

Gwenda Hughes was associate director at Birmingham Rep and is currently Artistic Director at the New Victoria Theatre, Stoke on Trent.

Polly Irvin is an actor, director and co-founder of Wild Irish Theatre Company.

Hazel Maycock is an actor.

Lizz Poulter is a stage manager and lighting designer.

Sandra Yaw is an actor and writer.

Lear's Daughters was first performed by the Women's Theatre Group on 12 September 1987, with the following cast:

Cordelia Polly Irvin
Regan Adjoa Andoh
Goneril Sandra Yaw
The Fool Hazel Maycock
The Nurse/Nanny Janys Chambers

Directed by Gwenda Hughes
Designed by Jane Linz Roberts
Lighting designed by Dee Kyne
Stage Manager Lizz Poulter

When speeches are interrupted by another character, the point in the sentence at which the interruption is made is marked with a solidus.

SCENE ONE – THE BEGINNING

Light up on the Fool.

Fool
There was an old man called Lear
whose daughters, da da da da, fear,
The Queen was their mum,
Da da da da son,
Da da da da da dada here.
(*She shakes her head.*)
Knock, knock.
Who's there?
Godfrey.
Godfrey who?
Godfrey tickets for
the play tonight.
(*Looks at audience.*)
Are you ready?
(*Thinks.*)
The play.
(*Holds up three fingers.*)
Three princesses.
(*Holds up two fingers.*)
Two servants.
(*Holds up one finger.*)
One king offstage.
(*Holds up one finger on other hand.*)
One Queen dead.
(*Thinks.*)
Or
(*some finger business*)
Three daughters,
Two mothers,
One father,

and the Fool.
(*Points to herself.*)
Now:
Six parts,
Four actors . . .
(*Looks at fingers, thinks.*)
The Fool.
(*Smiles.*)
Right.
One stage,
One audience,
One castle,
(*Stands up, moves centre stage, takes out blindfold.*)
One prop.
(*Puts it on.*)
Watch!
(*into game of blind man's bluff*)

All
One, Two, Three, One, Two, Three,
One, Two, Three.
Fool Goneril!
All
No. One, Two, Three, One, Two, Three,
One, Two, Three.
Fool Cordelia!

Cordelia turns to audience.

Cordelia I like words. Words are like stones, heavy and solid and every one different, you can feel their shape and their weight on your tongue. I like their roughness and their smoothness, and when I am silent, I am trying to get them right. Not just for beautiful things, like the feel of old lace, but for the smell of wet soil, or the tug of the brush through my hair. I learned to read by myself. The first thing I ever did on my own. And the voices were so rich and strong that now, I read all through the summer in a garden den of raspberry canes and blackberries, and I look up at the sky, and it's full of words.

All
  One, Two, Three, One, Two, Three,
  One, Two, Three.
Fool Regan!

Regan turns to audience.

Regan I love the feel of wood, of bark cracked and mutilated by
  lightning or curves smooth and worn by wind and rain. I love
  the musty smell of old wood decaying, or of new wood freshly
  cut. Sometimes when I touch it, I can almost feel the wood
  breathing still, its breath, my breath. When I carve, it is as if
  there is a shape lying within the wood already, waiting to be
  released, moving my knife independent of the hand that holds
  it. So on some days I carve slowly, carefully, holding my
  breath, frightened of what I might create, whilst on other days
  I carve passionately, wanting to release this shape, this being,
  because I know that one day the shape that appears will be
  particular – my shape, me.
All
  One, Two, Three, One, Two, Three,
  One, Two, Three.
Fool Goneril!

Goneril turns to audience.

Goneril When I look the world breaks into colours. When I was
  small – finding paints and brushes in the chest, opening tiny
  pots and setting them out, taking water – I couldn't believe
  how the colours sharpened under the wet brush! And now I
  paint all the time, every minute, big canvas, big strokes, getting
  it right. Self-portrait . . . on a throne . . . scarlet, gold, black
  . . . it's outside. Trees cracked by lightning, a knot of raspberry
  canes and blackberries . . . and my sisters, beside me, our faces
  upward, smiling – sky full of stars. My painting. And one day,
  I'll get it right.
All
  One, Two, Three, One, Two, Three,
  One, Two, Three.

Fool turns to audience.

Fool I like money. And myself. And money.

Fool moves down right. Nanny moves upstage centre, sits, and sisters gather upstage centre around her.

Three princesses, living in a castle, listening to fairy-tales in the nursery.

SCENE TWO – THREE SISTERS, THE NURSE TOGETHER

Nurse (*to Goneril*) When you were born, the Queen wore nothing but her crown.
Cordelia What, nothing?
Nurse Lear was not there. He was in the library looking at something. You came out like a dart, head first, then body, all over scarlet, covered in blood. The crown fell off and over you, encircling you, your whole body.
Goneril What then?
Nurse And then a comet rushed through the sky, leaving a red trail in the black. (*Whispers.*) And it was twelve o'clock midday.
Goneril I remember it. I remember it quite clearly. I remember being born quite clearly. I heard music.
Regan What about me?
Nurse When you were born, the Queen was sitting on her throne. At midnight you dropped out on to the velvet plush like a ruby.
Cordelia Where was Daddy this time?
Nurse Still in the library.
Regan And then what happened?
Nurse A volcano erupted.
Regan A volcano?
Nurse Yes, the lava got everywhere. We were cleaning for days.
Regan I remember it. I heard music too.
Nurse And was it beautiful?
Regan Yes, oh yes.
Cordelia Now me. What happened when I was born?
Nurse When you were born . . . (*Nurse looks at her. She draws Cordelia to her, whispers in her ear.*)
Goneril What?

Regan What?
Goneril What did she say?
Regan What did she say?

Cordelia and Nurse look at each other.

Goneril Nothing. Nothing happened, did it? Nothing.
Nurse And afterwards we had cake. Victoria sponge on a doily
in the parlour with the clock ticking. The cake was cut into
three.
Regan A piece for each of us.
Nurse A piece for Lear. A piece for the Queen. And a piece for me.
Regan Did it taste nice?
Nurse Ask Lear. (*She moves away.*)
Regan What did she say?
Goneril What did she say?
Regan Come on, Cordelia!
Cordelia (*slowly*) She said that the Queen was outdoors. And I
grew like a red rose out of her legs. And there was a hurricane.
Regan It's the same, it's the same.
Cordelia And Lear was there.

Lights down. Light up on Fool down right.

Fool When she came, there was just a note. It said, 'I'm coming
soon. Nanny.' So I went about my business. If the note had any
significance it was wasted on me. Two weeks later there was
another note, pinned under my cereal bowl. 'There's been a
setback, but wait for me there. Nanny.' I was seven or maybe
twelve, I can't be certain, but Goneril was definitely two. The
Queen, their mother then, had taken to spooning honey over
the flower beds. She wore a peg on each finger and had ordered
the hair to be removed from all over her body. Everyone said
there was something wrong. She'd tipped the scales. She
needed a friend or a nurse or 'at least something to cheer her
up a bit', everyone said. A third note came. 'Sorry it's taken so
long, but I shall be with you by midday tomorrow. Can I bring
my ducks?' Signed Nanny or Nurse.

By eleven o'clock next day I was at the city walls watching
for a new face. At midday she came, riding sideways on a
donkey. I knew it must be her.

Nurse moves into space as if entering for the first time.

Nurse Sorry I'm late.

Fool She said.

Nurse But these things take time.

Fool 'Oh, don't worry, no matter,' I said and I helped her carry her things to her room. 'Will you be stopping long?' I asked.

Nurse That's not really up to me.

Fool She said.

Nurse I do as I'm told.

Fool I don't know if you're expected, that's the trouble.

Nurse I'll make myself indispensable. Soon they'll come to rely. You know how these folks are, always make the same mistakes.

Fool holds out hand for money. Nurse places gloves in Fool's hand. Fool throws bag to Nurse.

Fool Three daughters. With two mothers – one buying, one selling. One paying, one paid. (*Fool picks up the Queen's veil.*)

SCENE THREE – THE FOOL IS THE QUEEN

Fool sits on box upstage. Arranges veil as the Queen. During this scene Fool speaks as Fool and Queen.

Fool (*Queen*) Nurse! Nurse!

Nurse Yes, your majesty.

Fool (*Queen*) Is it nearly morning?

Nurse The birds are just beginning.

Fool (*Queen*) Don't talk to me about birds. The doctor was putting live pigeons on my feet all day yesterday.

Fool To help her conceive.

Nurse What is this? (*Picks up cup.*)

Fool (*Queen*) The doctor gave it to me.

Nurse What for?

Fool (*Queen*) To help me sleep.

Nurse He's a fake. What are you doing with these? (*Picks up ledgers.*)

Fool (*Queen*) Keeping the accounts/

Fool The budget is in chaos. Taxes aren't being paid, and there's no income from the fields.

Nurse You should leave all that business to him.

Fool (*Queen*) He is very distressed by reading documents like these/

Fool so by and large he doesn't read them.

Nurse About your children.

Fool (*Queen*) I want them taken away.

Nurse You don't see them enough.

Fool (*Queen*) South.

Nurse He won't like that.

Fool (*Queen*) I could go with them. For a holiday.

Both He won't like that.

Fool (*Queen*) No, he won't, he likes to have me near him.

Nurse I'll bring them in to see you then, shall I?

Fool (*Queen*) I'm too tired.

Nurse Later on this afternoon.

Fool (*Queen*) They wear me out.

Nurse That's settled then. I'll go and arrange it. Good.

> *Nurse crosses down left, pauses at exit. Curtsies. Fool dumps Queen and moves down centre.*

Fool Lear's daughters. Three princesses creeping down the stairs, learning about a father, who is also a king.

Going downstairs.

Goneril, Regan, Cordelia centre stage. Fool circles the sisters and as each one speaks mirrors actions and words. Fool first looks at Goneril then turns suddenly and points to Cordelia.

Cordelia The first time I go downstairs, I run, barefoot cold on the stone steps. Careful, I tell myself. Slow down. Don't slip. But I have to run because of the shadows. In my new white shift, satin rustling as I go downstairs. Looking up, there is a huge oak door, with a handle high above my head. I reach up, wanting to be let in, banging my hands on the door until it opens. There are too many lights and too many faces. And then the one face, clear and sharp, stooping right down and swinging me high above the floor, up to the ceiling, up to the rafters. In a giant's arms, my feet are touching the sky, and then . . . down. The smell of a breath, warm and sweet, soft lips wet on my cheek, bristles scratching my chin and neck, and down on to the table, and I turn, holding my skirt, round and round. Look, Daddy, look, Daddy, look, look, look.

Fool touches Regan.

Regan I'm not scared going downstairs. It's dark and very late. Goneril is asleep, lying across her bed, with one hand and foot hanging over the side, frowning and talking in her sleep, like she always does. Cordelia is sleeping curled up tight in a ball. Sheets and blankets wrapped tight around her. And I am on my own. Downstairs I go, breathing shallow and seeing nobody. The stairs are rough on my feet. Passing a door I hear men's voices shouting and calling. The door is open and looking in, I can see my father. He is singing, banging his fist on the table, not quite in tune, not quite in time. And his arm is around Mother's neck. I think it's Mother. He has a hand inside her dress, holding her breast. Not tender, he's just holding her. And Mother's face. It is Mother. I'm certain it is. Her face is blank, without expression, like a figure made of wax. I'm scared now. (*Turns back to mirror.*)

Fool touches Goneril.

Goneril The first time I go downstairs, I sit on his throne to see what it is like. It has a high back, carved and uncomfortable. He likes that, likes to feel its weight behind his back. It is so big my feet cannot reach the edge. I stay on a long time, sitting quietly, looking about me. When he comes in, I am smiling, and he is angry because he knows what I am thinking and I smile on – because I want him to know.

Fool (*to audience*) The first time I went downstairs I was pushed. And it bloody hurt. I broke my finger (*Holds up little finger – it is straight.*) and it's never been straight since. Look. (*Bends little finger.*) (*Fool moves downstage. Looks at notes – the running order.*) The Guided Tour. (*Fool walks round centre stage.*) The nursery. Books, paints, a knife – for carving – and a

Nanny. Down the stairs the parlour – lace, cake, a knife – for slicing – medicines, honey, account books – to keep things in order.

Nurse (*interjects*) And the Nurse.

Fool Down the stairs. The dining room. The kitchen. The storeroom. The Counting House – for the king! A knife – for the guard. And (*Points.*) the Fool's room. (*Moves to its spot.*) And underneath, the sewers, full of Rats. Now. (*Gets comfy.*) The Fool.

When I was born, nothing happened. There was no bright star, no hurricane, no visitors came from afar. Obviously my parents hadn't read the right books so my arrival was completely overlooked.

SCENE FOUR – THE FOOL AND SISTERS

Fool moves centre stage and joins sisters and Nanny. Goneril stands at the back looking out of window. Fool is counting its money.

Cordelia What was your father like?

Fool Don't know.

Regan What was your mother like?

Fool (*concentrating*) Don't know.

Cordelia How long have you been here?

Fool Not long.

Regan How old are you?

Fool Work or pleasure?

Regan What?

Fool Is this question work or pleasure?

Regan Pleasure.

Fool Don't know.

Regan Work then.

Fool holds out hand. Regan gives it a coin.

Fool What was the question?

Regan How old are you?

Fool Seventeen.

Cordelia How do you know?

Fool It's a feeling I've got.

Regan And what's that feel like?

Fool Time for a change.

Cordelia What were you before you came here?

Fool I was a singer called Somers. Not with a 'U' you understand, as in summer and winter, but with an 'O', as in some and none.

Goneril You're lying.

Fool I am not. I was a singer of filthy and wanton songs and I heard voices. For money.

Goneril I meant it's a lie that you haven't been here long. You were here when I was little.

Fool That was some other Fool.

Goneril That Fool looked exactly like you.

Fool It's the clothes, they come with the job. And the expression. (*It smiles brightly.*) It's a tradition, there's always been a Fool.

Goneril is about to speak but returns instead to the window.

Regan What did you mean, you heard voices for money?

Fool Heard voices, had fits, saw devils, foamed at the mouth. Standard stuff. I did it to frighten the godless into returning to the faith. Sometimes I fell backwards into fires, but that cost extra.

Regan You did that for money?

Fool Of course. Skilled work. Did you expect me to do it for the good of my soul and a bowl of soup?

Cordelia Are you a man or a woman?

Fool Depends who's asking.

Regan Well, which?

Fool Which would you rather? It's all the same to me.

Goneril How can you?

Fool looks at her.

How can you be so . . . accommodating?

Fool It's what I'm paid for. Time's up.

Cordelia If you weren't a Fool, what would you be?

Fool Time's up.

Regan hands Fool another coin.

What was the question?
Cordelia If you weren't a Fool, what would you be?
Fool A dog with no masters.

SCENE FIVE – LEAR RETURNS TRIUMPHANT FROM A SPORTING TOURNAMENT

It starts to rain. Fool mimes getting wet.

Fool Three princesses sitting in a room, listening to the rain fall and hoping for the sun.
    Lear returns triumphant from some sporting tournament. At sixty-five he is still the most agile horseman and best archer. The title 'king' demeans his status – he is a demi-god. He has competed against the best and won. His countrymen weep with pride, and disbelief. Nanny woke Fool at 4 a.m.
Nurse (*interjects*) It's time.
Fool It practised smiling in the mirror (*Mimes smiling in a mirror.*) and put on its man's man suit.

Lights up on centre stage. Goneril at window, Regan stands on trunk. Cordelia crosses to mirror.

Goneril He's been away for a very long time.
Regan I am up even before Nurse, watching a watery sun creep up over the fields.
Cordelia Nanny makes me spit on her apron so she can wipe a piece of dirt from my cheek.
Goneril I am so excited. I have missed him so much.
Regan We are going to get out.

Cordelia crosses down to left stage. Goneril moves downstage to centre. Regan stands to right of Goneril.

Goneril I am going to see him again. Touch him again. Smell him. He always smells lovely.
Regan It is drizzling.
Goneril It is November but it is mild. The sky is clear, crisp blue. No rain – all dry.

Cordelia Goneril and Regan look beautiful.

Regan Cordelia chatters like some excited lace-covered guinea-fowl.

Cordelia Nanny holds me high above her head. It makes me laugh.

Goneril Cordelia isn't very well – sniffy and crying at the slightest thing.

Regan Goneril sits with her hands, two tight fists balled up in her lap. She doesn't want him home.

Goneril Regan keeps wriggling at my side.

Regan There are crowds of people in the streets, mud-spattered and sodden.

Goneril So many ordinary people have turned out to greet him.

Cordelia I can see nothing but people's backs as they leap and stretch higher and higher.

Regan When they see our coach they surge forward.

Goneril Cheering and singing.

Regan Something soft and rotten-smelling hits the side of my face.

Goneril They love him.

Regan It slides slowly down my jaw and neck. They are still shouting, but their faces have changed.

Goneril It is a holiday. He has come home.

Regan The coach begins to rock violently.

Cordelia The people cheer and cry so I do as well.

Goneril I can see him in the distance.

Cordelia The crowd slowly parts and there he is.

Goneril He is so upright.

Cordelia I'd forgotten his face.

Goneril I can see no one else in this huge crowd – just him.

Cordelia He reaches towards Mother and kisses her. She lets go of my hand.

Goneril He smiles, parts his lips, shows his teeth. He puts one hand on my shoulder and pushes me away.

Cordelia He puts his hand on our heads one at a time as if he is healing us.

Goneril And then he lifts Cordelia high into the air and kisses her on each cheek.

Regan We don't even get out of the coach.

Cordelia He lifts me back into the coach and Father, Mother, my sisters and I are all together again.

Regan Mother leaves our coach and joins him in his.

Goneril Throughout the drive back to the castle I look out of the window.

Regan I want to lay my head on Goneril's lap, but that space is still occupied by her fists.

Goneril As Nanny takes us away he touches my cheek.

Cordelia We all love each other.

Goneril I don't feel it.

Cordelia I don't remember everything, but when I do, I remember *exactly*.

Fool There are only three things I can't remember. I can't remember names. I can't remember faces and I've forgotten what the third thing is.

If they'd only been the two instead of three, things might have been different.

'Cos two is nice, it's manageable.

It's more easily understandable.

Two is one – holding hands with another.

First and last,

Bottom and top,

Master and servant,

Mother and child.

Two is what one is, and the other isn't, a pair.

Whereas three. You're asking for trouble.

Bad news travels in threes.

Three splits two into half, leaving piggy in the middle.

Two against one.

'If she isn't with me then she must be with . . .'

Three means a private detective.

Three sisters, playing in the nursery, with the mother who sells, but not the mother who buys.

Three daughters, visiting in the parlour, with the mother who's paid and the mother who's paying.

SCENE SIX — THE SISTERS AND THE THEIR MOTHER

*Fool is Queen. Stands centre stage with veil. Sisters and Nanny
enter. Nanny stands to side. Sisters stand around Queen. As they
ask their questions, the sisters circle the Queen. Nanny claps her
hands as sisters enter.*

Goneril Hello, majesty.
Regan Mother.
Cordelia Majesty.
Nurse Curtsy to the Queen.
Cordelia Hello, Mother.
Regan Majesty.
Goneril Mother.
Nurse Kiss your mother.

Sisters kiss Queen. She flinches.

Regan Do you like my hair?
Cordelia Daddy likes my hair.
Regan Do you like it?
Fool (*Queen*) Do I like it? (*Looks at Nanny.*) Do I like it?
Cordelia Do you like my dress?
Goneril Come and see my painting.
Cordelia Do you like it?
Goneril I'm painting heaven.
Cordelia Do you like the colour of it?
Goneril Why do we have a sun and a moon?
Regan Do you like it?
Cordelia Am I too young to wear black?
Nurse You are tiring the Queen!
Regan Can I go out?
Goneril Why are we always shut in?
Cordelia Do you like it?
Goneril Can we go out with you?
Regan Can we go out?
Cordelia Can I do a handstand?
Regan Can I go out?
Cordelia I can stand on my head?
Goneril Do you ever go out?

358

Nurse Keep your voice down.
Cordelia Can you stand on your head?
Goneril Do you ever go out?
Fool (*Queen*) He doesn't like shouting.
Cordelia Do you stand on your head for Daddy?
Fool (*Queen*) Keep your voice down.
Cordelia Do you like it?
Nurse He won't like these boys' manners.
Cordelia Why are you always in bed?
Fool (*Queen*) I don't like these boys' manners.
Regan Do you like it?
Cordelia Does he like you in bed?
Fool (*Queen*) Stop these boys' manners!
Cordelia Are you going to have a baby?
Nurse You are not a boy.
Goneril Why does he want a boy?
Fool (*Queen*) You are not a boy.
Goneril Why do you want a boy?
Fool (*Queen*) You are not a boy.
Regan Do you want a boy?
Fool (*Queen*) Do I want a boy? (*Looks at Nanny.*)
Regan Are you sick?
Cordelia Why don't you have a boy?
Goneril Are you sick?
Cordelia Will he be cross?
Regan Is that why you're sick?
Cordelia Is he cross with you?
Goneril Is that why you're sick?
Cordelia Does he like you?
Goneril He likes Cordelia.
Regan Is that why you're sick?
Cordelia Does he love you?
Goneril Do you love him?
Regan Are you sick?

Sisters stop circling Queen. Start pulling at veil.

Cordelia Will you die?
Regan What will happen to us?
Goneril If you die?

Cordelia Are you going to die?
Regan Who will be Queen?
Goneril If you die?
Regan Will it be Goneril?
Cordelia What will happen to us?
Goneril If you die?
Cordelia Will Nanny be our mother?
Goneril If you die?
Regan Mother?
Cordelia Mother, will you die?
Fool (*Queen*) Stop!
Nanny Stop!

Queen collapses to floor.

Fool Knock, knock, who's there? (*Fool shrugs shoulders in answer then picks up veil and carries it carefully, draped over its arms, back to its spot.*) Three princesses listening down the stairs with the mother who lives – for the mother who is dying.

SCENE SEVEN – THE NURSE AND THE SISTERS

Goneril stands looking out of window. Regan is sitting on trunk, Nanny brushes Cordelia's hair downstage.

Regan Tell us about when we were little.
Goneril Cordelia's still little.
Nurse You are all still small.
Regan Smaller then.
Nurse When Goneril was very small you weren't there. (*Looks at Cordelia.*) And neither were you.
Regan No, do when we were all three there.
Nurse Even Lear?

Pause.

Regan Yes.
Nurse Once, Lear had not been there, and then suddenly he was. It rained for forty days and nights before he came home and

when he did, the sun came out. The King walked over the water to meet us.

Cordelia Over the water?

Goneril (*To Cordelia*) Over a bridge.

Nurse Yes. That's better. Over a bridge. We had to build a bridge to get to him. The Queen crossed the bridge and everybody had to cheer.

Goneril Had to?

Nurse Yes. (*smoothly*) Because it was important to see the Queen at Lear's side.

Cordelia Then did we cross over?

Nurse I think so, yes.

Regan Who went first?

Nurse I can't remember.

Regan I bet I did.

Goneril In order of age.

Cordelia Youngest first.

Regan We went across the bridge together. Everybody cheered. Nanny went quite deaf with the cheering.

Nurse Did I?

Regan Daddy gave you a present.

Nurse (*laughing*) Did he?

Cordelia It was cake.

Nurse Was it?

Regan You were there.

Nurse Was I? (*Pause.*) If you want me there.

Goneril No. (*Slowly, concentrating, she moves to Nanny.*) Nanny stayed on this side of the bridge.

Nurse That is my place.

She curtsies to Goneril. Silence.

Goneril (*measured*) I stayed with Nanny. (*Smiles at Nanny.*)

Regan So did I.

Cordelia And so did the Queen. So Daddy must have come to us.

Nurse Yes, he must have come to us.

Cordelia (*satisfied*) One big happy family.

Fool (*Queen*) (*off centre stage*) Nurse! Nurse!

They all look off. Know Queen has died. Nurse goes off. Goneril takes over brushing Cordelia's hair. Cordelia shows pain.

Cordelia Stop it, Goneril, you're hurting me.

Goneril stops brushing. Pain continues.

Goneril stop it! It's pulling. Goneril, please, stop it, you're hurting me! Stop it, Goneril, stop it!

SCENE EIGHT — FUNERAL PREPARATIONS

Fool (*putting veil down in bundle*) The Queen is dead! Long live the Queen! But who will take her place at the King's right hand? Cordelia the favourite, Goneril the eldest, or Regan the outsider?

Cordelia leaves centre stage. Goneril goes to trunk and puts head on hands. Regan picks up hair brush from floor.

Regan We'd better get changed. We can't go downstairs dressed like this.

Goneril is shaking. Regan crosses to her.

Don't cry. (*Regan comforts her.*) Don't cry . . . you're laughing! Stop it! Why are you laughing?

Goneril stops. Shakes head.

Goneril He'll be very upset. He'll have to manage on his own now.

They both start to laugh. Fool laughs quietly with them offstage. They stop laughing.

Regan How will we manage without her?
Goneril Don't worry. I'll take care of everything now.
Regan We should change.
Goneril No. He'll be down there all in black. Dressed for sorrow. We'll be fine as we are.

They smile. Regan turns away.

Regan. I feel sick. (*Goneril holds her stomach. Cries.*)

Regan You'll be fine. You'll be fine.

Goneril Will it take long?

Regan No, I don't think so.

Cordelia enters.

Cordelia He said I'm his special girl and I've got to look after him. I'm not going with you, I've got to hold his hand.

Goneril goes to trunk. Regan slumps on bench.

Nanny!

Nurse enters.

Daddy says Mummy's gone to live with God and I can wear a long black dress with gloves. Get me ready.

Nurse Turn around.

Cordelia He said Mummy would be pleased to know she'd left everything in such good hands. Do you think she can see us now?

Nurse Keep your head still.

Cordelia He said when we come out of the church all the people will cheer when I stand next to him because I will be so brave. Do you think they will?

Nurse There you are. You'll do.

Cordelia (*turns to look in mirror*) Oh. Look, Nanny, look. I look really grown up. Just like a Queen.

Regan (*sharply*) Goneril. Look.

Goneril crosses to window. Looks at Nurse. Nurse goes to window.

Cordelia What is it?

Goneril indicates to Nanny to take Cordelia away quickly. Nanny looks out of the window.

Nurse Come with me.

When Nurse and Cordelia have gone, Regan and Goneril look to the window again. After a while Regan turns away.

Goneril How can he? Today.

Regan He's disgusting.

Goneril He's got his hand right up her skirt.

Regan Anyone can see him. Not just us. Doesn't he care?

Goneril He's unbuttoning himself.

Regan Come away.

Goneril He's so . . . How dare he?

Regan Who is she?

Goneril I don't know.

Regan Doesn't she mind him pawing her like that?

They turn away from window.

Goneril What will happen now? Do you think he will marry her?

Regan I don't know.

Goneril If he does he'll have a son. I know it. He'll try until he does. I'll never be Queen.

Fool enters from left, whistling 'Sing a Song of Sixpence'. Circles centre stage and then looks out of window over shoulders of Goneril and Regan.

Fool (*laughing; sings*) Wasn't that a dainty dish to set before the King? (*Fool returns to its spot. Whistles.*) Time passes. (*Whistles.*) It rains. And every spring the river outside the castle overflows, flooding the sewers and disturbing the rats. (*Pause.*) One morning a stone is thrown through the window, breaking the glass and cracking the mirror. It lands in the middle of the floor.

Fool makes popping sound. Sisters centre stage look at spot and then turn away in boredom.

Lear takes to riding his carriage with the shutters down and going the long way round to avoid the crowds. And the Fool amuses the Nanny, and the Nanny amuses the Fool, as they wait for the rain to stop.

SCENE NINE – THE NURSE TELLS THE FOOL THE STORY OF THE PIED PIPER

Fool crosses to stage right to the Nanny's spot.

Fool (*sings*)
Nanny put the kettle on,
Nanny put the kettle on,
Nanny put the kettle on,
We'll all have tea?

Nanny is sitting darning veil. Pause.

Nurse Who's there?
Fool Nanny.
Nurse Nanny who?
Fool Nanny your business.

Nurse snorts. Fool laughs.

I'm tired and I'm hungry. (*fed-up*) Is there anything in the pantry?
Nurse Empty.
Fool Game?
Nurse Out of season.
Fool No! Word game. Empty.
Nurse Full.
Fool Stomach.
Nurse Pregnant.
Fool Queen.
Nurse Princess.
Fool Goneril.
Nurse (*triumphantly*) Regan.

Fool is astonished. Mouth falls open.

Time's up. You lose.
Fool Not fair. Not fair.
Nurse You lose. You owe me one favour.
Fool Can't make me.
Nurse True. But you've got an aptitude for servitude.
Fool Oh! A rhyming game. Snotty.
Nurse Botty.

Fool (*hooting and laughing*) Potty.

Nurse Clotty.

Fool Not a word. 'S not a word. You lose, I win! Oh, Nanny, Nanny. Can I sleep in your bed tonight? (*Leans backwards across Nurse's lap.*)

Nurse Can I afford it?

Fool I'll waive the fee.

Nurse (*to audience*) Now that's what I call a joke.

Fool Would you prefer it if I set a price? It can be arranged.

Nurse Well, at least I could complain then if I wasn't pleased.

Fool turns from her, sulking.

Fool feeling hurt?

Fool sulks.

I thought Fool was above such things. You're a funny Fool. What are you after?

Fool I'm after everyone else. I'm an afterthought. Oh, tell me a story, Nanny. Tell me the one about the Fool who becomes rich and famous, inherits the earth and travels the sky on a magic carpet. That's my favourite.

Nurse Oh, that one.

Fool There's no such tale.

Nurse Please yourself.

Fool Nanneeey. (*begging*) Nanny, Nanny.

Nurse All right. A very long way from here there is a land that is very beautiful, but where it is always raining. The land is full of tiny towns and villages. If you look at it from above they are scattered about like crumbs of cake. And in the middle of it all there is a river, and by the river a castle.

Fool I know the very spot.

Nurse And over the castle the sun always shines. And in the castle there lives a king and all his court. Landowners, merchants, clerics, bankers.

Fool Yes, yes, what about me?

Nurse And every so often the people look up from their work in the fields and hold their babies up high to see the castle because it looks so beautiful. But each day it gets harder for them to do this because of one thing.

Fool The debris of a passing swan. (*Whistles, mimes splat in eye.*)

Nurse Rats.

Fool Rats?

Nurse Big, hungry rats, scavenging for food, trampling down the meagre crops, scampering in and out of the mean houses. And one day there comes a terrible famine. And then the rats move.

Fool Move? Move where?

Nurse Into the castle, where food is still plentiful. And by day the king and his men struggle with the poor that batter against their gates, begging for food, and by night with the rats that run through their stores and kitchens, gnaw even at the king's throne.

Fool Yes, yes, gnaw, gnaw, nibble, nibble, what about me?

Nurse This is you now.

Fool Good.

Nurse But then one day there comes into the castle a strange figure who is called the

Fool Fool.

Nurse No one knows whether this

Fool Fool

Nurse is a woman or a man, for it has a woman's voice, but walks with the carriage and stature of a man. The

Fool Fool

Nurse announces itself as a rat-catcher.

Fool (*triumphantly*) Ha-Ha!

Nurse and offers to rid the place of the vermin. The king and his men agree and ask the

Fool Fool

Nurse what the

Fool Fool

Nurse would like in return and the

Fool Fool

Nurse replies

Fool money.

Nurse So it is agreed.

Fool Lots of it.

Nurse Whereupon the

Fool Fool
Nurse draws out its pipe

   Fool mimes smoking pipe.

and begins to play,

   Fool changes to playing a pipe.

so that the rats swarm to follow, out of the castle, into the river,
   into which they all plunge and drown.
Fool Ha Ha! And now I get paid.
Nurse No sooner has this happened than the king and his court
   repent of their bargain, refusing to pay the –
Fool Swine!
Nurse – Fool its fee, saying, 'Why should we pay this creature,
   neither man nor woman?' and they drive it from the land.
Fool Never!
Nurse But that evening the
Fool Fool
Nurse is back –
Fool Good!
Nurse – outside the castle, playing a different tune, and out of
   the wet fields and ditches, out of the mean houses, come the
   children, mud-spattered and sodden.
Fool No.
Nurse And as the king and his men look out of the castle
   windows, they see the shadows fill with this dark army, and,
   strangest of all in this strange story, as they look at the
   children's teeth glinting in the moonlight, at the long fingers
   scratching at the doors, the men see not children but –

   Fool gags Nurse.

Fool Rabbits.
Nurse – rats. Clambering up the walls, scrabbling through the
   slits in the windows, chewing their way up through the thick
   walls and floors, whetting their teeth against the stones.
Fool No!
Nurse And soon they have gnawed the flesh from the bodies of
   the king and his men, picking over the bones and leaving every
   one bare.

Fool (*angrily*) What about my money? You've forgotten about my money.

Nurse As dawn breaks over the town, the song of the

Fool Fool

Nurse changes

Fool to one of demand

Nurse and, chattering and tumbling, the –

Fool gold coins

Nurse – children –

Fool fall into

Nurse – run into –

Fool the Fool's lap.

Nurse – the fields where the Fool waits for them and they follow across the fields and are never seen again.

Fool No, no, no.

Nurse But sometimes –

Fool No.

Nurse – at night –

Fool No.

Nurse – the sound of music –

Fool No.

Nurse – and laughter –

Fool No.

Nurse –can be heard –

Fool No.

Nurse – as though from a –

Fool No!

Nurse (*shouting*) – Better World.

Fool It's stopped. The rain's stopped. (*triumphantly*) Ha, ha, ha.

Fool crosses back to down left.

SCENE TEN – INVESTMENT

Fool takes pieces of paper. Reads.

Fool Scene One, Fool introduces play. Good. (*Reads. Keeps paper.*) Scene Two, Nanny and the princesses. Scene Three, Nanny and the Queen, Fool is Queen. Good. (*Keeps paper.*)

Scene Four. (*Reads paper.*) Princess, princess, princess. Scene Ten. Nanny tells all about her love life? (*Spits. Crumples paper and throws it aside.*) Scene Eleven, princess, prin. . . (*Reads quickly.*) Ah. Scene Thirteen. Fool talks about investment. Investment is . . . (*Thinks.*) Investment is . . . Money, cash, dosh, lolly, crinks, ackers, makes the world go round, doubloons, duckets, crowns, pieces of eight, muck and brass. Money – Investment. (*Puts coin down front of skirt. Mimes rubbing tummy.*) Nest egg, pension, taken care of, rainy day, looked after, old age. (*Smiles, waits, starts to wriggle as if eruption under skirt. Looks under skirt. Gasps with delight. Gasps. Reaches under skirt and pulls out fool doll. Cradles it as child.*) Investment. Three princesses all grown older, thinking about their father and counting the cost.

Cordelia centre stage, looking in mirror. Fool stays in its place. Cordelia humming 'Polly Put the Kettle on'.

Fool (*Lear*) Cordelia, where's my Cordelia?
Cordelia Here, Father – here I am.
Fool (*Lear*) Oh, see my pretty chick. Come my pretty, dance for Daddy.
Cordelia For you, only for you?
Fool (*Lear*) Of course for me.
Cordelia But everyone is watching.
Fool (*Lear*) Don't be silly.
Cordelia I'm shy.
Fool (*Lear*) You're not trying.
Cordelia I'm too big.
Fool (*Lear*) Spin for Daddy.
Cordelia I can't.
Fool (*Lear*) Spin!

Cordelia picks up skirt.

Gather round gentlemen, please. Show them Lear's baby.
Cordelia I'm not your baby.
Fool (*Lear*) What? Pardon?
Cordelia I'm . . . (*Going to repeat above but resists.*) I'm tired, Daddy. Cordelia tired.
Fool (*Lear*) Spin. Spin. Spin.

Cordelia Spin for Daddy. (*Begins to spin.*)

Fool (*Lear*) Don't let me down, darling. There's my peach.

Cordelia There's my peach.

Fool (*Lear*) Such lovely hair and lips.

Cordelia And tongues –

Fool (*Lear*) Spin.

Cordelia – and bulging eyes,

Fool (*Lear*) Spin.

Cordelia – shouting and cheering.

Fool (*Lear*) Shouting and cheering.

Cordelia I'm falling. No. I don't want to. Cordelia not want to be Daddy's girl.

Cordelia collapses on floor. Regan enters up right. Crosses to down centre, then back to window.

Regan Nurse!

Nurse enters.

What happened the night Mother died?

Nurse I don't understand.

Regan The night she died. I can't remember. You and us, what happened?

Nurse I put you all to bed, you were over-tired. I sat up watching in case you were disturbed. Cordelia cried out, but you slept soundly.

Regan What else?

Nurse You wanted a story, so I told you one.

Regan About what, about Mother?

Nurse About all of you.

Regan Tell me.

Nurse does not respond.

Tell me!

Nurse crosses to trunk and sits.

Nurse I told you of the time your Father came home and you all went to meet him.

Regan Over the bridge.

Nurse Yes.

Regan I remember. You brushed our hair.

Nurse I often did.

Regan You brushed our hair and you were lying.

Nurse No.

Regan He came to us. It rained for forty days. When he came home the sun came out. It was lies.

Nurse It was a story. You were all upset. It was for comfort.

Regan Tell me about Mother.

Nurse How?

Regan What was she like?

Nurse She was a beautiful woman, but delicate. All perfume and lace.

Regan Yes.

Nurse When she married your father, it was a love-match.

Regan You're lying again.

Nurse She meant the world to him.

Regan How did she die?

Nurse She was delicate.

Regan What did Father do?

Nurse It was a love-match.

Regan Tell me the truth. Tell me the truth. Tell me the truth!
(*Regan walks towards Nurse.*)

Nurse All right. I used to hear him in the room below, whining on at her to let him fuck her. He wouldn't give up on her having a son. She always gave in, that's why she was always tired.

Regan A love-match.

Nurse She brought a large dowry. Substantial. She was beautiful.

Regan And when she died?

Nurse Miscarriage. Her third. Cordelia had finished it for her. She died in the night so he was spared a bedside scene. I was not. I had been up all night. I was tired. He came in the morning to look at the Queen, lying in her white dress. I'd cleaned her up and laid her out. He looked at her for a long moment and then he stormed out.

Regan We saw him, Goneril and I, out of the window. The day of the funeral.

Nurse Yes. She *was* important to him. She organized the budget.

Looked after his interests. Night after night when he wasn't
with her, adding and subtracting to balance the figures.

Regan Did she love us?

Nurse Oh, yes, when she had the time. She took you all away
once. She came in here with his light all around her, like a net.
We sat in the shadows and she told me she wanted to leave him
and take all of you with her. I said nothing – packed our
belongings in the trunk. I should have guessed but I never did
until the time came that I wasn't to go as well. I took my cloak
from the trunk and came in here and I never moved for three
days. But in the end she had to bring you back. And then it was
all up with us and no one ever left again except by his say-so.
She didn't have long after that.

Regan No.

*Nurse gets up and moves to Regan. Holds her face and
examines it.*

Nurse How long?

Regan Two months.

*Nurse puts hand on Regan's stomach. Shakes head. Regan
exits. Goneril enters.*

Goneril Nurse! Where's Cordelia?

Nurse Downstairs, with your father.

Goneril Regan?

Nurse Downstairs.

Goneril looks.

In the cellars looking for wood. Why don't you paint?

Goneril It's raining too hard. I can't see the colours. (*Silence.*)
Have you been down there?

Nurse Where?

Goneril The cellars.

Nurse Of course.

Goneril I went down there once. When I was very small. Father
took me. I couldn't believe it. Rooms and rooms of food, all
those cheeses and flour and racks of meat hanging from the
ceiling.

Nurse We're well provided for against the bad weather.

Goneril He took me down all these corridors, I could hardly keep up and then he stopped and fumbled in his pocket and took out a key. He opened a door and pushed me inside. And the room was full of gold. Everywhere crowns, coins, breastplates, gold bars, all glowing in the candlelight. I never knew that gold had so many colours. He shut the door and bent down to me and whispered, 'When you are Queen, this will be yours. This will be our secret – just you and me – and you mustn't tell.' And then he put his hand (*Silence.*) on my shoulder. I never did tell anyone. (*She smiles.*) Until now.

Nurse says nothing.

I went looking for that room again, once. The night Father came home and the crowds cheered and he pushed me away to kiss Cordelia. I couldn't find it. I must have taken a wrong turning and I came into this corridor, with a torch shining at the end of it, and set into the floor . . .

Nurse Yes.

Goneril Bars. As I walked past, these hands came out from them, clawing and scratching. Nanny. There were people in there. Shut in. I don't know how many. By him. he's the king. He must know they're there. (*Goneril moves back to the window.*)

Nurse He knows.

Goneril I can't put it all together. This is our secret. Just you and me. And the cheering crowds and those people. Can you?

The Nurse can't speak.

And now this.

Nurse What?

Goneril (*Holds out ledger.*) He came in last night and pushed it at me. 'Your mother used to do this so you can now.' It's the accounts. Columns and columns of figures.

Nurse I know.

Silence.

Goneril I have to get out of this place soon.

Nurse You will.

Goneril (*at window*) There he is now. Going out riding. Something must have annoyed him, to go out riding in this

374

weather. How small he looks from up here. A wooden man on a wooden horse.

Nurse exits. Curtsies to Goneril. Lights down centre stage. Lights up on Fool.

SCENE ELEVEN – FOOL INTRODUCES MARRIAGE

Fool Lear returns triumphant from yet another sporting tournament . . . Grouse-shooting! Lear's countrymen grow thin, his coffers fat. So. Plenty of grouse about. And remember that at seventy-five he is still the most agile horseman and (*Mimes flying an arrow.*) archer. Nanny! If a trap's caught three rats, can the one in the middle survive?

Nurse looks coldly at Fool.

No, because it's dead – centre! The river is rising again. But how to stop the tide of unrest? What did one king say to another when the flood came in? I can't stop it, can ute? Three daughters alone can't plug a dyke. We need a finger. Three fingers! (*Holds up three fingers. As Lear*) Not my little Cordelia. (*as Fool*) Well, two then. (*Holds up two fingers.*) Two fingers to plug the dyke! One called Albany, one called Cornwall.

Lights down on Fool. Up on centre stage.

SCENE TWELVE – SISTERS DISCUSS GETTING MARRIED

Goneril and Regan on stage. Goneril is reading ledger.

Regan Are you getting changed?
Goneril No.
Regan Aren't you coming down?
Goneril No.
Regan Why not?
Goneril I'm too busy.

Regan You have to come. It's our celebration.
Goneril I must finish this.
Regan Come down with me.
Goneril No.

Silence.

Regan Goneril.
Goneril What?
Regan This wedding. (*Silence.*) What do you feel about it?
Goneril Nothing.
Regan I don't understand.
Goneril I feel nothing about it.
Regan Do you want this marriage?
Goneril Wanting doesn't come into it.
Regan When I lie in bed at night, I can feel my heart beating so
  fast, it's like I'm living at twice the pace. I'm running out of life.
  How can you feel nothing about it?
Goneril It's our job. It's what we're here for. To marry and breed.
Regan Like dogs?
Goneril Like dogs. Valuable merchandise. I can show you the
  figures here if you like.
Regan I'm scared.
Goneril It's what we're here for.
Regan I'm going to have a baby. Seven months' time. Nurse
  says.
Goneril How could you be so stupid?
Regan Oh Goneril! I'm not stupid, but I'm not stone, not dead.
  You, you've always been the first, the cleverest, the best, and
  Cordelia, she's the . . . the pretty, the lovable, Lear's darling.
  Then there's me, in the middle, neither fish nor fowl, do you
  see? I've had nothing that's, that's for me, just for me. I've been
  number two, between one and three, but nothing. So I've taken
  everything, everything that I can feel or touch or smell or do or
  be, everything to try and find something, to find me, do you
  see?
Goneril Come here, Regan. You see these ledgers? What do they
  say to you?
Regan Listen to me!
Goneril You see these figures!

376

Regan turns away, goes to mirror, Goneril pulls her back to trunk. Forces her to look at ledger.

Regan (*struggling*) Let go of my arm.

Goneril They say Regan, Second Daughter of Lear, is worth this much, and these figures here . . .

Regan tries to look away.

Look at them! These figures say My Lord Duke of Cornwall owns this much. These figures say Regan will marry Cornwall and then Cornwall will own more and Lear will get a grandson, a legitimate heir and they will all be contented men. However, Regan, Second Daughter of Lear, with bastard child, is worth *this* much!

Goneril rips out page from ledger, crumples it and throws it on floor. Regan pulls away to mirror, staring hard into it.

Get rid of it!

Regan (*looking in mirror*) I can't see your features. Your expression in the mirror. Your face is blank.

Goneril You're imagining things.

Regan It's him. You've got his face.

Goneril exits. Lighting change. Regan pacing floor. Nurse enters carrying cup and cloth.

Will it take long?

Nurse No, I don't think so. It will hurt.

Regan nods. It is hurting already.

Regan What was it?

Nurse Rue and pennyroyal.

There is pain. Regan groans aloud.

You mustn't scream. Bite on this.

Nurse hands Regan cloth. There is pain. Nurse goes to Regan and holds her.

Regan I'm going to die. You've poisoned me.

Nurse You're not going to die yet.

Regan (*in pain*) Please let it be over. (*pain*) Please.

Nurse puts rag in Regan's mouth. Regan groans. Nurse stands behind Regan. Holds her.

Nurse Breathe. Breathe. You have to push.
Regan Oh, Jesus.
Nurse You have to.
Regan I'm frightened.
Nurse Push. Push.

Pause.

Regan What do I look like?
Nurse You look as if you're laughing.

There is no more pushing. Regan collapses on floor. Nurse looks down.

It would have been a boy.
Regan I'll get out of here soon.
Nurse You will.

Lights down. Lights up on Fool.

SCENE THIRTEEN – THE WEDDINGS

Fool Two bridegrooms waiting downstairs. Two brides waiting to be swept off their feet.

Fool walks to window, humming the Wedding March. Goneril and Regan kneeling at altar. Fool stands on window seat. Nurse and Cordelia watch.

Who gives this woman?

When answering questions Regan, Cordelia, Goneril and Nurse all speak together and take different poses. The first three responses are all made happily, with big smiles, until Fool becomes menacing.

Cordelia So beautiful.
Goneril/Regan I promise, I do, I will.

Nurse Lear triumphant.
Fool To love, honour and obey.
Nurse That is my place. That is my place.
Goneril/Regan I promise, I do, I will.
Cordelia Spin for Daddy.
Fool Just cause or impediment?
Nurse And you mustn't tell. And you mustn't tell.
Goneril/Regan I promise, I do, I will.
Cordelia Just the two of us.
Fool (*menacing*) Who gives this woman?
Nurse (*loud*) Lear triumphant.
Cordelia (*whispered*) So beautiful.
Goneril/Regan (*whispered*) I swear to.
Fool Love, honour and obey?
Nurse (*whispered*) That is my place, that is my place.
Goneril/Regan (*whispered*) I promise, I do, I will.
Cordelia (*loud*) Spin for Daddy.
Fool Just cause or impediment?
Nurse (*loud*) And you mustn't tell.
Cordelia (*whispered*) Just the two of us.
Goneril/Regan (*whispered*) Triumphant.
Fool (*happily*) Kiss the bride.

> *The women's responses are loud and happy from here until, again, Fool becomes menacing.*

Cordelia She means the world to him.
Nurse She brings a large dowry.
Goneril/Regan To love and cherish.
Fool Catch the flowers.
Cordelia Daddy's girl.
Nurse Cordelia the favourite.
Goneril/Regan To love and cherish.
Fool Cut the cake.
Cordelia Together again.
Nurse A knife for slicing.
Goneril/Regan To love and cherish.
Goneril/Regan To love and cherish.
Fool (*menacing*) Kiss the bride.
Nurse (*loud*) She brings a large dowry.

Cordelia (*whispered*) She means the world to him.
Goneril/Regan (*whispered*) To love and cherish.
Fool Catch the flowers.
Cordelia (*loud*) Daddy's girl.
Nurse (*whispered*) Cordelia the favourite.
Goneril/Regan (*whispered*) To love and cherish.
Fool Cut the cake.
Cordelia Together again.
Nurse (*loud*) A knife for slicing.
Goneril/Regan Cherish.

Goneril goes for Lear's (Fool's) eyes with knife. Action freezes. All turn to audience, begin to walk downstage. Chattering, repeating sections of above plus:

Goneril Thank you for coming. Yes, he is handsome, isn't he?
Nurse With his light shining all around her, like a net.
Cordelia As they came out of the church the people cheered and cried so I did as well.
Fool One day this will all be yours. (*pushing way to front*) And the King said, 'I have decided I cannot part with you both yet. Live here a while longer.'

Silence. Then all begin to speak again. Goneril holding knife moves upstage. Goneril drops knife.

Regan Goneril.

Chatter starts again. Goneril slowly moves to window. In the chatter we hear the name 'Goneril' emerging until it turns into a collective cry.

All Goneril!
Goneril (*on window seat, as though to throw herself out*) Nanny! I can't see! The lace is scoring into my eyes. I can't see anything. Nanny! Nanny!

Nanny catches Goneril. Fool runs away. Lights out. Goneril and Regan move off-centre. Nanny returns to her spot. Fool walks from its spot across stage to Nanny.

SCENE FOURTEEN – THE NURSE REVEALS ALL

Fool scuttles across to Nurse's spot. Has letter behind its back.

Fool Knock, knock.

Nurse Who's there?

Fool Letters.

Nurse Letters who?

Fool Let us in, I've got a note for you. (*Hands letter to Nurse. Hurries back to Fool's spot.*)

Nurse (*opening letter, finds money inside*) My services are no longer required. Who does he think he is? Who is he to throw me aside when he no longer wants me to do the job he chose for me in the first place! Oh no, I didn't choose it; I was poor. Just like the Queen when she didn't make the right sort of boy-child for him – finished. Well, she died, didn't she? (*Mimics.*) Yes, but . . . Yes, but what? Why did she die? how? You don't know. I do. I was there. And now me. How many more? How many more of us will he throw away when we no longer suit? Goneril? Regan? Cordelia even? (*Mimics.*) Oh-no-not-Cordelia-she'll-always-fit. Will she though? I could have dropped her on the castle steps and her head would have cracked open like an egg. I could have taught them bad things. Have I? I've nearly bitten my tongue in two. And sometimes I haven't bothered. Well, they've learned. From-me-with-me-without-me. All but her. Cordelia. Well, we'll see. Money he gives me. Pieces of silver. What do I want with his gold? I had a baby once. Did you know? I had to give my baby away so that I had milk for his. Milk. When his Queen died I looked at my shrunken breasts in the bit of mirror I had and then I put it in the coffin. What to do? Eat farewell cake in the parlour? Stab it to crumbs! Leave him a note, 'Cordelia's mine – I swapped her at birth for your son. Love Nanny.' That would rock his little world. But is it true? You'll never know. I do. Walk down the stairs, out of the castle, through the city, out of the city, beyond into the countryside, back to where I belong, people I know. Lear! There are rats gnawing at your throne and I'll not be in it but I'll watch the spectacle from afar, smiling, knowing it is what I've always wanted to happen.

Nurse gathers her belongings. Takes off apron. Walks to centre stage. Cordelia is looking through window.

Cordelia They've gone. I saw Goneril stop on the skyline and I thought for a moment they were turning and coming back. But they didn't. (*Walks round room.*) She's left her paints behind. I suppose I can give her them when they visit. She can get some more. Just us now, Nanny. You and me, and the Fool. You're very quiet.

Nurse I'm leaving.

Cordelia Leaving?

Nurse They've gone . . . you're to be married soon – when he's decided on your husband. I'm not needed any more. He says. (*Nurse goes to exit.*)

Cordelia Nanny!

Nanny turns.

You never liked me, did you?

Nurse doesn't answer.

No. No one does but him.

Nurse turns to go.

Nanny, listen. I've got two voices. Ever since going downstairs and Daddy lifting me on to the table, I've talked like a child, used the words of a child. No one likes it but him. But I do have another voice. In my head I have words I never say to anyone – never have said to anyone. Till now. I can do it, you see. (*Goes up to Nanny.*) Nanny, don't go. I could go and see him, he listens to me. I'm his little girl . . . (*Trails off. Realizes the difficulty. Starts again.*) I could speak to him as a woman, as one adult to another, he'd listen, he'd . . . (*Stops. Knows.*)

Nurse It doesn't matter, Cordelia. (*Turns. Whispers something to Cordelia. Exits, walks to Fool.*) Money he gives me! Pieces of silver! What do I want with his gold? Here, Fool. Grovel for it, Fool, for that I shall never do!

Nanny tempts Fool with money. Throws it up in the air and hits the Fool around the face with fist, flattening Fool to ground. Nanny exits through audience. Banging doors. Fool gets up.

Cordelia Fool!

Fool gathers money. Goes to Cordelia who is sitting at window seat, crying. Fool tosses coin in air. Decides. Sits next to Cordelia and starts to cry, aping it badly. A caricature of Cordelia. Cordelia looks at Fool and stops crying.
Fool moves quickly to front stage. Lights up on Fool.

Fool That very night the Fool went downstairs, stood on the table and began its turn.
How many kisses does it take to keep a king happy?
103.
One to kiss his tears away.
One to kiss his fevered brow.
One to kiss him deep in passion and a hundred to kiss his arse!
(*Mimes being hit in face.*)
And the King doesn't laugh.
Who's the biggest stinker in the world?
King Pong! (*Laughs again and mimes being hit in face.*)
And the King doesn't laugh.
A man goes up to a woman in the street. 'How much?' he says. She is outraged. 'What do you think I am?' and the man says, 'We know what you are, love, we're just discussing the price.' And the King laughs – and he laughs. He laughs as though he would burst. Taking the Fool's ear he twists it to open its mouth. He places a coin on the edge of its tongue and the Fool – (*Mimes swallowing coin, gulps.*) – three, two, one and the Fool – standing on the table looking after number one. A Father waiting outside. Two mothers, one dead or gone missing, the other leaving. Three daughters, paying the price.

Lights up centre stage. Goneril, Regan, Cordelia stand in line, Goneril in middle.

Goneril Looking up, I can't see the sky. There's too much red. Red in my eyes. Red on my hands. They touched and felt but I cannot recognize them. My father's daughter, and still he gives me stop and start. Controlling by my hatred, the order of my life. Lear's daughter. Blood in my eyes and lost to heaven.

Regan I used to carve with my knife, create beauty from distortion, soft curves from the knottiest, most gnarled woods.

When life was at its dullest, most suffocating, I would be full of energy, curiosity. And then 'Get rid of it,' she said, 'Get rid of it,' and that was all. The veil was pulled away from my eyes and I could see what he had done to her, had done to me. And so I shall set my face to a new game which will not be beautiful, but there'll be a passion still and I'll be there with it till the end, my end, carved out at her hands – and I would not have it any other way.

Cordelia Words are like stones, heavy and solid and every one different. I hold two in my hands, testing their weight. 'Yes', to please, 'no', to please myself, 'yes', I shall and 'no', I will not. 'Yes' for you and 'no' for me. I love words. I like their roughness and their smoothness, and when I'm silent I'm trying to get them right. I shall be silent now, weighing these words, and when I choose to speak, I shall choose the right one.

Lights on Fool on its spot. Bows to audience.

Fool An ending. A beginning.

Throws crown into circle, the sisters all reach up and catch it. Freeze.

Time's up.

Holds out hand for money.
Blackout.

Acknowledgements

Thanks to the students and actors who worked with me as I chose different texts and teaching/performance contexts. To the directors, playwrights and academics who provided contacts, ideas and feedback, especially: Beau Coleman and The Wild Women, Fiona Shaw, Pam Gems, Annie Castledine, Miki Flockemann, Jill Greenhalgh and Magdalena, The Maenads. To Jane de Gay, research assistant, and Stephen Regan, collaborator, on The Gender Politics, Performance Research Project. And to Mags Noble, Tony Coe, Huw Williams, Jenny Bardwell and Amanda Willett: BBC colleagues who produced the audio/visual programmes which support this book. Thanks for support to the Open University Arts Faculty, and to the following institutions which provided space and funds allowing this anthology to be completed: the Schlesinger Library for the History of Women in America (Radcliffe, Harvard), the Centre for Research in Women's Studies and Gender Relations (University of British Columbia), and the British Academy.

Lizbeth Goodman